Roman Defeat, Christian Response, and the Literary Construction of the Jew

University of Pennsylvania Press
MIDDLE AGES SERIES
Edited by
Edward Peters
Henry Charles Lea Professor
of Medieval History
University of Pennsylvania

A listing of the available books
in the series appears at the
back of this volume

Roman Defeat, Christian Response, and the Literary Construction of the Jew

David M. Olster

University of Pennsylvania Press

Philadelphia

Copyright © 1994 by the University of Pennsylvania Press
Printed in the United States of America

Library of Congress Cataloging-in-Publication Data
Olster, David Michael, 1954–
    Roman defeat, Christian response, and the literary construction of
the Jew / David M. Olster.
        p.   cm. — (Middle Ages series)
    Includes bibliographical references and index.
    ISBN 0-8122-3152-X
    1. Church and state — Byzantine Empire.   2. Christianity — Byzantine
Empire — History — Middle Ages, 600–1500.   3. Christianity and
antisemitism — History.   4. Judaism — Controversial literature —
History and criticism.   5. Christian literature, Byzantine — History
and criticism.   I. Title.   II. Series.
BR232.O47   1994
949.5'013 — dc20   93–42841
                                                            CIP

For Alice

Contents

Acknowledgments

This book has two beginnings. It was initially conceived as part of my dissertation, which was to be a study of the effects of seventh-century political collapse on imperial thought and institutions. As dissertations usually do, my dissertation fell far short of this grand design. Indeed, I found that the internal disorder of the first decade was a sufficient challenge. The study of that tumultuous decade now published, I have moved on to mid-century, and the reactions to the first shock of the Persian and Arab invasions. I hope to complete yet a third volume, on the institutional reaction to the Arab invasions and its implications for the Iconoclast controversy.

The second source from which this book springs is an NEH seminar organized by Professor Louis Feldman at Yeshiva University. There, I worked on the classical roots of Christian ethnography and its application to the problem of the anti-Jewish dialogues. Indeed, this book is in one sense the sequel to the pre-Constantinian material that I studied in New York. I am now working on Christian ethnography in pre-Constantinian Christianity, before the Romans emerged as the Christian "race."

I would like to thank the American Council of Learned Societies and the National Endowment for the Humanities, which supported much of the research for this book.

I have been fortunate to have Professor Walter E. Kaegi, Jr., as my advisor. He was my most exacting reader and most valuable critic. My work follows in his wake, and it is to his seminal article, "Initial Byzantine Reactions to the Arab Invasions," that I owe the inspiration for this work. I hope it measures up to the standards of his scholarship.

I extend my deepest gratitude to Professor Louis Feldman, under whose invaluable direction and critical eye I researched much of the material for the first and last chapters. He was ever giving of his time, extensive knowledge, and encouragement. I also owe a debt of gratitude to the participants in the NEH seminar, in particular Professors Frederick Krantz, Thomas Renna, and W. Barnes Tatum, who contributed greatly to this volume through their searching examination of my logic and their all-too-common discovery of its weaknesses.

The always insightful and incisive suggestions and criticisms of Professors Steven Bowman, George Dennis, and John Fine helped refine and improve the book. Its publication would not have been possible without them. And I would also like to thank Professor Mark Summers, whose demands for clarification and clarity compelled me to explain many things that I took for granted and assumed the readers would.

Last, but certainly not least, I would like to thank Professor Alice Christ. It was her misfortune and my good fortune to have had her as a captive audience for rambling discourses on seventh-century literature and confused initial drafts. In both cases, she not only listened and read, but often brought order to their confusion. Much of my argumentation was shaped by conversations with her.

These scholars have made my research far easier than it would have been had their help not been forthcoming and unstinting. What they have not contributed are its weaknesses. For those, I alone am responsible.

Abbreviations

AB	*Analecta Bollandiana*
Byz	*Byzantion*
Byzsl	*Byzantinoslavica*
BZ	*Byzantinische Zeitschrift*
DOP	*Dumbarton Oaks Papers*
FHG	*Fragmenta Historicorum Graecorum,* ed. C. Mueller (Paris, 1841–70).
JoeB	*Jahrbuch der oesterreichischen Byzantinistik*
PG	*Patrologia Graeca*
PO	*Patrologia Orientalis*
REB	*Revue des études byzantines*
ROC	*Revue de l'Orient Chrétien*

Introduction

Defeat and disaster seem to inspire witnesses to weave a historical pattern to explain them. And often this explanation is their contemporaries' only solace for failed hopes. From the bad luck that plagued Thucydides' Athens to the divine will that brought the Goths to Augustine's Rome, writers have created for themselves and their audiences historical schemes to give order to a world turned upside down and perhaps to offer some reassurance to the bewildered. And few disasters have called forth a greater effort to construct a fragile historical vision of order than the collapse of the Roman Empire in the East during the seventh century.

The Roman Empire in the year 600, buffeted by barbarian invasions and blighted with institutional rot, yet remained the most powerful realm of Europe. Justinian's conquests in Africa, Italy, and Spain had made the Mediterranean a Roman lake; Roman arms contested the Danube with Slavs and Avars; and in 590, the Persians, falling into civil war, made a peace that favored New Rome. The Constantinopolitan court retained many of its Latin roots; Augustus, not *basileus,* was the official imperial title; and a generation earlier the poet Corippus had written panegyrics in the language of Pliny and Claudian. The court's Christianity was challenged not by the pope, who had come to Constantinople to preside over the Fifth Ecumenical Council in 553, but by dissidents of still Christian Syria and Egypt.

Within a generation, as shocked and demoralized east Rome lurched from one defeat to another, the imperial order collapsed. By 650, Jerusalem, the pilgrimage center of Christianity, had been twice conquered by infidels (Persians and Arabs); the Levant, the Balkans, and Spain were lost; Italy and Africa nearly were lost; and Latin and Greek orthodoxy embarked on the roads that ultimately divided them. By 700, the empire emerged as a rump holding Asia Minor, Constantinople, a bit of Thrace, a few coastal fortresses in Europe, and a swiftly contracting area of Italy. Little wonder that later chroniclers imagined that the first imperial victim of the Arab conquests, Heraclius, went insane.[1]

So revolutionary were the social and political changes that followed the Arab invasions that scholars have baptized this truncated empire the Byzantine to distinguish it from the late Roman. But the Byzantines never ceased to think of themselves as Romans, nor of their empire as the empire of Augustus, which, as God's chosen instrument, had held universal, invincible rule for more than half a millenium. But as disasters mounted, a dilemma arose that engaged the Byzantines to the very end. Roman imperial rhetoric, drawn from Christian and classical sources, asserted that God's love and favor for the empire was demonstrated through victory. The reality of defeat painfully exposed this rhetoric's emptiness, but to abandon it was to abandon Christian claims to God's favor. Caught between obsolete rhetoric and inexplicable disasters, seventh-century authors required a new imperial rhetoric that could assure readers that God's favor had not been lost and explain how God would set imperial history, momentarily diverted, back on its hegemonic course.

Contemporaries constructed their answer with the rhetoric of older genres: martyrdom, apocalyptic, and Old Testament prophecies. Out of these arose a new imperial redemptive cycle of sin, punishment, repentance, and restoration. Defeat became God's chastisement of an erring but beloved people, and restoration, the result of divine forgiveness. Such rhetoric was hardly original; the Jews had long used it to assert their own eventual political restoration. What this book investigates is how the Byzantines transferred sin and restoration to an imperial context for the first time in Christian literature, and how its translation from one social, literary, and cultural context to another became the foundation of a new Byzantine historical self-definition that survived until the very end.

Scholarship has, however, largely ignored this literary and cultural transformation because of the still powerful influence of two nineteenth-century scholars, Karl Krumbacher and Adolf Harnack, whose interpretive frameworks still define for many scholars the historical and literary contexts of seventh-century Byzantine literature and in particular the anti-Jewish dialogues. Krumbacher and Harnack, in different ways, assumed two basic dichotomies in late Roman culture: one between Christian and classical literature and genres, and a second between Christian religious discourse and Roman political discourse. The first two chapters of this book illustrate how deeply rooted are these assumptions in modern scholarship, and how flawed.

In the next three chapters, I will examine the interweaving of Christian and classical genres and religious and political discourse in seventh-century literature. Genres as diverse as the panegyrics of the court poet George of

Pisidia and the homiletic corpus of the Patriarch Sophronius of Jerusalem reveal an obsession with imperial collapse that is not bounded or defined by genre but which shapes political and religious discourse. Their response to disaster inextricably binds religion and politics in framing a response to an immediate political and social crisis, a literary response that we can broadly (and without negative connotations) call apologetic.

The last three chapters examine the explosion of anti-Jewish texts in the seventh century in the light of this broader cultural response to crisis. These works constitute a sizable portion of the extant seventh-century Greek sources, and their prominence implies a significance beyond the narrow focus of Judeo-Christian social and theological conflict. In fact, these works reveal how this most "Christian" genre adhered to the same thematic complex of political and historical apologetic for Christian Roman defeat as other literary genres.

Were the anti-Jewish dialogues chosen as a vehicle to convey the political apologetic message of Christian Roman restoration? Other than *Jacob the Newly Baptized*, they addressed intra-Christian social and political issues. More importantly, they used the Jew as a rhetorical device to personify the doubts within their own community with a recognizable, evil, and most important, eminently defeatable, opponent. For this reason, the Jews' place in Christian society had relatively little to do with their sudden prominence in seventh-century literature. On the contrary, the imagined Jew represented something for Christian contemporaries that fit well into a new pattern of apologetic.

Note

1. Nicephorus, *Breviarium,* ed. C. deBoor (Leipzig, 1880), 25; cf. G. Ostrogorsky, *History of the Byzantine State,* 3d ed., trans. J. Hussey (New Brunswick, 1969), 111.

1. Politics and Theology: The Anachronism of Modern Scholarship

The Sources of Christian Doubt

The Syrian Melkite historian Agapius reported that in the year 593, the eleventh year of the emperor Maurice, an Antiochene Jew rented a Christian's house, and finding a Virgin icon, urinated on it. In the resulting uproar, the Jews were expelled from the city.[1] Twenty or thirty years later, the anonymous *Miracle of Berytus* told a similar tale, but with a very different ending. This time, the Jew renting a Christian's house found a Christ icon, upon which he and his fellow Jews reenacted the crucifixion. But when the Jews pierced Christ's side, the icon bled, a miracle that persuaded them to convert.[2]

What motivated the anonymous author to rework the Jews' expulsion into conversion?[3] The answer lies in *Miracle*'s paradoxical revelation of Christ's strength from seeming weakness. The injuries that the Jews inflicted on Christ called forth his power and were the very means by which they were forced to concede defeat. "Struck, he received all those who witnessed [his] powers and his amazing miracles."[4] The Jews' conversion confirmed that Christ needed no human allies to expel his enemies; he defended himself by turning the outrages of his enemies against themselves.

Miracle's assurance that Christ could redress infidel outrages was self-conscious, a direct response to a military, political, and spiritual crisis within eastern Christendom. Even as *Miracle* was being written, infidel Slavs, Avars, Persians, and Arabs not only desecrated Christ's icons but also burnt his churches, murdered his clergy and faithful, sacked his cities, and trampled on his "God-beloved" empire.[5] But Christ's victory over the Jews in *Miracle* held out hope of victory over these "others" as well, for the Jew personified all infidels. The Jew's defeat was a "refutation of every unbelieving infidel," and a "confirmation of those who have believed in [Christ] in the truth."[6]

But even such works as *Miracle* could not pacify its audience for long.

As heathen victories mounted, patience waned in the ravaged provinces. Some began to wonder why, if Christ's power was so great, he withheld it from his sorely oppressed followers. Some Christians began to worry that perhaps it was Christ's power, not his weakness, that was the mirage. A seed of doubt was planted, and a shrill note of desperation began to enter the sources as Christian authors tried to confront it.[7]

Some today might find it strange that Christians would measure Christ's power by his followers' material successes and reverses. But as A. D. Nock explained sixty years ago about the late antique religious sensibility, "*Sotereia* and kindred words carried no theological implications; they applied to deliverance from perils by sea and land and disease and darkness and false opinions."[8] Nock rightly recognized that material well-being was one of religion's prime concerns, but he failed to distinguish his own modern definition of abstract theology from theology in late antiquity. It would be far more accurate to say that protection from material peril was a theological subject. Christians and pagans were scrupulous judges of a god's powers; claims of Christ's material power fill early Christian literature. Men sought, as Peter Brown wrote, "where exactly this 'divine power' was to be found on earth and, consequently, on what terms access to it could be achieved."[9] Such power was needed to confront a nasty and brutish world, to gain "powers over the demons, and so over the diseases, the bad weather, the manifest disorders of a material world ruled by demons."[10] Christians saw Christ's will in every material accident and expected the power behind that will to be exercised on their behalf. This conjunction of natural and supernatural led them to seek divine causes for material events, and to expect divine resolution of material disasters. Just as uninterrupted victory confirmed Christ's power, unrelieved defeat raised doubts precisely because religion encompassed politics and history.

For this reason, "religious" as well as "secular" writings exhibit the same social, political, and psychological symptoms of defeat. The *Miracles of St. Demetrius,* written around 615–20 by John, the archbishop of Thessalonica, offers a sad testament to the city's futile requests for aid and to imperial impotence.[11] A generation earlier, Roman soldiers had held the Danube against Avars, Bulgars, and Slavs. Now John narrated how Christ's soldier Demetrius alone held them at bay. This was unusual—demons, not barbarians, were a saint's traditional opponents. But Demetrius's preoccupation with barbarians was an understandable concession to seventh-century conditions.[12]

This record of imperial collapse, barbarian threats, famine, and plague makes for depressing reading. It is painfully clear that its audience found bare survival miraculous. Bewildered, John's flock asked why they were subjected to an "all-consuming, all-destroying plague, transgressing beyond measure, by its abundance of evil, any previous lesson that God has sent." John could only answer, "Our provocations are worse; for if we are subjected to a punishment that causes us innumerable sufferings, still we do not have a punishment equal to our sin."[13] The only way to regain divine favor and restore the past would be "if one turns to repentance and admission of sin, and . . . lives a virtuous and Christ-loving way of life."[14]

But even John was forced to concede that divine punishments made some despair rather than repent:

> For the soul, weakened and suffering with various and assorted ills of the body, [at first] made ardent with the memory of God, ultimately becomes increasingly weaker in the faith, and falls, from a feeling of frustration into anger, even uttering and murmuring abominations against [God], the one giving him instruction, as the prophet says, "in judgment and not in wrath."[15]

The admission that for many God's pedagogy was too severe reveals all too clearly the mood at Thessalonica.[16] It was typical that *Miracles*'s continuator judged John's death just before an earthquake as an indication of God's singular favor; one's best hope was to die undisturbed.[17]

Thessalonians could at least take solace that God preserved them from the barbarians. Jerusalem was not so lucky. Antiochus Monachus, whose *Fall of Jerusalem to the Persians in 614* recorded the siege, fall, and sack of the city, was even more explicit than John about the corrosive effects of defeat on Christian morale:

> For the devil stands and tempts your hearts . . . and says to you, "Oh Christians, how you err and fool yourselves; for Christ has washed his hands of you and ignored you. . . . For you are hated by him and are his enemies, not his friends; for did he not aid your enemies and strengthen them more than you, and strip you of your armour, and take away from you his protection?"[18]

Defeat meant Christ had failed to protect his faithful, and at least some Christians concluded that weakness was the reason. Thus, we should not be surprised to hear from Antiochus that "a few weak-minded" Christians renounced Christ.[19]

Defeat not only tested a Christian's faith, but also led many to test their neighbors'. Maximus the Confessor's fanatical defense of Dyotheletism accompanied the conviction that the emperor's Monotheletism ensured defeat. Theological debate over Christ's energies and wills also urged either imperial unity or schism between Rome and Constantinople when the empire desperately confronted foreign invaders. Brought to trial, Maximus claimed that he was persecuted for his belief; his opponents asserted that he was prosecuted for treason.[20]

Maximus's defense may have been disingenuous. He was after all acutely aware that religious dissent, especially during the current crisis, was a political act with political consequences: "And now, for our sins, it is a time in which blood flows, but it is not a time for arguing about creeds! And it is a time of powerful sorrows sent from the frowning countenance of God, but not for sophistic squabbles that are more annoying troubles for ourselves."[21] Naturally, Maximus judged his opponents "squabblers," but he well understood that doctrinal debate did not take place in an intellectual vacuum. For both Maximus and his opponents, politics and religion were inextricable, and it was their entanglement that made Maximus doctrinally intransigent and politically dangerous.

Defeat left its mark not only on genres like *Miracula* or historical narratives, but also on genres that had been rare in the Christian Empire's triumphal centuries. Apocalypses, for example, suddenly flowered as authors sought literary vehicles that would allow them to place defeat into a comprehensible context and restore hope in the conquered Christian communities.

The mid-century Syrian author of the *Apocalypse of Pseudo-Methodius* knew the problem: "Why does God allow the faithful to undergo these trials?"[22] An answer was needed quickly because "all those weak in the faith [became] manifest and voluntarily separate[d] themselves from the holy churches."[23] The very mention of apostasy reveals the social as well as religious strain on provincial Christians. But the apocalyptic genre permitted the author to transform defeat and apostasy from an admission of Christian weakness into a divine plan wherein "the faithful will appear and the unfaithful become manifest, the wheat separated from the chaff; for this time is a fire of trial."[24] The explanation was not convincing for long; future glory could not compete with present disaster. Islam's victory demonstrated its truth and removed one of Christianity's most persuasive arguments, the social and political stability of the imperial order. By the ninth century, as the hope of imperial restoration died, so did many Christian communities of the Levant.

These diverse sources share two mutually dependent themes: a response to defeat and a defense of Christianity. Where the empire receded, the defense failed, revealing a faith so integrated into the intellectual, social, and political fabric of the imperial system that it could not survive its fall. Our task is to investigate the interweaving of Christianity and the imperial ideal as well as to explore the imperial Christian responses to political collapse and the challenge to Christianity's integrity.

On the whole, scholars have ignored the close ties that bind the political integrity of the empire and the religious integrity of Christianity. Some scholars even deny any integration of the religious and the political. This reluctance to see late antiquity in its own terms can be traced to the influence of two nineteenth-century scholars, Karl Krumbacher and Adolf Harnack, who shared the belief that Christianity enjoyed a spiritual autonomy that freed it from the profane influences of its late-classical cultural and, especially, political contexts.

Krumbacher: The Conflict of Christian and Classical

Karl Krumbacher's encyclopaedic *Geschichte der byzantinischen Literatur,* one of the great works of Byzantine scholarship, proposed that the period from Christianity's fourth-century victory to the Roman order's seventh-century collapse was "the time of the final struggle of the ancient Roman-Hellenistic spirit [*Geist*] with the medieval Christian-Byzantine spirit," a "transition period" in which the "Christian-theological" spirit of belief overcame the profane Hellenic to create an ideological "synthesis."[25] Simple and devout Christianity, impregnated by pagan Hellenism, produced a literature that inherited the one's profane, classical sophistication, but retained the other's anti-classical spirituality. With the culture thus divided, religion naturally fell to Christianity, politics to the classics. Typically, Krumbacher named the pagan Diocletian as the founder of Byzantine politics, whose spirit, so opposed to Christianity's, embraced "court intrigue, fawning cunning," and "ruthless cruelty and lust."[26]

One hundred years later, this conflict model still dominates the field.[27] Although far more sophisticated than Krumbacher's, Averil Cameron's interpretation of Byzantine culture rests on the same ideological conflict between the pagan classical and Christian. Christian literature did not "copy from, derive from or develop from classical forms."[28] Indeed, Christians rejected classical culture as they strove to create a literature purified of the tainted pagan ideology of the classical educational system.[29]

Only in the sixth century did Christian ideology enter pagan "classical" contexts; only in the seventh did George of Pisidia and Theophylact Simocatta, "in their clumsy way, [reach] a synthesis of contemporary Christian thinking and their classical heritage." Christianity triumphed "as the 'Roman' side of imperial ideology fell away," and "it became more normal for literary works of the highest level to express the Christian modes of thought."[30] The result of this process was the creation of a culture "based firmly on a unitary Christian world-view."[31] Profane classicism had its eye firmly on the material world; now spiritual or religious Christianity looked to the world beyond.

This perceived conflict of Christian and classical "modes of thought" has influenced not only the study of literature, but also the study of the political culture. Otto Treitinger, author of the most thorough study of Byzantine ceremonial, *Die ostroemische Kaiser- und Reichsidee,* examined Byzantine political culture through Krumbacher's dialectical prism. He saw a shift from a Roman ideology that exalted worldly power with military pomp, to a Christian ideology that exalted otherworldly power with liturgical pomp,[32] an evolution that illustrated "the power of the medieval soul at work that . . . reached for the Idea."[33]

Sixty years later, Michael McCormick's work on Byzantine ceremonial has not challenged Treitinger's dialectical model. He endows pagan Roman political culture with almost Machiavellian indifference to religion, but Byzantine political culture with sincere faith. Roman triumphs, purification rites, liturgies of the prosecution of war and the celebration of peace, were mere forms whose "religious significance had come to be eclipsed by its political value."[34] The rational Romans, forebears of the believing Byzantines, transcended religion. "The archaic sacral element of the triumph continued to be dominated and subsumed into its political dimension."[35] On the other hand, Christian Roman imperial ceremonies like victory celebrations, often structurally and thematically indistinguishable from their Roman predecessors, possess a new and distinct religious ethos.[36]

This nineteenth-century cultural conflict model, whether in a literary or political context, divides Byzantine culture into categories that designate "classical" sources for the study of political history and formal rhetoric, and relegate "Christian" sources to the study of spirituality and the devout expression of belief. But although Byzantine culture arose from diverse sources, it remained internally unified. What lends Byzantine literature its fascination is precisely the amalgam of Christian and classical, religion and politics, that all sources display.

As H. I. Marrou wrote, "Christianity is first and foremost a religion, . . . not a cultural ideal,"[37] and Christians and pagans differed little about what defined culture. For both, the term *paideia* meant not simply culture, but the education that distinguished the cultured. This education was almost exclusively rhetorical and literary; students learned to compose by following detailed outlines for well-defined genres, and by arranging citations, allusions and clichés from the classics, called *topoi*, that had been painstakingly memorized.[38] This compositional method of *mimēsis*, or imitation, produced a highly stylized, often artificial literature. Authors preferred to display their erudition by literary and rhetorical ornamentation, often to the detriment of accuracy or even truth, and a modern reader must be cautious about accepting such literature at face value.[39]

Yet despite its formalism, late antique literature possessed considerable flexibility. Authors adroitly manipulated genre and cliché to achieve very different thematic goals with very similar literary elements. Political themes were especially prominent, if not dominant; as Herbert Hunger wrote, "Rhetoric seems to have had its strongest foundation in its political role."[40] Pagans and Christians both manipulated the thousand-year mimetic tradition to meet contemporary political needs, constantly reinterpreting it to create what Hans-Georg Beck has called a "political theology."[41] Politics to the Byzantines, however, was something very different than for us moderns. They had little interest in institutions or theory; the study of politics (and history) concerned the moral causes of events and the character of historical actors.[42] For this reason, panegyric and invective dominated political rhetoric, and histories often tell us more about the virtues and vices than the legislation or reforms of a general or emperor.

Far from rejecting the classical foundations of late antique culture, Christians embraced them. From the pedantry of Justin Martyr to the graceful baroque style of Gregory of Nyssa, Christians shared *paideia* (in both senses) with pagans.[43] Even those Christians who complained most bitterly about the dangers of studying the classics relied on the thesaurus of classical education for their denunciation. The Apologists' claim of "Christian simplicity" was itself an allusion to Socrates' *Apology* and was itself a *topos*, employed to fit their apologetic needs.[44] After Constantine, when imperial and aristocratic patronage might have created an alternative educational system, Christians made no attempt to do so. Instead, they attempted to integrate Christian "classics" (like the Bible or Church Fathers) into the curriculum with Homer and Demosthenes.[45] Assimilation, not conflict, guided Christianity's relationship with the classics.

The victory of Christianity brought new "classics" into the classical tradition, but it did not radically alter the direction of late-antique literary evolution. Of course, Byzantine authors enjoyed the conceit that they perfectly reproduced their models, and modern scholars, as Cyril Mango has explained, "always on the look out for classical survivals, . . . inevitably fall into the trap that the Byzantine texts have set for them."[46] Late classical literature, despite its mimetic roots, was never static, and its evolution affected Christians as much as pagans. Literature in the Christian empire preserved the bonds of unity with the pagan past: the fourth-century panegyrics of the pagan Claudian have more in common with the sixth- and seventh-century panegyrics of the Christians Corippus and George of Pisidia than with those of the second-century pagans Dio, Pliny, or Aristides;[47] the fourth-century history of the pagan Ammianus has more in common with the sixth-century histories of the Christians Procopius and Agathias than with Thucydides.[48] Even genres closely identified with Christianity shared the thematic concerns that had evolved from earlier pagan authors: the third-century biographies of the pagans Diogenes Laertes and Porphyry share more themes with the fourth-century hagiography of the Patriarch Athanasius than with the *Lives* of the second-century pagan Plutarch;[49] and the fifth-century pagan historian Zosimus is best compared with the church historians.[50] Christianity was not a break in continuity, but a watershed in development.

Christians also embraced the mimetic aesthetic that informed all late-antique literature. By the sixth century, church history and hagiography had evolved generic qualities like the genres of history and biography. The church historians who succeeded the fourth-century bishop Eusebius made few changes in his juxtaposition of imperial and ecclesiastical historical narrative;[51] hagiography evolved into a sometimes repetitive string of miracles, prefaced with a narrative of the saint's youth and concluding with the saint's edifying last words and a doxology.[52]

Christianity also inherited the political rhetoric and perspective of the pagan past. When the third-century A.D. pagan Menander Rhetor outlined the proper panegyrical form, Christians and pagans alike followed his directions. Eusebius, who founded Christian panegyric, felt no hesitation about using the vocabulary of Hellenistic kingship for Constantine, Christ's chosen.[53] Bishops did not hesitate to praise emperors as a "new David" and a "new Augustus" simultaneously, or to wish them "eternal reigns" in the tradition of deified Augusti.[54] Especially at court, bishops raided the classical rhetorical thesaurus to promote their interests. For many, like Cyril of Alexandria, the defense of orthodoxy was never far removed from the more mundane pursuit of power and influence.[55]

The idea of a cultural conflict that divides Christian from classical is anachronistic. Through *paideia* Christians and pagans shared a common, but dynamic and evolving, literary tradition and culture. As culture and literary tradition evolved, the meaning of *topoi,* both Christian and classical, also evolved. There should be nothing surprising about this. "Liberal" and "conservative" have been basic *topoi* of American political rhetoric since the Second World War, but their meaning varies with the historical context; liberalism in 1962 meant something very different than in 1992.

Nonetheless, the conservatism of the Byzantine mimetic style made topical themes like imperial collapse or Christian apostasy difficult to introduce into well-defined genres. Consequently, stretched beyond its generic limits, much of Byzantine literature displays a literary tension that Krumbacher's successors view as an ideological struggle between Christian and classical cultural elements. But "Christian" genres exhibit this tension just as much as "classical" precisely because it arose out of a shared literary culture and socio-political context.

Thus, when Arab victory compromised Christianity, the Byzantines, guided by their literary training, turned increasingly to genres that already possessed an apologetic apparatus. Apocalyptic became popular; the anti-Jewish dialogue became perhaps even more popular. At first, this seems an odd choice. Monotonous, generic arguments over the virgin birth or Christ's divinity are banal and easy to dismiss.[56] And the dialogues' seeming goal — often made explicit, but by their nature always implicit — was to convert or refute Jews, not address the Arab invasions.

In fact, the dialogues make no effort to convert Jews. One monk even mocked the Jews, "I have no desire to make you all Christians; in fact, I cannot do so, but I can make you bad Jews."[57] Nor were the dialogues designed to refute Jewish attacks so much as to convince Christian audiences that "we are 'prepared' and 'anxious' to 'make a defense to *all* who question us about the cause of the hope that is in us [1 Peter 3:15].'"[58] As one author explained, "Our discourse is not to Jews alone, but to every sort who does not believe in Christ."[59] As in *Miracle of Berytus,* the Jew is no simple theological opponent but a witness to Christ's power and Christian superiority, a proxy for those whose argument was victory.

Nor can the dialogues' claim to seek "the improvement of our Christian faith and the refutation of Jewish slanders and blasphemies,"[60] mask

Christian anxiety over the *Arab* threat. As one monk, confronted with the fact of Christian defeats, responded: "I, enslaved, oppressed and murdered, condemned to many punishments, have not denied my God. And if some Christians have denied him, they are not as many as you [Jews] have had apostasize, even though you are not being murdered for being Christian."[61] An admission of Christian apostasy is rare; more revealing is that apostates clearly were *not* converting to Judaism. The claim that although less perse-cuted—an obvious reference to the Arabs—more Jews than Christians apostasized implies *both* were turning to Islam. Confronted by this threat, authors reminded their readers, "Those who guard the Christians' com-mandments are alone Christians, those who do not, do not deserve the name."[62]

The dialogues' insulting tone toward Jews and Judaism, and the patent artificiality of Jewish characters and arguments, suggest strongly that the authors had little interest in converting Jews. On the contrary, the response to defeat that dominates all seventh-century literature so dominates these dialogues that one must doubt whether they were intended to address Jews or their objections at all. When seen in their socio-political context, these dialogues offer views of Byzantine social and psychological reaction to defeat, not a record of Judeo-Christian debate. Christians had often ad-dressed works intended for a Christian audience to non-Christians: *Apolo-gies* to emperors who were never meant to read them, or responses to authors long dead. A parallel case should be made for the dialogues.

But scholars, laboring under an assumed dichotomy of Christian and classical culture, have accepted unquestioningly the dialogues' generic claims. They have devalued historical context to mere background to a theological debate, not a means of understanding the authors' motivation or the dialogues' thematic thrust. M. Waegemann's recent analysis of *Tro-phies of Damascus* typifies this determination to fix the anti-Jewish dialogues within their narrow literal bounds: "The *Trophies of Damascus* is written at the moment when a great number of Christians were converting to Islam, and the church was divided over the question of iconoclasm. All this made Judaism a redoubtable rival."[63] Why should Islam's success, or more, the conversion of Christians to Islam, make *Judaism* a more redoubtable rival to Christianity? Why, when Islam, not Judaism, undercut Christianity, did no Greek anti-Islamic work appear until the mid-eighth century, while the seventh century saw a flood of anti-Jewish works? Scholars have ignored such questions partly because an assumed conflict between classical and Christian has obscured the social and political themes that unify Byzantine literature. But a second assumption has also prevented them from setting works considered Christian, in our case, anti-Jewish dialogues, into their proper historical contexts. It is to this assumption that we now turn.

Harnack: The Dichotomy of Religion and Politics

Adolf Harnack, who founded modern historical study of Christianity, saw theology as the source of Christian dynamism, and the historical study of Christianity as the study of theology, or "history of dogma." But theology for Harnack was not the same as for the ancients. As we have seen, late-antique theology devoted much attention to a deity's care for the body, perhaps even more than to its care for the soul. But Harnack, wishing to raise spiritual Christianity above inferior materialist pagan competitors, used a nineteenth-century definition of theology to distinguish them. Christianity had a "rational" theology; "in fact only by this means did [it] expect to make an impression on [the] audience."[64] Christianity addressed morality and salvation; failed paganism addressed politics and other mundane topics. When early Christian authors incorporated worldly themes, Harnack dismissed such writings as "apologetic rhetoric," a superficial concession to a pagan audience's taste, divorced from the true religious sensibility of Christianity.[65]

When Harnack read the anti-Jewish dialogues, he saw at once the gap between their generic claims and their contrived, straw-man portrayal of the Jews. To resolve this paradox, he first demonstrated that the theology of the dialogues was no different than that of contemporary Christian literature which made no claims to refute Jews. Harnack determined the audience from the theology that the author used. A "gentile" theology must have been written for a gentile audience; a "Jewish" theology would have been employed to appeal to Jews.[66] Harnack further argued that this theologically inaccurate portrait of Jews proved that Christians had no social contact with them; otherwise, Christians would not have represented them so poorly. But if Jews and gentiles were so estranged, why should a Jew appear at all? Harnack answered that the Jew was a rhetorical device, that he was "the Jew as the Christians feared him."[67] It was no Jewish challenge, theological or otherwise, that dictated the choice of a Jew, but the Jew's rhetorical usefulness in conveying a "rational," "gentile," theology.

Harnack's assumptions about the nature of Christianity have defined its study up to today. Modern scholars might reject Harnack's solution to the problem of the anti-Jewish dialogue, but many have accepted his anachronistic view of early Christian theology, and even intensified the division between theology (in Harnack's sense) and its secular (especially political) context. Equally important, they inherited his distaste for and dismissal of topical apologetic as an obtrusion of social and political concerns into the Christian realm of religion.

Harnack's influence on the analysis of seventh-century dialogues is immediately apparent in A. C. McGiffert's nineteenth-century edition and commentary of *Dispute of the Jews Papiscus and Philo with Some Monk*. He also saw Jews as straw men, and the Christians' true opponent as "not the Jew, but the unbeliever in general, as the Christian imagines him." Thus, the dialogue did not aim to refute Jews, "but the whole non-Christian world . . . for the confirmation of the faith."[68] But while Harnack, analyzing pre-Constantinian dialogues, could point to a hostile pagan environment that made confirmation (and refutation) necessary, McGiffert denied that heathens threatened Christianity by the seventh century.[69] He simply ignored the Arab and Persian invasions because secular history had no place in Christian discourse. "Only when Christianity had history behind it, could it make use of that history as a [prophetic] argument."[70]

In the 1930s, Lukyn Williams, who wrote the first survey of anti-Jewish literature, and Amos Hulen, who first studied the seventh-century *Debate of Saint Gregentius with the Jew Herbanus,* disagreed with Harnack about the dialogues' purpose and audience. Whereas Harnack had understood the dialogues' Jews to be rhetorical devices employed to make the arguments more persuasive, Hulen and Williams insisted that the dialogues' Jews were historical, recorded literally in order to be refuted.[71] For Harnack, the dialogues' "gentile" theology indicated no Jewish theological threat and thus Jewish social insignificance; for Williams and Hulen, the dialogues' "Jewish" theology indicated a Jewish theological threat and thus Jewish social aggression. But Williams's and Hulen's distinctive "Jewish" themes in Christian literature — a defense of the Incarnation, and the refutation of Jewish claims to Old Testament restoration prophecy[72] — are prominent throughout early Christian literature, anti-Jewish or not.[73] Thus Hulen could only declare the prophetic argument "Jewish" because it appeared in a dialogue, but McGiffert, with equal logic, could declare it "gentile" because it appeared throughout early Christian literature.[74]

But the argument for "Jewish" theology in the dialogues is circular. The Jewish characters' theology makes them historical; their historicity guarantees the theology's authenticity.[75] But what else, Hulen and Williams asked, could explain the dialogues? "It [is] evident that the Christian apologists were not making a needless display of their eloquence."[76] But they could offer no other explanation for Jewish characters or references to Jews than that the authors were "those who had Jews around them," and "feared the influence of Jews on others, if not on themselves."[77]

They could imagine no other reason for anti-Jewish dialogues because their literal interpretation retained Harnack's assumptions about the nature of Christianity, including his anachronistic exclusion of politics from the realm of religion. Hulen could identify Christian claims to Old Testament imperial restoration prophecies as a central theme of *Gregentius,* but he could neither integrate this theme into a historical context—the Persian and Arab invasions—that transcended the Jews, nor set *Gregentius*'s obsession with political restoration in the context of seventh-century literature.[78]

Hulen and Williams disagreed not with Harnack's assumptions about the nature of Christian literature, but with his failure to accept the dialogues as literal, albeit biased, records of Judeo-Christian theological debate. Their contemporary James Parkes went one step further to assert that they were literal records of Jewish–Christian social relations as well.[79] Parkes insisted that although the Jews of the seventh-century dialogues were "dummy figures,"[80] the dialogues remained "serious intellectual argument devoted either to converting the Jew, or at least to confirming the faith of the Christian [against the Jews]."[81] At times, this literal reading of the dialogues approaches the absurd. Of one "dialogue" (where the Jew never speaks), Parkes insisted, "Though the Jew never appears or produces any arguments, the author gives every appearance of having real Jews in mind in writing."[82]

Parkes's literalism did not lead him to abandon Harnack's separation of religion and historical context; that went no further than the material conditions of a theological debate (in Harnack's sense). When he found causes for the seventh-century popularity of anti-Jewish texts — "increasing severity of Byzantine legislation," "religious fanaticism of the oriental monastic orders," and "the political situation caused by the Persian War" — he maintained that the last could never inspire religious texts. "The political cause is secondary and the result of the first two causes, both of which are in their nature religious."[83] His perspective made it impossible for him to imagine that political tensions could achieve theological expression, and thus redefine the Jew as literary symbol or social target. Typically, he read a Jew's gloating recital of Christian defeats in the *Trophies of Damascus* as nothing more than a rhetorical flourish in an eschatological debate; a quibble that messianic peace had not arrived.[84] Without doubt, eschatology was a popular seventh-century theological topic, but as we have seen, seventh-century eschatology was inextricably tied to its social and political context.

At the end of the 1940s, Marcel Simon insisted even more than Parkes that anti-Jewish works aimed "to demonstrate from scripture the truth of Christianity, and by the same means to refute the claims of Judaism."[85] He denied the possibility that such texts might address intra-Christian political or social concerns. Employing Parkes's literalism and Harnack's separation of historical context and religion, Simon asserted that mundane politics could not intrude on anti-Jewish works because "the question with which we are faced is not one concerning legislation or politics; it concerns primarily a clash of religions."[86] The Roman sack of Jerusalem, a foundation of Eusebius's defense of Christian imperialism, had significance for Simon only as a trump card in the Judeo-Christian debate over the theology of covenants.[87]

Almost a half century after Simon, Robert Wilken lends the destruction of the temple no wider political significance; for him as well, it is only a part of a Judeo-Christian debate over the ritual efficacy of new and old covenants.[88] But for the Christian Romans, the destruction of the temple fit the same theological context of sin and divine retribution as the Persian defeat at Salamis, Cambyses' madness, or the Arab conquests. Thus Wilken judges the restoration of the Jewish temple to be Julian the Apostate's greatest threat to Christianity because it challenged the prophetic claims of Christianity.[89] He ignores Julian's military reputation, his limitation of Christian access to classical education, and his power of political patronage, all of which Christians feared far more.

Wilken has tried to return to the questions about rhetoric first raised by Harnack, but cannot escape Harnack's theological categories. Analyzing Cyril of Alexandria's claim, "the Jews are the most deranged of all men," he asks why Cyril engages in a polemic against Judaism.[90] But Cyril does not attack Judaism, he attacks Jews. His analysis of Chrysostom reveals even more his tendency to credit invective as theology:

> The Christian [rhetorical] language, used with particular reference to the Jews reflects a theological interpretation of Judaism. At times, its themes merge with those of the rhetorical tradition—for example, charging the Jews with immorality. In other places, however, Christian critics of the Jews and Judaizers speak of apostasy, faithlessness, rejection of God, and hardheartedness.[91]

This is no "theological interpretation of Judaism," but an invective against Jews, much of it inherited from the pagans.[92] Chrysostom impressed a

Christian label on much of it, and Wilken, the label of systematic theology on top of that. Like Harnack, Wilken divides his sources into rhetoric and theology in order to divine the "true" Christian message.

Kurt Hruby returned to Harnack's rhetorical method more successfully than Wilken, acknowledging that Christians used "pseudo-theological" rhetoric in the dialogues.[93] With Judaism no longer serious competition for converts,[94] Christians created an "un-Jewish" rhetoric alienated from a Judeo-Christian social or theological context, for a gentile audience with only a limited knowledge of Judaism.[95] But, Hruby continued, even if such Christian invective was "pseudo-theological," it was yet "the product of a theological situation."[96] And like Harnack himself, Hruby could not place this "pseudo-theological" invective in a broad literary or social context. Thus he concluded that anti-Jewish dialogues addressed theological problems that the presence of Jews raised, even if Jews did not raise them. Able to identify the dialogues' Jews as rhetorical constructs, their audience as Christian, and their theology as not directly related to Judeo-Christian debate, his adherence to Harnack's assumptions about context and religion prevented him from reaching the complementary conclusion that the Jews of the dialogues served intra-Christian concerns.

Vincent Déroche has gone even further than Wilken and Hruby in returning to Harnack's initial rhetorical approach to the anti-Jewish works, and so produced the most extensive analysis of seventh-century anti-Jewish literature.[97] For Déroche, the dialogues are fictive[98] and their Jew "a retouched image, an arranged portrait."[99] Recognizing that "rising intolerance" alone could not explain the seventh-century explosion of anti-Jewish literature, he looked to "the changing definition that the Christians held of themselves" for an explanation.[100] It was a crisis of *Christian* self-image "that meant that Jews could no longer be left in the isolation in which the first two centuries of the Christian Empire [had] tried to confine them."[101]

Déroche's logic should lead him toward the evolution of the contemporary Christian self-image as the key to understanding the Christian image of the Jew and use of the anti-Jewish dialogue. But he cannot escape the methodological fiat that the anti-Jewish works' mere existence proves that "these works are not all simple fictions where the Jew would be only a pretext for outlining the internal debates of the church."[102] Thus, Déroche suggests two aims for the dialogues: to address "real debates [with Jews]," and a "tendency toward internal use."[103] He reconciles these by introducing a "Jewish" theological threat, iconoclasm, to bridge Judeo-Christian and intra-Christian debate. The dialogues reflect historical debates with Jews, which at the same time sparked intra-Christian debate over icons.[104]

This elegant solution to the "paradox" of anti-Jewish literature, however, still incorporates the methodological weakness of earlier scholarship. Déroche explains how the Jew was used to define Christian self-image in a period of crisis, yet Harnack's rational theology, the debate over the ritual efficacy of icons, remains the context of that self-definition.[105] Not all seventh-century anti-Jewish tracts mention icons, but all refer to Christian defeat. Ultimately, Déroche fails to look beyond the intellectual and social context of Christianity's relationship with Jews to find an evolution of the Christian self-image. Evidence that defeat lay at the heart of the seventh-century Christian crisis of self-image has no place in his analysis.

Both Harnack and his detractors have assumed that the broadest socio-political question that the dialogues addressed was the relationship of Jews and Christians, and this only because it bore directly on the religious significance of the dialogues. And from Parkes to Déroche, scholars have asked the same question: How to read the dialogues so that their historicity can be preserved?[106] Even as scholars increasingly recognize the value of Harnack's rhetorical analysis, they persistently reject Harnack's conclusions about the dialogues' historicity. Yet they retain Harnack's separation of religion and politics, and so have often devalued socio-political context for the interpretation of this "Christian" literature.

Jews and Christians debated; Jews and Christians had extensive social contacts.[107] But for most Christians, a "Jew" signified much that was not theological in Harnack's sense. I suggest that Byzantine authors constructed an image of the Jew to meet contemporary social needs, and that these needs were not inspired by Jewish–Christian theological debate or social relations. The *Protocols of the Elders of Zion* or Nazi images of the Jew are not mere exaggerations of Jews. The Jew was a rhetorical tool to express gentile social and political obsessions, and we must ask how such fictions fit into the crises that produced these images.

Without doubt, manipulation of the image of the Jew can have horrifying social consequences, but one must first examine the image-makers' own cultural and social obsessions.[108] Perhaps the best examples of how the literary image of the Jew has served the needs of intra-Christian debate are those provided by modern scholars. Some scholars found the Jews a convenient rhetorical device for interdenominational polemic. While Harnack found Jewish oppression of early Christians a fine parallel to Catholic oppression of Protestants,[109] F. Murawski thought the church fathers fair to the Jews because they, like Protestants, deserved their reputation.[110]

Other scholars project obsessions with the Jews onto the past. Wilken's neglect of a broader historical context of Christian literature goes directly to his own theological belief that 'It was the Jews alone who had the capacity to prove Christianity false.'"[111] Williams even planned his book as a theological aid for the conversion or refutation of recalcitrant Jewry.[112] Perhaps his vision of the Jews' aggressiveness stemmed as much from his own missionary experience that "Jews have never been backward in attack" as from the sources.[113] H. Schreckenberg introduced his survey of anti-Jewish literature in the light of the bull *Nostra aetate*.[114] Like Williams, he blames unfortunate attacks on Jews by "Christian theologians, who were certainly not capable of personal hostility against individual Jews," on the Jews' "sometimes aggressively sarcastic anti-Christian apologetic."[115]

Perhaps the most common modern obsession is Christian anti-Semitism. D. Constantelos and J. Alvarez have argued that anti-Jewish polemic is not anti-Semitic because as Constantelos wrote, "The Jews as a people were treated no differently from other people."[116] In contrast, R. Reuther's argument that Christianity planted the "theological roots of anti-Semitism," places indirect responsibility for the Holocaust on Christianity.[117] On the other hand, Schreckenberg's book is in part written to answer those who believe "traditional theological anti-Judaism is at least partly responsible for secular hatred of Jews."[118] Interestingly, Schreckenberg's argument rests on Harnack's separation of secular and religious:[119] "The statement of M. Simon, 'True anti-semitism is theological,' is . . . misguided, because he . . . assumes the existence of a Christian anti-semitism as if this was an independent phenomenon within Christianity, and not, far more, a deprivation of Christianity."[120] Thus Christian anti-Semitism could not exist because Christianity, by its nature religious, could not include a socio-political phenomenon like anti-semitism.[121]

From Harnack to Wilken, scholars have contributed greatly to our understanding of early Christianity, but they continue to privilege modern theology in judging the niceties of theological anti-Semitism and confuse the historical analysis of early Christian polemic against the Jews. What the debate whether early Christian authors were anti-Judaic or anti-Semitic reveals is how modern Christian scholars, like the authors of the anti-Jewish dialogues, have used the image of the Jew to pursue agendas at once social, political and religious.

For seventh-century authors, words spoken by a Jew were more than "rational" theology, for the image of the Jew contained more than the academic tradition's narrow definition of theology. The image of the Jew also held social, political, and racial significance.[122] Classical ethnography identified social and political organization, as well as religion, with race, and theology shared this cultural assumption. For the seventh century, the historical question is not whether early Christianity left a heritage of so-called theological anti-Semitism — a category of investigation that is anachronistic — but how the racial stereotype, unflattering as it is, was used by Christian authors to address their own contemporary social and political problems.

To understand the cultural transformation that the traumas of the seventh century initiated, one must first remove the barriers erected by Krumbacher and his successors against integrating "Christian" literature into its historical context, and then one must break the chain forged by Harnack's successors between the presence of Jews in so-called dialogues and Christian social or religious confrontation with Jews or Jewish theology. The refutation of the Jew was more than the defense of Christianity, it was the assertion of the superiority of the Christian Roman "race." The ad hominem argument that runs through early Christian literature, over which contemporary theologians have agonized, was the foundation not only of a theological refutation of the Jews but also of a racial vindication and political legitimation of the Christian Romans, their religion, and their Empire in a time of crisis.

Four dialogues will command our attention. The first two, *The Dispute of the Jews Papiscus and Philo with Some Monk* and *The Trophies of Damascus*, were Syrian Melkite products, the first from about 650, the second from about 690. Their authors clung desperately to the hope that the empire would return to rescue them from the twin dangers of Moslem domination and Monophysite social pressure. *The Dialogue of St. Gregentius and Herbanus the Jew* is a Jerusalemite product from about 650–80, whose author, disillusioned by defeat and the heresy of the imperial house, began to redefine Christian society outside an imperial framework. Finally, *The Doctrine of Jacob the Newly Baptized*, composed between 634 and the early 640s, is a rare anti-Jewish treatise, one written by a converted Jew for Jews. Its value lies not only in its insight into Jewish life, but also in its theological divergence from the other dialogues, whose artificiality it highlights.

The subject of these dialogues was not Judaism, but Christianity; their aim was theological, but their theology embraced politics. Indeed, for these Christians, the empire was indistinguishable from its religion. Mostly they showed little interest in the Jews except as a rhetorical image to defend the racial and political, as well as religious, legitimacy of Christian Romans: they created a social and political caricature that, like all caricatures, tells more about the author than the subject.

Notes

1. Agapius of Menbidj, *Kitab al-'Unvan,* trans. A. A. Vasiliev (Paris, 1912), [*PO* 8], 438–39; see also John Moschus, *Spiritual Meadow, PG* 87, t.3:2861, for fighting between Christians and Jews.

2. Anonymous, *Sermo de Meracula Beryti, PG* 28: 797–805.

3. Possibly, Agapius's report is itself mythical. See J. Parkes, *The Conflict of Church and Synagogue: A Study in the Origins of Anti-Semitism* (New York, 1979 [1934]), 291–94, for the popularity of "crucified icon" tales in the sixth and seventh centuries. Of course, icons, even when not insulted, could persuade Jews to convert.

4. *Miracle,* col. 801.

5. See P. Alexander, "The Strength of Empire and Capital as Seen through Byzantine Eyes," *Speculum* 37 (1962): 339–57; for the empire as "God-beloved," see O. Treitinger, *Die ostroemische Kaiser- und Reichsidee nach ihrer Gestaltung in hoefischen Zeremoniell* (Darmstadt, 1956 [Jena, 1938]), 158–97. Needless to say, there was nothing particularly Christian about the idea that the gods loved the empire; see W. Ensslin, *Gottkaiser und Kaiser von Gottesgnaden* [Sitzungsberichte der bayerischen Akademie der Wissenschaften, phil. hist. Abt.,] (Munich, 1943), 53–61; H. Hunger, *Prooimion: Elemente der byzantinischen Kaiseridee in den Arengen der Urkunden,* [*Wiener byzantinische Studien* 1] (Vienna, 1964), 63–73. Indeed, the motivation of the persecutors was to avert gods' anger for the Christians' sacrilege and thus avoid disaster; see R. Wilken, "Pagan Criticism of Christianity: Greek Religion and Christian Faith," in *Early Christian Literature and the Classical Intellectual Tradition in Honorem Robert M. Grant,* ed. W. Schoedel and R. Wilken, [*Théologie historique* 54] (Paris, 1979), 122–25. See especially below, Chapter 2.

6. *Miracle,* col. 801.

7. For the literary traces of this psychological tension, see W. E. Kaegi, Jr., "Initial Byzantine Reactions to the Arab Invasions," *Church History* 10 (1969): 139–49; Paul Alexander, *The Byzantine Apocalyptic Tradition* (Berkeley, 1985), 32–33, 61–62, 72–77, 155–58; G. Podskalsky, *Die byzantinische Reichseschatologie* (Munich, 1972), 47–49, 53–56, and especially 70–76; *Apokalypse des Ps.-Methodios,* [*Beitraege zur klassischen Philologie* 83], ed. A. Lolos (Meisenheim am Glan, 1976), 16–22; K. Berger, *Die griechische Daniel-Diegēsis* (Leiden, 1976), 32–39; and especially P. Speck, "Versuch einer Charakterisierung der sogenannten Makedonischen Renaissance," *Les pays du nord et Byzance (Scandanavie et Byzance),* [*Acta universitatis Uppsalensis,* Figura n.s. 19], ed. R. Zeitler (Uppsala, 1981), 239–41. It is instructive to compare the seventh-century Byzantine reaction to disaster with earlier reverses; see W. E. Kaegi, *Byzantium and the Decline of Rome* (Princeton, 1969), esp. 176–223.

8. *Conversion: The Old and New in Religion from Alexander the Great to Augustine of Hippo* (Oxford, 1933), 9.

9. *The Making of Late Antiquity* (Cambridge, 1978), 11.

10. "The Rise and Function of the Holy Man in Late Antiquity," *Society and the Holy in Late Antiquity* (Berkeley, 1982), 106.

11. *Les plus anciens recueils des Miracles de Saint Démétrius,* ed. P. Lemerle, vol.

1 (Paris, 1979); ibid., 102.31, 120.1–4; see 106.6 for the threat of famine, 112.11–20 for the threat of civil war.

12. Ibid., 51.15. See P. Brown, "A Dark Age Crisis: Aspects of the Iconoclast Controversy," *Society and the Holy*, 276–84.

13. Ibid., 76.8–11.

14. Ibid., 70.28–71.7. Earlier writers had also occasionally called barbarian invasions "lessons"; see "Theognis, Bishop of Betelia (+522)," ed. I. van den Gheyn, *AB* 10 (1891): 108, "He taught us through barbarian invasions."

15. Ibid., 76.20–24; see also 149.11–12, for the description of God as pedagogue.

16. See also ibid., 150.18–27, for another response to the problem of God's seemingly insatiable anger.

17. Ibid., 194.10–18.

18. Antiochus Monachus, ed./trans. G. Garitte, *La Prise de Jerusalem par les Perses* [*Corpus scriptorum christianorum orientalium* 203] (Louvain, 1952), ch. 13.65.

19. Ibid., ch. 18.6.

20. For the accusations against Maximus, see his trial notes, *PG* 90, col. 109–29; also J. Haldon, "Ideology and the Byzantine State in the Seventh Century: The 'Trial' of Maximus Confessor," *From Late Antiquity to Early Byzantium*, [*Proceedings of the Byzantinological Symposium in the Sixteenth International Eirene Conference*] (Prague, 1985), 87–91.

21. *Opuscula polemica et theologica*, *PG* 91: 197c.

22. *Die Apokalypse des Ps.-Methodios*, ed. A. Lolos, [*Beitraege zur klassischen Philologie* 83] (Meisenheim am Glan, 1976), 118. Not only are apocalypses conspicuously absent from post-Constantinian Greek literature, but after Eusebius apocalypticism rarely appears in any literary context; see G. Podskalsky, *Byzantinische Reichseschatologie: Die Periodisierung der tausendjaehrigen Weltgeschichte in den vier Grossreichen (Daniel 2 und 7) und dem Friedensreiche (Apok. 20)* (Munich, 1972), 70–76; B. Lewis, "An Apocalyptic Vision of Islamic History," *Bulletin of the School of Oriental and African Studies* 13 (1949–51): 308–38; and S. Brock, "Syriac Views of Emergent Islam," *Studies on the First Century of Islamic Society*, ed. G. H. A. Juynboll (Carbondale, Ill., 1982), 9–21, 199–203. P. Alexander, *The Byzantine Apocalyptic Tradition* (Berkeley, 1985), 151–84, argues Christians adopted an earlier Jewish apocalyptic tradition, but the evidence is drawn almost exclusively from the seventh and later centuries.

23. Ibid., 114. Ibid., 116–18 is explicit that apostates convert to Islam, not Judaism. See also F. J. Martinez, "Eastern Christian Apocalyptic in the Early Islamic Period: Pseudo-Methodius and Pseudo-Athanasius" (Ph.D. diss., Catholic University of America, 1985).

24. Ibid., 118.

25. K. Krumbacher, *Geschichte der byzantinischen Literatur von Justinian bis zum Ende des ostroemischen Reiches (527–1453)*, 2d ed. (Munich, 1897), 5–15, 709–12.

26. Ibid., 7–8.

27. Naturally, Krumbacher's cultural conflict model has not gone unchallenged; see below pp. 9–10 for modern critiques.

28. "New and Old in Christian Literature," *The Seventeenth International Byzantine Congress: Major Papers* (New Rochelle, 1986), 48.

29. Av. Cameron, *Procopius and the Sixth Century* (London, 1985), 23. Cameron explains that they "could free themselves only with difficulty." M. Whitby on the seventh-century historian Theophylact Simocatta is typical. He asserts, in *The Emperor Maurice and his Historian: Theophylact Simocatta on Persian and Balkan Warfare* (Oxford, 1988), 347, that "the biblical allusions, Septuagint and patristic language, and religious stories . . . most accurately reflect the direction of Theophylact's and his audience's interests, not the classical patina." It is much more likely that Theophylact's patrons expected both.

30. "Images of Authority: Elites and Icons in Late Sixth-Century Byzantium," *Past and Present* 84 (1979): 24–25, 26.

31. Av. Cameron, *Procopius,* 27. Christianity's ideological victory was finally completed when the emperors eliminated the classical "élite" culture, and the "free thinking" associated with it.

32. *Die ostroemische Kaiser- und Reichsidee nach ihrer Gestaltung in hoefischen Zeremoniell* (Darmstadt, 1956), 27–32. The result of this evolution was that the imperial office came to resemble the priestly; a synthesis of Christian and classical.

33. Ibid, 33. Naturally, Treitinger's political categories have not gone unchallenged; see below, pp. 9–11, for modern critiques.

34. M. McCormick, *Eternal Victory: Triumphal Rulership in Late Antiquity, Byzantium and the Early Medieval West* (Cambridge, 1986), 12. McCormick mentions Roman religion's role in the ceremonial iconography of victory, ibid., 28–29, but almost entirely in the context of the ruler cult.

35. Ibid., 20.

36. For thanksgiving ceremonies, see ibid, 108–11; for purification rites, see ibid., 76–78.

37. *A History of Education in Antiquity,* trans. G. Lamb, (Madison, Wis., 1982), 318.

38. See H. Hunger, *Die hochsprachliche profane Literatur der Byzantiner,* 2 vols. (Munich, 1978,) 1:69–74; Marrou, *History of Education,* 340–42; G. A. Kennedy, *Greek Rhetoric under Christian Emperors* (Princeton, 1983), 52–132.

39. See C. Mango, *Byzantine Literature as a Distorting Mirror, Inaugural Lecture, University of Oxford, May, 1974* (Oxford, 1975), 10–16, for the difficulties that the artificiality of Byzantine literature raises for the modern reader.

40. Hunger, *Literatur,* 1: 71.

41. See H.-G. Beck, *Res publica romana. Vom Staatsdenken der Byzantiner* (Munich, 1970), especially 5–11; Beck, *Senat und Volk von Konstantinopel* (Munich, 1966), esp. 51–54.

42. For the antiquarian and moral perspective of Byzantine literature, see J. Karayanopoulos, "Der fruehbyzantinische Kaiser," *BZ* 49 (1956): 369–84, especially 369–71; H. Hunger, *Prooimion: Elemente der byzantinischen Kaiseridee in den Arengen der Urkunden,* [*Wiener byzantinische Studien* 1] (Vienna, 1964), 15–18, 36–45. For modern examples of this "moral" interpretation of history, see D. Olster, *The Politics of Usurpation: Rhetoric and Revolution in Byzantium in the Seventh Century* (Amsterdam, 1992), 4–13.

43. See W. Jaeger, *Early Christianity and Greek Paideia* (Oxford, 1961), 84–100.

44. See ibid., 28–35; on the Christian rhetoric of anti-classicism, and the Christian enthusiasm for classical rhetoric, see C. Mango, *Byzantium: The Empire of New Rome* (New York, 1980), 131–35.

45. Christian responses to Julian the Apostate's attempt to close the Christian schools illustrates their determination to participate fully in the classical tradition.

46. *Distorting Mirror*, 18.

47. See T. Nissen, "Historisches Epos und Panegyrikos in der Spaetantike," *Hermes* 75: 298–325; Av. Cameron, *In laudem Iustini Augusti minoris* (London, 1976), 7.

48. As J. Matthews, "Ammianus' Historical Evolution," in *History and Historians in Late Antiquity*, ed. B. Croke and A. Emmett (Sydney, 1983), 39, explains, "It was the career of Julian, not the writings of Tacitus, that turned Ammianus' mind to the history of the earlier Roman Empire." R. L. Rike, *Apex Omnium: Religion in the Res Gestae of Ammianus* (Berkeley, 1987), esp. 8–36, tries to show that Ammianus's "political" history was equally "religious." For Agathias, see K. Adshead, "Thucydides and Agathias," in *History and Historians in Late Antiquity*, ed. B. Croke and A. Emmett, 82–87.

49. See P. Cox, *Biography in Late Antiquity: The Quest for the Holy Man* (Berkeley, 1984), esp. 45–67. Such themes are the place of the demonic, the sayings of the wise, and the importance of discipleship.

50. See *Byzantium and the Decline of Rome* (Princeton, 1968), 99–145. Both share an obsession with divine intervention and the importance of proper propitiation of the divine in imperial success and failure.

51. See the differing views of A. Momigliano, "Pagan and Christian Historiography in the Fourth Century A.D.," in *The Conflict between Paganism and Christianity in the Fourth Century*, ed. A. Momigliano (Oxford, 1963), 79–99, and esp. 89–93; and R. Grant, *Eusebius as Church Historian* (Oxford, 1980), 164–69, and G. F. Chesnut, *The First Christian Historians: Eusebius, Socrates, Sozomen, Theodoret and Evagrius*, [*Théologie historique* 46] (Paris, 1977), 133–66, on the genre of church history.

52. This is not to deny that hagiographies are fertile sources; see P. Brown, "Rise and Function of the Holy Man in Late Antiquity," *Journal of Roman Studies* 61 (1971): 80–101; H. Chadwick, "John Moschus and his Friend Sophronius the Sophist," *Journal of Theological Studies* n.s. 25 (1974): 41–74.

53. See N. H. Baynes, "Eusebius and the Christian Empire," *Annuaire de l'institut de philologie et d'histoire orientales* 2 (1933): 13–18; and especially the philological analysis of M. Anastos, "The Ancient Greek Sources of Byzantine Absolutism," *Harry Austryn Wolfson Jubilee Volume* (Jerusalem, 1965), 89–109.

54. W. Ensslin, *Gottkaiser und Kaiser von Gottesgnaden*, 83–108; F. Dvornik, *Early Christian and Byzantine Political Philosophy*, 2 vols. (Washington, D.C., 1966), 2: 645–58.

55. The cases of John Chrysostom and Nestorius illustrate how theological rhetoric advanced ecclesiastical political ambitions; see M. Anastos, "Nestorius was Orthodox!" *DOP* 16 (1962): 119–40; T. Gregory, *Vox Populi: Popular Opinion and*

Violence in the Religious Controversies of the Fifth Century A.D., (Columbus, Ohio, 1979).

56. On the development of the anti-Jewish genres, their *topoi* and the image of the Jew, see Parkes, *Conflict,* esp. 273–308; M. Simon, *Verus Israel: A Study in the Relations between Christians and Jews in the Roman Empire (A.D. 135–425),* trans. H. McKeating (Oxford, 1986 [1964]), esp. 135–78; R. Reuther, *Faith and Fratricide: The Theological Roots of Anti-Semitism* (Minneapolis, 1974), esp. 117–82.

57. *Les Trophées de Damas, controverse judéo-chrétienne du VIIe siècle,* ed. G. Bardy, [*PO* 15] (Paris, 1927), 190.

58. Ibid., 233.

59. Ibid., 269.

60. *Dialogue between a Christian and a Jew entitled Antibolē Papiskou kai Philōnos Ioudaiōn pros monaxon tina,* ed. A. C. McGiffert (New York, 1889), 82.

61. Ibid., 75.

62. *Disputatio Gregentii cum Herbano Iudaeo, PG* 86: 693c–d.

63. "Les traités *adversus Judaeos:* Aspects des relations Judéo-Chrétiennes dans le monde grec," *Byzantion* 56 (1986): 313; for her analysis of *Trophies,* see 309–13.

64. A. Harnack, "Die Altercatio Simonis Iudaei et Theophili Christiani nebst Untersuchungen ueber die antijuedische Polemik in der alten Kirche," *Texte und Untersuchungen zur Geschichte der altchristlichen Literatur* 1 (1883): 65.

65. Ibid., 65, 71.

66. Harnack thought the audience either pagans who desired instruction, or faithful who confronted a "gentile" theological threat.

67. "Altercatio," 63; see also Harnack's somewhat modified analysis of the Jewish participant Trypho in Justin Martyr's work "Judentum und Judenchristentum in Justins *Dialog mit Trypho,*" *Texte und Untersuchungen zur Geschichte der altchristlichen Literatur* 39 (1913): 47–92, esp. 53–55, 91–92. Specifically, Harnack identified Trypho as artificial "Hellenized" Jew.

68. *Papiscus,* ed. McGiffert, 3. The influence of Harnack is also apparent in the analysis of *Papiscus*'s sources, see ibid., 34–35.

69. Ibid., 3–4. For McGiffert, ibid., 2–4, *Papiscus* was an anachronism, written long after any threat to Christianity had passed, especially one by the Jews. Like Harnack, McGiffert thought the dialogue's straw-man Jew proved the Jews had no social presence.

70. Ibid., 9–10.

71. Literalism led Hulen to claim the most artificial literary Jews as historical. Typically he argued the historicity of the Jew in Celsus's *True Doctrine,* yet conceded that while Celsus tried "to reproduce with fidelity the Jewish approach," his "chief handicap" was "his ignorance of the Old Testament." Hulen, "The 'Dialogues with the Jews' as Sources for the Early Jewish Argument against Christianity," *Journal of Biblical Literature* 51 (1932): 59.

72. Ibid., 58–65.

73. Of course, all Christian theology could be called a response to Judaism. But Hulen did not assert this, since then there would be no distinction between "gentile" and "Jewish" theology.

74. See McGiffert, *Dialogue*, 3–7.

75. Williams, *Adversus Judaeos: A Bird's Eye View of Christian Apologetics* (Cambridge, 1935), 162–63, thought the Jewish characters were historical, but the dialogues fictive. He thought that *The Trophies of Damascus* and *The Doctrine of Jacob the Newly Baptised* were based on actual events.

76. Hulen, "'Dialogues,'" 70.

77. Williams, *Adversus Judaeos*, 161. In particular, monks authored the dialogues.

78. Ibid., 65–70 for Hulen's analysis of *Gregentius*; see also below, Chapter 2, for the Byzantine interest in restoration.

79. Parkes relied on J. Juster, *Les Juifs dans l'empire romain*, 2 vols. (Paris, 1914), and S. Krauss, *Studien zur byzantinisch-judischen Geschichte* (Vienna, 1914), but went further in demonstrating Judaism's influence on Christianity, and in challenging Harnack's opinion on the social relations of Jews and Christians.

80. *The Conflict of the Church and the Synagogue: A Study in the Origins of Anti-Semitism* (New York, 1979 [1934]), 280.

81. Ibid., 282.

82. Ibid., 282.

83. Ibid., 305.

84. Ibid., 288.

85. *Verus Israel*, trans. McKeating, 156, 138–40.

86. Ibid., 132; see also Parkes, *Conflict*, 160–62.

87. Parkes, *Conflict*, 169–72. R. Grant has shown how Christians used the Jews' political disasters to answer political problems of the conversion of Constantine; see "Eusebius, Josephus and the Fate of the Jews," *Society of Biblical Literature Seminar Papers* 2 (1979): 69–86; idem, *Eusebius as Church Historian* (Oxford, 1980), 97–113. See also Chapter 2, below.

88. *John Chrysostom and the Jews: Rhetoric and Reality in the Late Fourth Century* (Berkeley, 1983), 125–26.

89. Ibid., 160.

90. *Judaism and the Early Christian Mind: A Study of Cyril of Alexandria's Exegesis and Theology* (New Haven, 1971), 1; also 60–61 for ad hominem attacks Wilken thinks theological. He claims, ibid., ix, that Cyril's theology was "shaped by the polemic against Judaism," and concludes, ibid., 67, "Though Cyril's statements on Judaism drip with venom, he constantly turns the discussion to the larger theological and exegetical issues."

91. *Chrysostom*, 123.

92. See L. H. Feldman, "Anti-Semitism in the Ancient World," in *History and Hate: The Dimensions of Anti-Semitism*, ed. D. Berger (Philadelphia, 1986), 15–42.

93. "Zum Buch von R. Richardson, *Israel in the Apostolic Church*," *Judaica* 28 (1972): 30.

94. *Juden and Judentum bei den Kirchenvaetern*, [*Schriften zur Judentumskunde* 2] (Zurich 1971), 9. "From early on, Christian missionary zeal against Jews seems to have been seriously decreasing even before Judaism had ceased to exert some appeal to the [gentile] Christians."

95. "Zum Buch," 9–10.

96. Hruby, *Juden and Judentum bei den Kirchenvaetern,* 7.

97. For the related work of Gilbert Dagron, see below, Chapter 5.

98. "La polémique anti-judaique au VIᵉ et au VIIᵉ siècle: Un mémento inédit, les *Képhalaia,*" *Travaux et Mémoires* 11 (1991): 275–311. As Déroche explains, ibid., 282, the fundamental question of the anti-Jewish literature is "What is its relationship to reality?" And the answer, ibid., 283, is that "the first examination immediately reveals [its] fictive character."

99. Ibid., 288.

100. Ibid., 294.

101. Ibid., 294.

102. Ibid., 283. He continues, "Their form is only justified by the existence of an anti-Jewish polemic." In fact, it was a *generic* form. Thus, generic *topoi,* like the prominence of Old Testament citations, ibid., 283, does not demonstrate historicity.

103. Ibid., 288.

104. Ibid., 290–92; "L'authenticité de *L'Apologie contre les Juifs* de Léontios de Néapolis," *Bulletin de Correspondence Hellénique* 110 (1986): 663–64, 667–69.

105. There is no credible evidence that iconoclasm was inspired by Christian contacts with Jews. Christians had debated the legitimacy of icons since the fourth century, and there is more iconoclastic material from the fourth century than from the seventh; see E. Kitzinger, "The Cult of Images in the Age before Iconoclasm," *DOP* 8 (1954): 85–87. Nor was iconoclasm the result of theological debate. Leo's imperial rescript ordering icons' removal from churches (which precipitated the crisis) was not a theological tract, nor was Leo a theologian.

106. For Déroche, ibid., 283, the historiographic problem is finding a mean between Williams's and Harnack's views of Jewish–Christian social relations and their impact on Christianity. In this, he echoes Simon, *Verus Israel,* 138, "Just as Lukyn Williams takes for granted that Judaism was aggressive and evangelistic, Harnack assumes, without any evidence, that it was withdrawn and indifferent."

107. See the bibliography (for the seventh century), in G. Dagron, "Introduction historique," *Juifs et Chrétiens dans l'orient du VIIᵉ siècle,* [*Travaux et Mémoires* 11], 17–38.

108. Of course, the Black Hundreds and the Nazi treatment of Jews are hardly comparable to the Christian Romans'. But in both cases, rhetoric generated a political agenda of its own. See below, Chapter 4, for the forced baptism inspired by Roman propaganda in the Persian War.

109. Harnack, "Judentum," 91. The critique of Catholic formalism in *History of Dogma* echoes the Pauline critique of Jewish formalism.

110. F. Murawski, *Die Juden bei den Kirchenvaetern und Scholastikern* (Berlin, 1925), 65.

111. *Chrysostom,* 159.

112. Williams, *Adversus Judaeos,* xvi.

113. Ibid., xvi.

114. H. Schreckenberg, *Die christliche Adversus-Judaeos-Texte und ihr literarisches und historisches Umfeld (1–11. Jh.)* (Frankfurt, 1982), 17–20.

115. Ibid., 20; see also ibid., 19, where he reminds the reader that the Jews are not without their own polemics, and that one must judge Christian polemics in the light of the Jew's own.

116. "Jews and Judaism in the Early Church Fathers," *Greek Orthodox Theological Review* 23 (1978): 156. This is simply wrong; the acerbity of Christian anti-Jewish invective has been amply documented, from Parkes to Simon to Reuther. Alvarez goes even further than Constantelos. He wrote of the *Epistle of Barnabus,* a racial attack and the first extant deicide charge, "Apostolic Writings and the Roots of Anti-Semitism," *Studia Patristica* 13.2 (1975): 76, "The Pseudo-Barnabus attributes Jesus' death to the Jews, even crucifixion, lance, insults, spits, which the Gospels attribute to the Romans. Yet apart from this historical inexactitude, he seems not offended." On the contrary, Barnabus created the image of the Christ-killing Jew, rejected by God, the enemy of all good.

117. R. Reuther, *Faith and Fratricide: The Theological Roots of Anti-Semitism* (Minneapolis, 1974), esp. 223–25, where she argues that Christian theology prepared the way for the Holocaust, and 226–61, in which she denounces the inherent theological anti-Semitism of Christianity.

118. Ibid., 31. See also ibid., 15, "the vast majority of these sorts of texts do not have an anti-Jewish intent"; rather, anti-Jewish texts "desire to outline the content of Christian faith in legitimate apologetic or establish theological claims."

119. See ibid., 23.

120. Ibid., 31.

121. His apologetic hinders his interpretation of the seventh-century anti-Jewish sources. He dismisses, ibid., 437, *The Doctrine of Jacob the Newly Baptised* as another work "in the tradition of the anti-Jewish apologetic since Justin Martyr," ignoring its mention of the Arab invasions and Mohammed. His description of *Trophies of Damascus against the Jews,* ibid., 449–50, summarizes some commonplace objections to Christianity made by Jews, but does not mention what its original apologetic says about why the victories of Islam did not compromise Christianity's legitimacy.

122. The use of the term *race* here in no way implies that Jews were or are a race in the modern genetic sense. It is the sources themselves that speak of Jews as a race. Race for these authors meant an ethnic group that descended from a single progenitor, inhabiting a geographic area with a cult center, and finally, and for our purposes perhaps most importantly, possessed its own distinctive relationship with a diety. (I am currently preparing a book on Christianity and classical ethnography.)

2. Christianity: The Imperial Religion

Christian Imperial Triumphalism

In the fourth century the Christians acquired an empire, and with it a religio-political rhetoric called triumphalism that expressed Christian Roman imperial pretensions. Evolving from Hellenistic and Roman rhetorical models, late Roman triumphalism employed three main themes: that victory demonstrated divine power, that divine favor guaranteed victory, and that the emperor was the empire's mediator for, and personal recipient of, divine favor.[1] Of course, the imperial Christian Romans adjusted these ideas to suit their own religious practices and scruples, but these principles continued to inform their imperial rhetoric. It was this triumphalist association of victory, divine power, and divine favor that seventh-century defeats challenged.

Before Constantine, the Christian rhetoric of victory was limited to the victories of Christ and his *milites,* the martyrs. But in a culture that judged a god by the material benefits he bestowed, martyrdom impressed most pagans as a sign of Christ's weakness.[2] Before Christianity, Cicero mocked the Jews for the claim that their defeat and death showed their god's power. "How dear that race was to the immortal gods is shown by the fact that it has been conquered, subjected to taxes, enslaved."[3] To defend their god's power, therefore, Christians carefully distinguished their own judicial, *individual* martyrdom from the Jews' military, *collective* defeat. As the second-century Justin Martyr explained to the "Jew" Trypho: "But you say [persecution and martyrdom] has befallen your own nation. Now if you have been exiled after defeat in battle, you have suffered such treatment justly. . . . But we, together with Christ, are taken out of this world."[4] Justin attacked the Jews using the same evidence, defeat, that Cicero had, because Christians shared with pagans the view that battlefield defeat indicated divine retribution or weakness.[5] To Christians, the Roman sack of Jerusalem resulted from the Jews' rejection of Christ and his punishment of the Jews.[6] Christians thus shared the cultural denial of military defeat as collective martyrdom, substituting a model of individual martyrdom.

The military victory that ended the Great Persecution, however, brought a new theme into the Christian rhetoric of persecution and martyrdom. The early books of the *Church History* by the fourth-century bishop Eusebius, which narrate the period before the Great Persecution, reaffirmed the distinction between God's judgment on the battlefield and Christian individual martyrdom: "Others who write histories pursue victories in war. . . . But our work of the community dedicated to God narrates those most peaceful warriors of the soul's peace itself, and more on behalf of truth than the fatherland."[7] Neither here, nor in any description of martyrdoms *before the Great Persecution*, did Eusebius hint that persecution was in any way a divine punishment of the Christian community. Following Justin's lead, Eusebius lauded persecution as an opportunity for martyrdom, an individual's triumph and itself a reward.[8]

This presentation of persecution abruptly changed when Eusebius came to the Great Persecution. Here, for the only time in the *Church History*, persecution was deemed a punishment of the Christian community rather than a triumph of an individual: "God himself has at all times been the guide of our affairs, at the right time punishing and correcting his people through misfortunes, and again thereafter, following sufficient punishment, showing mercy and goodwill to those holding their hopes in him."[9] In the wake of Constantine's victory, Christians looked to military victory as the means by which Christ would end or prevent persecution. Martyrdom retained the rhetoric of victory, but now that Christ possessed an empire and the martial might to protect his people, Christians slowly realized that persecution had to be *permitted* by Christ and thus could only be a punishment for sin.[10]

These reactions to the Milvian Bridge were the first step toward Christian triumphalism. As Christians conflated imperial wars and pagan persecutions, they began to measure God's power, and his believers' faith, through military, not martyrial victory. The civil wars of Constantine were recast so that love of Christ inspired Constantine; hatred of Christians, his enemies.[11] Above their earthly champions, Christ and the demons worshipped by the persecutors struggled for victory.[12] Maxentius trusted in demonic magic; Constantine trusted in Christ's power.[13] The civil war between Theodosius and Eugenius was equally a conflict between their respective divine patrons, Christ and Hercules. The battle of the Frigidus was no less a demonstration and vindication of Christian truth and Christ's might than was the Milvian Bridge.[14]

Although this conflation of persecution and war was applied less often to foreign wars, the sixth-century historian Procopius still claimed that the

Persian king Chosroes warred "not against Justinian, the Roman emperor, nor against any other man, but only against the God whom the Christians worship."[15] Not only did Christ destroy domestic persecutors in battle, but the fifth-century church historian Socrates asserted that through Roman arms "Christ took vengeance upon the Persians . . . since they had shed the blood of so many of his pious worshippers."[16] His contemporary, the bishop Theodoret, linked persecution and foreign war so that *any* attack on the empire was also a persecution. "Wars [against Christians] and the victory of the church have been predicted by the Lord, and the event teaches us that war brings us more blessings than peace."[17] A Christian empire meant that "wars against Christians" included not only persecutions, but also civil and foreign wars, so that military victory became as much a part of Christian history as martyrdom. Predictably, Theodoret proudly concluded that military victory was the seal of Christ's favor.[18]

The conflation of war and persecution, however, did not long dominate Christian imperial rhetoric. As Christians settled more firmly into power, persecution and martyrdom faded from the rhetoric of victory as Christians privileged Christ's martial might rather than his followers' patient endurance.[19] Christian Romans, just like pagan, congratulated themselves on their piety and attributed victory to divine guidance.[20] Roman victory and rule clearly demonstrated Christianity's efficacy and Christ's power;[21] the empire proved Christ's superiority over the gods of Rome's enemies.[22] The fifth-century church historian Sozomen boasted that a plague struck barbarians with fear, "not so much because they dared to attack a race of such valor as the Romans, as that they perceived them to be aided by a mighty God."[23] Just as pagan gods employed such natural agents as geese or dreams to aid their clients, Christ too rarely personally intervened in battle.[24] With the exception of Constantine's vision, his aid was rarely more supernatural than desertion of enemy mercenaries to the Romans,[25] the appearance of timely reinforcements,[26] or the passage of a lake.[27]

Not only did Christ evolve into the patron of Roman victory, but the Christian community of martyrs itself evolved. The marriage of Roman and Christian universalism merged "every race into one unity and concord," to create a Christian Roman race whose divine patron was Christ, god of battles.[28] The foil for this transformation was the Jews. The Christian Romans' victory proved them to be Christ's chosen and favored race; the Jews' defeat proved them to be a reprobate race.[29] As Romans and Christians joined in imperial union, the end of the Jewish kingdom came to prove God's favor not simply to the Christians, but to the Christian Romans. Gregory Nazianzenus claimed that Vespasian's victory over the Jews was a sign that even when pagan, the Romans were God's chosen people, and that the destruction of Jerusalem foreshadowed the Romans' greater glory to come as Christians.[30]

The blend of Christian and Roman also fused the *pax romana,* created by the Roman race's god-given victories, with the Christian mission so that "as knowledge of one God was given to all men . . . a single sovereign arose for the entire Roman Empire, and a deep peace took hold of all."[31] Of course, religion had long been identified with imperial order. Two centuries before Constantine, Plutarch wrote that, along with armed force, Alexander brought "the power of religion: oh wondrous power of Philosophic Instruction that brought the Indians to worship Greek gods."[32] Barbarians were civilized not only through Roman law and letters, but through the gods that gave their conquerors victory.[33] Rome's universal empire was not only the bringer of civilized order, but also Christ's instrument to missionize the world, to bring the religion of Rome to "all those not yet united [with the Empire] up to the limits of the inhabited world."[34]

Just as the Christian initial conflation of persecution and war increasingly assimilated and identified itself with the traditional Roman rhetoric of victory, the missionary aspect of Christian Roman universalism also evolved. Christians rarely spoke of barbarians as a pagan threat to Christianity, or of a need to convert them.[35] For Christians, as for previous generations, barbarism threatened the divinely ordained imperial order, civilization itself.[36] Duplicitous, "insolent to some, servile to others,"[37] barbarians' sole desire was to destroy.[38] They had human form, but no other human qualities;[39] as Aristotle explained, "The saying of the poets, 'It is right that Greeks rule barbarians,' means that barbarian and slave are the same in nature."[40] Christians found to their dismay that those worthy of mastery were enslaved by those worthy to be slaves.[41] So horrifying did Christians find barbarian cruelty that they hesitated to use them against Christian enemies.[42] Germans left desert where cities had stood;[43] Vandals plundered until nothing remained to loot;[44] Moors were even more destructive than Germans.[45] Perhaps the most depraved were Persians, who were marginally civilized, and whose duplicity and rapaciousness were thus doubly criminal.[46]

Barbarism threatened not souls, but the mundane primacy of Roman rule, and against it Christian Romans marshaled the same forces as their pagan predecessors. Justinian explained that the Roman order arose "from a double root, arms and laws."[47] In Africa, Christ's power enabled the Christians to restore "[the laws] that had lain abandoned in the time of the Vandals,"[48] and to bring civilized order to Armenia so that it "should in no way differ from the rest of our commonwealth" and should cease to live "according to the barbaric manner of life."[49] The uniformity and universality of Roman law and order, backed by arms and guaranteed by Christ's favor, was the antidote to the *barbarikos ethos.*

Without divine favor, Christian Roman laws and arms were powerless, and divine favor was dispensed not to the Romans, but to the emperor, their mediator with Christ. An emperor personified his subjects as if he had a multitude of souls.[50] His virtues turned aside disaster — "Thanks to a king's proper caution, catastrophe to both city and realm is avoided."[51] So central was the emperor to imperial well-being that the sixth-century church historian Evagrius illustrated God's favor to the empire by the stability of the imperial succession.[52]

In theory, the emperor mediated between heaven and earth as God's representative on earth.[53] As Pliny (the younger) explained, Jupiter committed the empire to Trajan so that the emperor could "fill [Jupiter's] role with regard to all humanity."[54] In practice, this meant that the emperor was the sole conduit of divine favor and aid to the empire.[55] Thus, the second-century rhetorician and orator Dio Chrysostom exhorted Trajan to "give first and chief place to religion" in order to insure divine favor.[56] Theodosius I echoed this advice three centuries later when he charged his sons to be pious Christians, "for in this way, peace is maintained, war ended, foes defeated, trophies raised, and victory proclaimed."[57] More than military might, the emperor's personal piety gained victory. The Christian emperor Theodosius II, "if at any time war was raised, trusted in God like David because he knew God was the judge of battles."[58] Even palace-bound, he repelled barbarian invasions because "according to his habit, he committed the direction of the affair to God, and continuing in sincere prayer, quickly received his desire."[59]

The Triumphalist Response to Defeat

Such was the outline of Christian triumphalism: Christ was the god of victory, patron of a Christian Roman race, whose favor guaranteed victory; the emperor was the Romans' mediator for, and recipient of, his aid. This rhetoric of victory, however, did not prevent defeat. Visigothic victory opened up the west to the Germans; fifth-century Huns and Ostrogoths ruined the Balkans; and sixth-century Persians even sacked Antioch in 540. Such reverses likely shook Christian confidence, but defeats in the west were distant, the Balkans expendable, and Persian incursions remained raids; Christian triumphalism bent but did not break.[60]

Another reason that Christians did not abandon triumphalism, however, was that an apologetic for defeat was built into the triumphal rhetoric of victory: the morals of the ruler. Since divine favor was the fulcrum on which imperial fortunes balanced, if a leader of an army or state offended the gods, disaster resulted. The *hubris* of Xerxes angered the gods, who destroyed his fleet at Salamis; the sacrilege of Appius Claudius condemned his fleet when he not only ignored the sacred chickens' refusal to eat, but then threw them into the Mediterranean, exclaiming, "If they will not eat, let them drink." Christians judged impiety according to their own religious practice, but an emperor's piety was a virtue no less important for Augustus than for his Christian descendents.

Christians agreed with such pagans as Livy and Herodotus that God punished a sinner's iniquity during his life; however, if the emperor sinned, then the empire that he personified and represented suffered punishment as well. Theodoret assured his audience that "Valens in his present life paid the penalty of his sins."[61] But the death of Valens at Adrianople embraced more than his personal chastisement; its consequence was imperial catastrophe. Indeed, Sozomen and Procopius attributed not only defeat but also natural calamities to God's displeasure with evil rulers like Julian and Justinian.[62] The emperor's moral virtue was the measure of imperial well-being, so that if he was pious and virtuous, the empire prospered, but if he was not, the empire suffered.

Thus, defeat need not compromise the triumphalist ideal. If one emperor's vice led to disaster, another's virtue could return God's favor and restore the empire.[63] Given this mind-set, Christians could identify weaknesses in the empire, but they could not recognize these as systemic causes of defeat or decline; the weakening of the army, the collapse or corruption of the bureaucracy, or the stretching of resources beyond the empire's capacity were all attributed to the emperor's vice. Perhaps the most extreme example of this moral causation is the *Secret History* of Procopius. Although the diatribe is grotesquely exaggerated, the idea that an emperor's vice caused defeat or decline was common. Agathias and Menander Protector also blamed Justinian's moral flaws for imperial decline; Menander included a moral critique of Justin II as well.[64] Agathias lamented the declining military, even recognizing that the Roman army would in the end succumb to numbers,[65] but he could discover no other cause for this than the aged timidity of Justinian. "He seemed to have wearied of vigorous policies . . . rather than rely on his own powers and expose himself to the hazards of a sustained struggle. So he allowed the qualities of the legions to deteriorate as if he thought he would have no further use for them."[66]

Church historians and hagiographers also found causality in the moral character of the emperors. And while heterodoxy or apostasy were more prominent vices in their works, they did not neglect the others. In addition to apostasy, the church historians accused Julian of pride, recklessness, and other perfectly conventional vices in the thesaurus of invective.[67] Valens was a heretic and persecutor, but the church historians did not forget his bloodthirstiness and arrogance, the same faults that the historian Ammianus Marcellinus criticized.[68] Theodore of Sykeon, the seventh-century saint, offered his explanation for the overthrow of Maurice and the troubles that followed it. "[Maurice] deserves his fate for he has in many things governed ill, and especially in the things that he is doing now." Typically, Maurice's fall involved not only his own ruin but imperial ruin as well. Theodore continued, "[Maurice], children, will shortly be removed, and after him worse things shall happen."[69] The *Life* even explained Heraclius's defeat by the Persians in 613 in similar terms. When the saint offered Heraclius gifts and dinner, and Heraclius, in haste to meet the Persians, rudely declined, his impiety resulted in a Persian victory.[70]

Just as an emperor's vice caused disaster, an emperor's virtue restored the empire. The vice and impiety of Valens nearly ruined the empire at Adrianople, but the virtue and piety of his successor, Theodosius, restored the empire.[71] Corippus's panegyric on the accession of Justin II, Justinian's successor, used this theme even within the same dynasty: "Many things were far too neglected while [Justinian] was alive. . . . Let the world rejoice that whatever was not done or put into practice because of our father's old age, will be corrected in the time of Justin."[72]

Corippus, writing for Justinian's nephew, was far more discreet in his criticism of Justinian than Agathias, but made clear that Justin's youthful vigor would restore whatever Justinian's aged exhaustion had weakened. For him, as for his contemporaries, the emperor remained the critical agent of renewal.[73] Indeed, even as Persian and Arab victory strained the triumphalist ideal, many Christians retained the emperor's vice as the cause.

As one might expect, initial explanations of seventh-century defeat, especially those originating from the court, retained triumphalist apologetic. The first extant response to Roman defeat by the Persians, a letter of the Constantinopolitan Senate to Chosroes II in 615, preserved in the seventh-century *Paschal Chronicle,* makes no mention of Byzantine sins or divine punishment, but relies on the emperor's vice to explain defeat.[74] This letter addresses Chosroes with the most ingratiating court rhetoric. Far from challenging him, it requests peace and blames the usurper Phocas for war.[75] It even excuses Chosroes' invasion as an understandable reaction to the usurper, who "failed to accord the proper honor to your exceeding Clemency, so that finally, angered by our faults, you brought the affairs of the Roman realm so low."[76] Now that Heraclius had assumed the throne, insults to Chosroes had been rectified.[77] The letter even concluded with the hope that Chosroes would treat Heraclius as a son.[78] The return to imperial virtue by Heraclius insured that the process of restoration of the empire had begun; now that the vicious Phocas had been removed, peace would surely follow.

Later chroniclers found the cause of Arab victory in Heraclius's incestuous marriage to his niece. The ninth-century chronicler Nicephorus wrote that even Heraclius's brother Theodore admitted that Heraclius was defeated because "through all [Heraclius's] affairs, his sin confronts him."[79] Since God inflicted punishment for an emperor's sin both on his person and on the realm he personified, chroniclers recorded not only Heraclius's defeat but also his hideous death. "This was the proof of his transgression."[80]

Two seventh-century groups of religious dissidents, who ironically opposed each other as well as the imperial religious establishment, found another sin of Heraclius to explain Arab victories.[81] One of the charges against Maximus the Confessor during his trial in the reign of Heraclius's grandson was that he attributed Arab victory to Heraclius's Monotheletism, and more, declared that so long as the dynasty of the heretical emperor held power, the empire would not recover.[82]

The Syrian Monophysites, bitter enemies of Maximus, but also heretics in the eyes of the court, differed little from Maximus in their understanding of imperial instability and disaster: "But the emperors of this time, Maurice, Phocas and Heraclius, on account of their estrangement from the true religion, were deprived of wisdom; they were abandoned to a hideous fate. God abandoned them, as it is written, to the pursuit of vanities, and each one destroyed the next."[83] Michael the Syrian drew no distinction between the "evil" emperor Phocas and the "good" emperor Heraclius because they were all heretical. But this view of the emperor's heterodoxy remained a minority opinion by authors who maintained a safe distance from Constantinople. The trial of Maximus showed how little emperors cared for such sentiments, and how imperial and ecclesiastical authorities punished those who promoted them.

Anastasius the Sinaite, a follower of Maximus, illustrates the other side of the triumphalist coin. Writing after the Sixth Ecumenical Council in 680–681 restored orthodoxy to the imperial office, he contrasted the successes of Heraclius's orthodox great-grandson to the sins of his Monothelete predecessors:

> What happened then? The reward of God for these misdeeds [of the Heraclian dynasty] fell upon us: that destruction of just about the entire army and navy in Phoenicia, and the obliteration, one after the other, of all the Christian people and places, which did not cease until the persecutor of [Pope] Martin, [Constans the father of Constantine], was killed by the sword. But Constantine, the pious son of this man, [returned to orthodoxy through the Ecumenical Council]. That holy Council, for the last twenty years, has brought to an end the sufferings of our people, turned the sword of our enemies against each other, brought peace to the land, smoothed the waves, and created consolation, cessation of trouble and peace beyond measure in the Roman lands.[84]

This characterization of the imperial condition, however, was not very convincing, at least to judge by its popularity. In fact, this rosy imperial vision is almost unique among sources outside the court.

Few seventh-century authors followed Anastasius's lead in pronouncing the empire restored; fewer still risked the imperial wrath that had fallen on Maximus for condemning the ruling house. Most authors trimmed their sails to the prevailing political winds. Typically, Socrates, Sozomen, and Theodoret proclaimed the reign of the incompetent Honorius (under whom Rome itself was sacked) an unbroken succession of victories, and Honorius himself a paragon of virtue.[85] But their praise had little to do with virtue. Honorius's nephew was Theodosius II, their imperial patron, and they had no desire to face his displeasure. One hundred years later, Procopius did not hesitate to attribute the sack of Rome to Honorius's vices,[86] and failure of imperial recovery in the west to the vices of the equally incompetent Valentinian III.[87] Unlike fifth-century writers, Procopius could criticize Theodosian emperors without fear, because by his time the dynasty had died out and such criticisms were no longer dangerous.

Unable to exploit the emperor's vice as cause for disasters in the west, Socrates proposed Alaric's barbaric destructiveness as the reason for the sack of Rome.[88] Sozomen and Theodoret, however, returned to the explanation used by Eusebius for the Great Persecution—collective sin. As Sozomen explained, "All sensible persons were aware that the calamities which this siege brought upon the Romans were manifestations of the divine wrath sent to chastise them."[89] Theodoret was even more explicit. Vandal depredations in Africa would never have happened "if men had respected the laws of God."[90] God responded to collective sin with collective punishment, sending "misfortunes as a potent medicine for sinners, as an exhortation to perseverance for the virtuous, and as a beneficial example for all observers."[91]

Thus, although the theme of collective sin and punishment that Eusebius introduced remained a minor theme of Christian historiography, it evolved in the thesaurus of Christian rhetoric. The very fact that one hundred years after Eusebius, military defeat, not persecution, had become the means of God's harsh pedagogy was itself indicative of how far Christianity had become imperialized. As Socrates explained, "calamities of the Empire and the difficulties of the church are intimately related. . . . I cannot believe that this constant overlapping is simply the effect of fortune, but I am convinced that our sins are the cause."[92] Far from abandoning triumphalism, he incorporated collective sin in the triumphalist imperial framework. Using the triumphalist identification of Christian community and empire, and the mediating role of the emperor as the means of retrieving divine favor,[93] Socrates declared, "We have continually included the emperors in these historical narratives, because, from the time they began to profess Christianity, the affairs of the church have depended on them."[94]

Thus, when an earthquake knocked down the dome of Hagia Sophia, the sixth-century hymnographer Romanus Melodus recognized this as a divine punishment for the Constantinopolitans' sins, and only "when [God] heard the voice of the [ruler] crying out" did he relent.[95] Romanus could claim God's forgiveness because, after all, the earthquake had stopped. But he found an even better proof of God's forgiveness of the Romans' sins through a contrast with the sins of a race that God had *not* forgiven. "The people of Israel were deprived of their temple, but we, standing in their place, have now the Holy Resurrection and Zion [churches]."[96]

Romanus's assertion of divine forgiveness and legitimation of the Christian Romans rested on the same foundation as all Christian apologetic that employed the Jews. From Justin to Romanus, the Jewish loss of kingdom and temple remained a demonstration of divine condemnation of

the Jews and of the Christian inheritance of God's favor. Romanus juxtaposed the Jews' condemnation with the Christians' temporary punishment
to lay the basis for restoration of God's favor.

In general, collective sin remained a secondary theme in the sources.[97]
But beneath the literary surface, this explanation of disaster had widespread
appeal. Agathias reports that after an earthquake:

> Fantastic stories and amazing predictions that the apocalypse was near began
> to circulate among the people. Charlatans and self-appointed prophets roamed
> the streets prophesying whatever came into their heads and terrifying the
> majority of the people. . . . Society indeed never fails to throw up a bewilder-
> ing variety of such persons in times of misfortune.[98]

Many sixth-century Christian authors took care to reject such an interpretation of events. Procopius artfully had the Vandal Gaiseric claim that he
sacked Rome since its citizens were those "against whom God is angered";[99] such a dubious proponent of this idea implicitly denied it as a
barbarian superstition. As noted above, elsewhere Procopius in his own
narrative voice employed the emperors' vices to offer the correct explanation of Roman reverses in the west.

John Lydus and Agathias were explicit in their rejection of collective
sin and divine anger as the cause of misfortunes. Lydus charged with
defeatism those who took refuge in religion.[100] Agathias was even more
dismissive of citizen sin as a cause, even poking fun at those who found
divine anger in every misfortune:

> According to the ancient oracles of the Egyptians and to the leading astrol-
> ogers of present-day Persia, there occurs in the course of endless time a
> succession of lucky and unlucky cycles. These luminaries would have us think
> that we are at present passing through one of the most disastrous and inaus-
> picious of such cycles. . . . Others hold the view that divine anger is responsi-
> ble for the destruction, exacting just retribution from mankind for its sins and
> decimating whole populations.[101]

Agathias contemptuously dismissed both sorts of superstition with an
ironic "It is not for me to judge."[102]

The viewpoint of these authors is not modern or in any way skeptical.
The moral order of the world required that "it is not at the moment of
sinning that we have punishment meted out to us, but for the most part
after some time has elapsed, and perhaps when we have forgotten all about
our past conduct."[103] Punishment of individual sin was assumed; it was

collective punishment that was rejected. Agathias thought it foolish that God would punish sins with an earthquake. "Undoubtedly, the earthquake would have been a very real boon if it could distinguish the wicked and the good."[104] It was ridiculous to suppose that God punished indiscriminately, so that sinners might escape while the innocent suffered.

If Christians found natural disasters perplexing, they could sometimes find no cause whatsoever for military disasters. Even Procopius conceded that he could not explain the fall of Antioch to the Persians in 540: "I am unable to understand why indeed it should be the will of God to exalt on high the fortunes of a man or a place, and then to cast them down for no cause which appears to us. For it is wrong to say that God does not do all things with reason."[105] Procopius's perplexity may be feigned. He might well have heard that the Antiochenes' sin had brought them to disaster, and simply ignored it. Antioch's fall also puzzled Menander Protector, but he found a rather different explanation than did Procopius. "This is God's way of punishing the excessive good fortune of the Romans, lest they think that they differ greatly from others."[106] Menander thus ascribed Persian victory to God's will as well, but hardly to the chastisement of sin.

Sixth-century authors from Procopius to the church historian Evagrius may have been loath to employ divine anger to explain Roman disasters because Zosimus, one of the last pagan historians of Rome, who wrote about fifty years after Sozomen, insisted that the Roman Empire had fallen on account of its citizens' sins, in particular the impiety of Christian worship. "Whereas Polybius tells us how the Romans won their empire in a short time, I intend to show how they lost it in an equally short time because of their sins."[107] His *New History* made a powerful impression on later Christian generations, perhaps because he touched a nerve of Christians already nervous about the imperial condition. Even one hundred years later, Christians were still writing refutations of the *New History*, trying to reassure their audience that the empire stood as rock solid as ever, and that Christianity was the source of its strength.[108]

Zosimus's accusations that Christianity was a false religion were not convincing because the empire did not seem threatened. Evagrius pointed with pride to Christ's achievements as patron of Roman arms: "Roman power has increased with the spread of our faith. At the exact time of the epiphany, [Macedonia] was crushed by the Romans . . . Egypt was added to the Roman realm. . . . How much territory of the Persians was taken by Corbulo, the general of Nero, Severus, Trajan, Carus?"[109] One should not be surprised that Evagrius set victories of pagan generals and emperors to

Christ's credit. His answer to Zosimus was delivered as a self-conscious Roman. What is remarkable about the passage is that no Christian emperor is included in the list. Augustus, as a Roman, was as Christian as Constantine, and his victories sufficed to prove Christ's power.

One hundred years after Zosimus, however, another pagan made claims against Christ that were less easy to dismiss. Chosroes II, king of the Persians, conqueror of Jerusalem, had a more substantial argument than an embittered pagan intellectual. In a letter to Heraclius, preserved in the late seventh- or early eighth-century *History of Heraclius* attributed to the Armenian bishop Sebeos, Chosroes put forward his case:

> I have thrashed the Greeks, and you pretend to rely on your God. Why has he not preserved from my hands Caesarea, Jerusalem and great Alexandria? Since your hope is vain, do not deceive yourself; for how can this Christ, who could not save himself from the hands of the Jews and was killed by them and attached to the cross, save you from my hands?[110]

Whether this letter is completely authentic or not, Chosroes did in fact send a letter of this sort, which made so great an impression that it was read publicly at Hagia Sophia and deposited on the altar as a direct challenge to Christ.[111] It reveals the unease that Christians were experiencing, especially in the provinces where evidence of Roman defeat could not be ignored. Defeat cast a shadow over Christ's power; if Christ was not a god of victory, then he was hardly a god at all. Byzantine defeat stripped away the victorious façade of Christian triumphalism and required Christians to seek an explanation of defeat that preserved Christ's power and the promise of Roman restoration.

Significantly, and for them ominously, the Jews occupied a central place in the letter of Chosroes. Even beyond the letter, Chosroes may even have systematically exploited Jewish "victory" over Christ to highlight Persian victory over the Christians as propaganda in the conquered provinces;[112] certainly works like the *Miracle of Berytus* and the anti-Jewish dialogues illustrate the contemporary Christian construction of the Jew as a living symbol of infidel attacks on Christ and his people, the Romans. The Jew in turn became the object of both Christian and Roman victory, an unenviable position fraught with dire social consequences.

The *History of Heraclius* offers evidence not only of the doubts that defeat raised, but of the answer Christian authors offered to assuage them. A speech, obviously invented, by Heraclius to the Persians occupying Chalcedon illustrates how seventh-century Christians molded the formerly dominant theme of barbarism with the themes of religious war, collective sin, punishment, and restoration to reassure an audience shaken by defeat.

The speech begins by contrasting the moral characters of the Romans and Persians. Heraclius rhetorically asks why Chosroes has not made peace with him, complaining, "Your king thirsts ever for blood. When will he be sated? . . . This is what I ask of him, to know peace and friendship."[113] This contrast in fact is traditional. Late antique writers repeatedly contrasted peace-loving Romans and warmongering Persians by personifying these qualities in their rulers. The third-century historian Herodian invented a speech in which Alexander Severus exhorted his troops to fight with the knowledge that Rome held the moral high ground: "I first endeavored by letters and persuasion to check [Artaxerxes'] mad greed and lust for the goods of others. But the king, with barbarian insolence, refuses to remain within his boundaries and challenges us to battle."[114]

The Constantinopolitan Senate's letter served the same function in the *Paschal Chronicle*'s narrative as Alexander's or Heraclius's speeches: to define war as a moral conflict between civilized Romans and barbarians. It permitted Chosroes a dignified opening to conduct peace negotiations, and when Chosroes responded by jailing the ambassadors, his barbarism became apparent.

All three works, from very different literary contexts, used the same rhetorical device to establish a moral context for war. But the *History of Heraclius* continued in a different vein, offering an explanation for Roman defeat that was very different from that of the Senate's letter. "For it is not on account of your piety that God has given you victory, but on account of our iniquity. It is our sins, not your valor, that has made you successful."[115] Heraclius was not using a royal "we;" he was not the evil ruler that had aroused God's anger. It was collective sin that caused defeat. That God would relent and forgive was certain; God had established the Roman Empire, and "no one can destroy that which is well-pleasing to God."[116] And then, when God had forgiven the Romans, Heraclius threatened, "Cannot the Romans put [Chosroes] to death, and destroy [his] empire when God places it in their hands?"[117]

Chosroes' letter and Heraclius's speech illustrate how defeat threw minor literary themes into prominence. Christian triumphalism, which proclaimed Roman history an unbroken march of conquest of the race chosen by God, foundered on unexpected, unprecedented, and thoroughly demoralizing Byzantine defeats at the hands of both traditional enemies like the Persians, and newer ones like the Arabs and Slavs. Constant, geographically close, and quite unprecedented, seventh-century defeat shattered the triumphalist association of Christian truth and Roman victory.

Christians did not reject triumphalism because it was insufficiently Christian, nor because of a long-standing dialectic of Greco-Roman and Christian ideologies. Defeat's bitter reality made triumphalism ludicrously out-of-step with experience, opening a gap between rhetoric and reality that Christians sought to close with a rhetoric that had long been available to them, but which they had not extensively exploited. Traditions explaining defeat as God's punishment of the Christian Roman community and treating war between Roman and barbarian as one between Christian and pagan were to dominate seventh-century literature. In the wake of defeat, Christians turned away from triumphalist claims of victory to a rhetoric that promised restoration of an increasingly idealized past.

Even worse, Christians could not turn to the traditional triumphalist response of the emperor's vice. The hundred-year tenure of the Heraclian dynasty through the worst of the Arab invasions further impelled writers to seek an explanation of imperial reverses that would not offend dynastic sensibilities. Religious dissidents like Maximus or the Monophysites accused the emperor of heresy, but their view hardly represented an official, or even a majority, view. On the other hand, Constantinopolitan and Melkite authors had an interest in the success of the ruling house that did not allow them to accuse it of heresy or other vices. It is not surprising that in these circumstances, they turned away from the emperor's vice to the same explanation as Eusebius or Sozomen: God's punishment of the citizens' collective sin.

As a corollary of this, the veritable explosion of anti-Jewish works in the seventh century coincided with the widespread adoption of the sin-punishment-repentance-restoration cycle that came to dominate explanations of contemporary Christian defeat. As discussed above, the Jews were a rhetorical foil for both Christian triumphalism and restoration. As I will show, anti-Jewish literature does not represent a systematic polemic against the Jews, but rather, an elaboration of a theme that complemented the new imperial rhetorical model. The anti-Jewish works are not directed outward to counter a Jewish polemic against Christianity. They are a necessary corollary to seventh-century Christian apologetics, an integral part of a new imperial model that could withstand a century of steady and calamitous defeat. The Jews were chosen as a rhetorical foil by Christian apologists because they were the example by contrast to whom the promise of Christian recovery could be certified.

The following chapters will trace this transformation of Byzantine imperial rhetoric, and in the course of this examination follow the critical role that the Jews played in the resolution of the Byzantines' self-doubt, and the legitimization of an empire whose legitimacy had for centuries been based on its victories.

Notes

1. Modern discussions of triumphalism are legion, and only some main works are noted here; see A. Alfoeldi, *Insignien und Tracht der roemischen Kaiser, Mitteilungen der Deutschen Archaeologischen Instituts* 50 (1935): 3–158; W. Ensslin, *Gottkaiser und Kaiser von Gottesgnaden,* [Sitzungsberichte der bayerischen Akademie der Wissenschaften,* phil.-hist. Abt.] (Munich, 1943), esp. 15–61; H. Hunger, *Prooimion: Elemente der byzantinischen Kaiseridee in den Arengen der Urkunden,* [Wiener byzantenische Studien 1] (Vienna, 1964); F. Dvornik, *Early Christian and Byzantine Political Philosophy,* 2 vols. (Washington, D.C., 1966), especially 1:205–78; G. Roesch, *Onoma Basileias* (Vienna, 1978), especially 41–61; S. MacCormack, *Art and Ceremony in Late Antiquity* (Berkeley, 1981); M. McCormick, *Eternal Victory: Triumphal Rulership in Late Antiquity, Byzantium and the Medieval West* (Cambridge, 1986).

2. See R. Wilken, *The Christians as the Romans Saw Them* (New Haven, 1984), 23–24. Martyrdom may not have even appeared victorious to many Christians. The great number of *lapsi* likely illustrates doubts inspired by Christ's inability to protect his faithful; see G. Ricotti, *The Age of the Martyrs: Christianity from Diocletian to Constantine,* trans. A. Bull (Milwaukee, 1959), 72–85.

3. *Pro Flacco,* 28.69; discussed by M. Stern, *Greek and Latin Authors on Jews and Judaism,* vol. 1 (Jerusalem, 1976), 196–201.

4. Justin Martyr, *Dialogue with Trypho,* ed. G. Archambault (Paris, 1909), ch. 110.

5. See L. Bonniec, "Aspects réligieux de la guerre à Rome," in *Problèmes de la guerre à Rome,* [*Civilisations et Sociétés* 12], (Paris, 1969), 101–15, esp. 111–15; A. Michel, "Les lois de la guerre et les problèmes romains dans la philosophie de Cicéron," in ibid., 171–77; R. Grant, "War — Just, Holy, Unjust — in Hellenistic and Early Christian Thought," *Augustinianum* 20 (1980): 174–78. Origen was this view's most forceful proponent, and greatly influenced Eusebius in his evaluation of the empire.

6. Eusebius, *Church History,* ed. E. Schwartz (Leipzig, 1903–09), III.7.1, 8–9.

7. Ibid., V.1.3–4. This is from the introduction the *Martyrs of Vienne and Lyons,* a second-century *acta* that Eusebius included in the *Church History.*

8. See ibid., IV.15.4.–5; IV.16.1; VI.1.1.

9. Ibid., IX.8.15. This explanation of disaster was neither new nor unique to Christians, see A. Pertusi, "L'atteggiamento spirituale della più antica storiografia byzantina," *Aevum* 30 (1956): 144–47.

10. Persecution in pagan countries retained the rhetoric of victory rather than punishment; for Persian martyrs, see Theodoret, V.38, or "La Passion Georgienne de St. Golinduch," ed. G. Garitte, *AB* 74 (1956): 405–40.

11. See Eusebius, *Church History,* IX.4.2–3, IX.9.1–3.

12. Ibid., VIII.14.8–9, VII.10.4. Maximin persecuted Christians so he could conduct divinations, and his Egyptian priests, their rites, without interference.

13. Ibid., IX.9.3.

14. Cf. Theodoret of Cyrus, *Ecclesiastical History,* ed. L. Parmentier and F. Schweidweiler, 2d ed. (Berlin, 1954), V.24. It was also a contest of ritual efficacy; both pretenders consulted their own soothsayers, and the Thebaid monk John proved superior; see Sozomen, *Ecclesiastical History,* ed. G. Hansen (Berlin, 1960), VII.22; Theodoret, V.24.

15. *Wars,* ed. J. Haury and G. Werth, *Opera Omnia* (Leipzig, 1962), II.26.2.

16. Socrates Scholasticus, *Ecclesiastical History,* VII.20. The war was fought, Socrates, VII.18, to protect Persian Christians. It is worth noting that all these conflations of foreign war and persecution take place in Persia.

17. Theodoret, *History,* V.38.

18. Ibid., V.24; see S. MacCormack, "Christ and Emperor, Time and Ceremonial in Sixth Century Byzantium and Beyond," *Byzantion* 52 (1982): 303–04.

19. See A. Michel, "Les lois de guerre," 180–83. See, however, F. Dvornik, *Early Christian and Byzantine Philosophy,* 737–45, on the "Athanasian" opposition in the fourth century. Augustine illustrates the cultural gulf between east and west.

20. Ironically, Christians were indebted to the Tetrarchs and their predecessors, who had exaggerated victory clichés during the political crises of the third century in order to establish legitimacy; see R. H. Storch, "The 'Absolutist' Theology of Victory: Its Place in the Late Empire," *Classica et mediaevalia* 29 (1968): 197–211; McCormick, *Eternal Victory,* 43–45.

21. Eusebius, *Life of Constantine,* ed. I. A. Heikel (Leipzig, 1904), 1.28–38.

22. Eusebius, *Tricennalia Oration,* ed. I. A. Heikel (Leipzig, 1902), 16.7.

23. Sozomen, *History,* VII.43; see also VII.23, where God opens a path for Theodosius II's army. Even Christian barbarians like Burgundians or Franks received victory; see Socrates, *History,* VII.30.

24. One time angels announce victory; see Socrates, VII.18. Castor and Pollux appear most commonly, but interestingly, they are almost never recognized during battle.

25. Sozomen, *History,* IX.5.

26. Socrates, *History,* VII.20.

27. Ibid., VII.24.

28. Eusebius, *Tricennalia Oration,* 16.6. See A. Harnack, *The Expansion of Christianity in the First Three Centuries,* trans. J. Moffatt, 2 vols. (New York, 1972), 1: 300–35, for the Christian expression, the "third race." I am now working on a book on Christian ethnography before Constantine.

29. See Eusebius, *Tricennalia Oration,* 16.5; see also M. Simon *Verus Israel: A Study of the Relations between Christians and Jews in the Roman Empire (135–425),* trans. H. McKeating (Oxford, 1986), 68, 169–73; R. Wilken, *John Chrysostom and the Jews: Rhetoric and Reality in the Late Fourth Century* (Berkeley, 1983), 145–58; R. Grant, *Eusebius as Church Historian* (Oxford, 1980), 97–113; Grant, "Eusebius, Josephus

and the Fate of the Jews," *Society of Biblical Literature 1979 Seminar Papers*, ed. P. J. Achtemeier, vol. 2 (Missoula, Mont., 1979), 69–86.

30. *PG* 38, cols. 261–62.

31. Eusebius, *Tricennalia Oration*, 16.4–5.

32. Plutarch, "The Fortune of Alexander," ed. and trans. F. Babbitt (Cambridge, Mass., 1957), 4:393.

33. Strabo, *Geographica*, vol. 1, ed. A. Meineke (Graz, 1969 [Leipzig, 1877]), IV.4.4.

34. Eusebius, *Tricennalia Oration*, 16.6.

35. See C. Lacy, "The Greek View of Barbarians in the Hellenistic Age, as Derived from Representative Literary and Artistic Evidence from the Hellenistic Period," diss., University of Colorado, 1976, esp. 196–209; J. P. V. D. Balsdon, *Romans and Aliens* (Chapel Hill, 1979), 59–73, 214–59; A. N. Sherwin-White, *Racial Prejudice in Imperial Rome* (Cambridge, 1967). Lacy, "Greek View," 196, concludes, "The entire range of barbarians . . . are lumped together under the single heading 'the barbarians.'"

36. *Wars*, VI.14.9; VI.28.26, where Procopius contrasts the pagan Persians and Christian Lazi; see H. Chadwick, "The Relativity of Moral Codes: Rome and Persia in Late Antiquity," in *Early Christian Literature and the Classical Intellectual Tradition, In honorem Robert M. Grant*, ed. E. Schoedel and R. Wilken (Paris 1979), 135–53.

37. Strabo, *Geographica*, IV.4.5, on the Celts; Isocrates, *Panegyricus*, vol. 1, ed. G. Benseler and F. Blass (Leipzig, 1913), 151.

38. Strabo, *Geographica*, IV.4.2, on the Celts.

39. Velleius Paterculus, *History*, ed. K. Holm (Leipzig, 1863, 1875), 2:117.3, 118.1; see Balsdon, *Romans and Aliens*, 62–63; Sherwin-White, *Racial Prejudice*, 36–61 (for the Germans especially); Lacy, "Greek View," 211–212.

40. *Politics*, I.1.5.

41. Claudius Mamertinus, *Gratiarum actio, XII panegyrici latini*, ed. R. Mynors (Oxford, 1964), 4.1–2.

42. Procopius, *Wars*, V.9.27.

43. Ibid., III.2.11

44. Ibid., III.5.22–23.

45. Ibid., IV.12.1.

46. More to the point, the Byzantines had endured one of their greatest humiliations when the Persians compelled them to sign treaties making territorial concessions; see E. Chrysos, "The Title *Basileus* in Early Byzantine International Relations," *DOP* 32 (1978): 29–45; idem, "Der Kaiser und die Koenige," *Die Voelker an der mittleren und unteren Donau im fuenften und sechsten Jahrhundert*, ed. H. Wolfram and F. Daim (Vienna, 1980), 143–48.

47. *Corpus iuris civilis*, ed. P. Krueger (Dublin/Zurich, 1972), 2:2.

48. *Corpus iuris civilis*, ed. R. Schoell and G. Kroll (Dublin/Zurich, 1972), 3:243.

49. Ibid., 144–45.

50. Dio Chrysostom, *First Discourse on Kingship*, ed. G. de Budé (Leipzig, 1916, 1919), 32.

51. Theophylact Simocatta, *On the Predestined Terms of Life*, ed. and trans. C. Garton and L. G. Westerink, [*Arethusa Monographs* 6] (Buffalo, 1978), 28.

52. See Evagrius, *Ecclesiastical History,* ed. J. Bidez and L. Parmentier (London, 1898), III.41.

53. This idea was thoroughly Hellenistic; see H. Hunger, *Kaiser Justinian I (527–65),* [*Anzeiger der oesterreichischen Akademie der Wissenschaften,* phil.-hist. Klasse, 102] (Vienna, 1965), 339–56.

54. Pliny the Younger, *Panegyricus,* ed. R. T. A./B. Mynors (Oxford, 1964), 80.4; see the comments of W. Ensslin, *Gottkaiser und Kaiser von Gottesgnaden,* 21–53.

55. See H. Hunger, *Prooimion: Elemente der byzantinischen Kaiseridee in der Arengen der Urkunden,* [*Wiener byzantinische Studien* 1] (Vienna, 1964), 49–63; D. Olster, "The Politics of Usurpation in the Seventh Century: The Reign of Phocas (602–10)," diss., University of Chicago, 1986, 312–57.

56. *Third Discourse on Kingship,* 51.

57. Theodoret, *History,* V.25; see the guarantees of victory that Theodosius receives for his faith; Socrates, *History,* VIII.18, 20; Sozomen, *History,* IX.16.

58. Socrates, *History,* 7.22.

59. Ibid., 7.43.

60. See W. Kaegi, *Byzantium and the Decline of Rome* (Princeton, 1968), 176–223; G. C. Chestnut, *The First Christian Historians: Eusebius, Socrates, Sozomen, Theodoret and Evagrius,* [*Théologie historique* 46] (Paris, 1977), 223–42. E. Kitzinger, "The Cult of Images Before Iconoclasm," *DOP* 8 (1954): 125–28, and Av. Cameron, "Corippus' Poem on Justin II: A Terminus of Antique Art," *Annali della Scuola Normale Superiore di Pisa* 5, t.3, (1975): 160–65; Cameron, "Images of Authority: Elites and Icons in Late Sixth-Century Byzantium," *Past and Present* 84 (1979): 29–35, assume that a sense of decline followed Justinian's death, an assertion that merely projects our own hindsight.

61. Theodoret, *History,* IV.32.

62. Sozomen, *History,* VI.2.

63. See Hunger, *Prooimion,* 123–54.

64. Agathias, see below; Menander Protector, *Historia, FHG* 4, fr. 5.1, 9.1 for Justinian; fr. 18.6 for Justin II.

65. Ibid., V.13.7–8.

66. Ibid., V.14.1–2.

67. Socrates, *History,* III.20; Sozomen, *History,* VI.1–3, boasted that Julian's Christian assassin was a "tyrannicide," and that Julian's arrogance led to Persian victory; Theodoret, *History,* III.22, IV.1, attributed the Roman defeat to Julian's impiety and tyranny.

68. Sozomen, *History,* VI.40; Socrates, *History,* IV.15, 21, 24; Ammianus Marcellinus, *Res gestae,* ed. C. V. Clark, 2 vols. (Berlin, 1910–15), XXVI.10. Socrates, *History,* IV.35 suggested that Valens's death at Adrianople was God's method for ending his Arian persecution.

69. *Vie de Théodore Sykéôn* [*Subsidia hagiographica* 48], 2 vols., ed. A. J. Festugière (Brussels, 1970), ch. 119.

70. Ibid., ch. 166. Such a negative contemporary view of Heraclius is quite rare. The Byzantine chronicle tradition from Theophanes on attributed the success of the Persian invasions to the vices of the emperor Phocas, and New Rome's victory to the virtues of Heraclius; see Olster, "Usurpation," 2–7.

71. See Socrates, *History*, V.2.

72. Flavius Cresconius Corippus, *In laudem Justini Augusti minoris libri iv*, ed. and trans. Av. Cameron (London, 1976), II.26–65.

73. See J. Haldon, "Some Remarks to the Background of the Iconoclast Controversy," *Byzsl* 38 (1977): 161–84; F. Tinnefeld, *Kategorien der Kaiserkritik in der byzantinischen Historiographie von Prokop bis Niketas Choniates* (Munich, 1971), 11–16; see below, and Chapter 2 on George of Pisidia.

74. See Olster, "Usurpation," for the chronology of the correspondence between Heraclius and Chosroes; see also George of Pisidia, in *Heraclius*, ed. A. Pertusi, *Georgio di Pisidia, Poemi: I. Panegyrici epici* (Ettal, 1959), 3, fr. 50; cf. Theophanes, *Chronographia*, 2 vols., ed. C. de Bon (Leipzig, 1883), 324.17–20.

75. Paschal Chronicle, ed. L. Dindorf (Bonn, 1832), 707.15–16; 707.9–10; 708.9–13; see also W. Kaegi, "New Evidence on the Early Reign of Heraclius," *BZ* 66 (1973): 308–30; Kaegi, "Two Notes on Heraclius," *REB* 37 (1979):221–24.

76. *Pasch. Chron.*, 707:18–22.

77. Ibid., 708:13–16.

78. Ibid., 709.14–16. Chosroes had himself been "adopted" by Phocas's predecessor Maurice.

79. Nicephorus the Patriarch, *Breviarum*, ed. C. de Boor (Leipzig, 1880), 23.

80. Ibid., 27; George the Monk, *Chronicon*, 2 vols., ed. C. de Boor (Leipzig, 1904), 673.

81. The chronicle tradition has far less to say about Heraclius's heterodoxy, since they relied on the tradition that Heraclius had been duped by evil ecclesiastical advisors like Sergius and Athanasius; see Theophanes, *Chronographia*, 329.21–30.27.

82. Anastasius Apocrisarius, *Relatio motionis inter Maximum et principes*, PG 90.112a–c; see also Chapter 4 for a more detailed discussion of Maximus.

83. Michael the Syrian, *Chronique*, 4 vols., tr. J.-B. Chabot (Paris, 1899–1910), 402; for the Monophysite view of the Arab invasions, see J. Moorhead, "The Monophysite Response to the Arab Invasions," *Byz* 51 (1981): 580–91.

84. *PG*, 1156–57.

85. See Kaegi, *Byzantium*, 185–87, for the ecclesiastical historians' view of Honorius.

86. Procopius, *Wars*, III.2.25–26, see Kaegi, *Byzantium*, 214–16.

87. Procopius, *Wars*, III.3.10–11.

88. Socrates, *History*, VII.10.

89. Sozomen, *History*, IX.6. Significantly, the argument that the citizens' sins were responsible for defeat was limited to the west.

90. Theodoret, Letter 22.

91. Ibid., Letter 52.

92. Socrates, *History*, V:intro.

93. This integration of collective sin into a decidedly imperial context in which the emperor retains his role as mediator finds its most explicit expression in the seventh-century court authors George of Pisidia and Theodore Syncellus; see below, Chapters 3 and 4.

94. Socrates, *History*, V:intro. As Theodoret, V.24, explained, "The peace of

the churches was secured by the most religious emperor." For the role of the emperor as the "protector" of the church and leader of the Christian community, see D. Olster, "Justinian, Imperial Rhetoric and the Church," *Byzsl* 50 (1989): 165–75.

95. *Sancti Romani melodi cantica: Cantica genuina* (Oxford, 1963), 469; see also E. Topping, "On Earthquakes and Fires," *BZ* 71 (1978): 22–35.

96. Romanus, *Sancti Romani melodi*, 470.

97. For the church historians, see G. F. Chesnut, *The First Christian Historians: Eusebius, Socrates, Sozomen, Theodoret and Evagrius,* [*Théologie historique* 46] (Paris, 1977), 207–12; Kaegi, *Byzantium,* 176–204.

98. Agathias, *Historiarum libri quinque,* ed. R. Keydell (Berlin, 1967), IV.5.1–3.

99. *Wars,* III.5.25.

100. *De magistratibus populi romani libri tres,* ed. R. Wuensch (Leipzig, 1903), I.3.8.

101. Agathias, *Historiarum,* V.5.5–6.

102. See the insightful remarks of A. Pertusi, "L'atteggiamento spirituale della più antica storiografica byzantina," *Aevum* 30 (1956): 150–52.

103. Agathias, *Historiarum,* IV.22.8.

104. Ibid., V.4.3.

105. *Wars,* II.10.4–5.

106. Menander, *Historia,* fr. 6.1; see also Chosroes' speech in Procopius on the fall of Antioch that sorrows must necessarily accompany good fortune; see also Av. Cameron, *Procopius,* 117.

107. Zosimus, *New History,* ed. L. Mendelssohn (Leipzig, 1887; reprint, Hildesheim, 1963), I.57.

108. Evagrius, *History,* III.41.

109. Ibid.

110. Ibid., 79–80. Dated to 623, ibid., 79, it responds to the invasion of Persia by Heraclius and his "brigand bands."

111. Pseudo-Sebeos, *Histoire d'Heraclius,* trans. F. Macler (Paris, 1904), 80. Doubtless reworked, this letter nonetheless bears a close similarity to one that Theophanes, 301, describes being set on the altar of Hagia Sophia.

112. M. Avi-Yonah, *The Jews under Roman and Byzantine Rule: A Political History of Palestine from the Bar Kokhba War to the Arab Conquest* (New York, 1984), 265–70. The Persians even established a Palestinian Jewish state; see F. Dexinger and W. Seibt, "A Hebrew Lead Seal from the Period of the Sassanian Occupation of Palestine (614–629 A.D.)," *Revue des Études Juives* 140 (1981): 303–17.

113. Sebeos, *Histoire,* 78.

114. Herodian, *Ab excessu divi Marci libri octo,* ed. C. Stavenhagen (Stuttgart, 1969), "Severus Alexander," III.5.

115. Sebeos, *Histoire,* 78.

116. Ibid.

117. Ibid.

3. Crisis and Response: The "New" Rhetoric of George of Pisidia

The preceding chapter revealed two minor themes of Christian Roman rhetoric: the transformation of *Roman* defeat at the hands of the barbarians into the first step of the process of *Christian* victory over heathen enemies, and the causal role of collective sin in defeat. In the seventh century, these themes became dominant as the triumphalist vocabulary of war evolved. This evolution, which became more pronounced as pagan victories mounted, can be best seen in the works of George of Pisidia, arguably Byzantium's greatest poet, whose poems recorded Heraclius's victory in the last war between Sassanid Persia and Byzantium (604–28).[1]

George is best known to scholarship as the poet who thoroughly assimilated Christian rhetoric and theology into the classical genre of panegyric. George, however, never thought of himself as a Christian poet, much less a theologian. In one of his rare glimpses into his art, George addressed his patron Heraclius, "I have not possessed the well-versed words of dogmas, but always reveling in your military prowess, have I portrayed the fall of tyrants, the flight of enemies, and the variegated and diverse tales of your labors."[2] George advertised his own inadequacy in order better to praise Heraclius's universal wisdom; he had no desire to engage in theological speculation.[3] The business of praising one's patron was a precise rhetorical exercise; panegyric was one of the most circumscribed and structured literary genres of late Roman literature.[4] But as we shall see, George could not ignore the growing gap between triumphalist clichés and the defeats that made such clichés obsolete. His so-called Christianization of panegyric must be seen against this historical background.

Thus, it is not surprising to find George's earliest dated poem, on Heraclius's overthrow of Phocas, is also his most conservative. Writing some years before the fall of Jerusalem, George only briefly mentioned the Persian and Avar threats and simply referred to the Persians as "images of beasts," and Avars as "barbarians."[5]

In the tradition of earlier panegyrists, George predicted that the advent of the virtuous Heraclius would repair the damage done by the vices of Phocas. "For if the citizenry was often being destroyed, falling through the negligence of the rulers, even now the citizenry have been saved by God through the noble deeds of those who rule blessedly."[6] Nowhere in this poem is there the least hint that Christian reverses were due either to sinfulness or to God's punishment. George simply followed the customary formula of imperial setback and recovery. Certainly, Heraclius was helped and guarded by God, but so was every emperor, both Christian and pagan alike.[7]

The dominant rhetorical image of Heraclius in the poem is that of the hunter. Even greater than the hunters of old, he is the hunter of the enemies of Rome, bestial men and bestial passions.[8] This imperial image was nearly as old as Roman panegyric. Five hundred years before, Pliny had praised Trajan for being a great hunter, locking the barbarians in their lairs.[9] This first poem, written before the fall of Jerusalem and Egypt — that is, before the full disaster of the Persian wars had unfolded — was largely a compendium of older *topoi,* often cunningly rearranged, but hardly original. The war of Persians and Romans is not one between heathens and Christians, but the traditional conflict of civilized Romans and uncivilized barbarians.

Even a decade later, after the loss of Jerusalem and Egypt, George's poetry retained the rhetoric of Roman–barbarian conflict, with all its attendant cultural implications. In the *Persian Expedition,* from the early 620s, Heraclius was compared to a Homeric hero[10] and judged superior to Alexander,[11] while Chosroes was compared to Xerxes.[12] George dwells on Heraclius's restoration of order in the army after the *ataksia* caused by his "evil" predecessor,[13] and on his presence in battle, fighting almost as a simple soldier.[14] George followed the lead of Pliny, who had written five centuries earlier, "How wonderful it was of you . . . to rekindle the dying flame of military discipline by destroying [the evils] of the preceding reign."[15]

No less conventional is the description of Heraclius's victory against the Persians. When George described the passage of arms between them, Heraclius's victory was a Roman victory over barbarians, not a Christian victory over heathen:

> For who expected that the almost unconquerable race of the Persians would give their backs to the sword of the Romans? Who expected, among so many waves of misfortunes to joy in their midst? Who was persuaded, in the midst of such a great dearth of necessities, that the cities would furnish provisions, unless the weigher of all things had driven away the evil ones from the lands that are near to us through you [Heraclius].[16]

This victory of the Christians against their age-old enemies was hardly a demonstration of Christianity's truth.[17] Naturally, God aided the pious emperor Heraclius, but the gods of Rome, whether Jupiter or Christ, had aided every emperor, pagan and Christian. The Christian god remained a god of victory who maintained the empire in the face of the barbarians,[18] and the emperor his earthly imitation: "How fine is the monarchy which rules with God. For it was not a many-headed anarchy, but rather the monarchy that rules with God that cherishes and corrects all through its reason, and throws aside their confused twistings."[19] Victory alone ensured the mimetic order of heaven on earth, and George concluded his poem with the prayer that Heraclius might "raise a trophy over both passions and barbarians!"[20] Thus his second poem ended on the same note as his first, remaining fixed in its traditional thematic framework.

No less important for the usurper Heraclius, George prayed to God to extend the reign of his patron's dynasty to eternity,[21] another convention of panegyric. The third-century pagan Menander Rhetor had specifically recommended just the concluding sentiments that George expressed.[22]

But alongside the *Persian Expedition*'s largely traditional triumphalism, George begins to introduce the rhetoric of Christian victory against heathens. For the most part, the Persians' paganism follows classical ethnographic lines. On one occasion, George berated the Persians for worshipping the created rather than the creator, and continued, "Among whom some god is insanely thought to be an armoured horse," another classical ethnographic *topos* adopted by George.[23]

Later in the poem, however, George first raises what will eventually become his most dominant theme of victory: the struggle against the violators of Christian holy places and rites, a war against pagan persecutors of Christians. Heraclius inspired his troops with the idea that they marched forth not against barbarians, but against persecutors: "For it is proper that we, as the creations of God, march against the enemies who bow to created things; who defile the altars that were undefiled with blood, with gory murders full of blood; who sully the churches, pure of unworthy passions, with passionate pleasure."[24] In earlier Byzantine literature, wars with barbarians had generally not been fought for the sake of the Christian religion.[25] Nor is the conflict of Christian and heathen very prominent in *Persian Expedition*. But this poem first hints at the theme that will come to dominate George's treatment of the Persian War.

The *Persian Expedition* introduces a second theme that would also become prominent in George's later poetry, the single combat of Heraclius and Chosroes, the personifications of their respective empires and cults. George began to adapt the traditional identification of emperor and empire to the new religious dimension of war so as to narrow the scope of the war to two combatants: "That one had the fire to which he bowed down, but you, most powerful, had the Wood [of the Cross] that raised you up."[26]

Scholars have noted both these themes in George's poetry, but not their relative obscurity in the early poetry. In *The Persian Expedition*, these themes are poorly integrated and secondary to the more traditional themes; in George's first poem, they do not appear. As we approach his more mature work, it is necessary to remember, first, these themes do *not* appear uniformly in George's poetry; second, they have a long literary history; and third, that their use before the seventh century implies that George was inspired not by a sudden religious upsurge (although there may well have been one) but from the conscious choice of a client artist to compose material that suited his patron.

The impact that immediate political circumstances made on George's poetry explains the sharply distinct thematic emphases of his two poems about the Avar siege of Constantinople in the summer of 626. *On Bonus the Patrician*, which only mentions the looming Avar threat, was probably written at the beginning of the summer of 626, ostensibly to praise Heraclius's regent while the emperor campaigned against the Persians.[27] *On the Attack and Defeat of the Barbarians* was written in the next couple of years after the end of the siege, to record the victory of the city during the absence of its emperor[28] and to praise the Patriarch Sergius, Bonus's co-regent and Heraclius's main source of money.[29]

Bonus also retains the traditional perspective of George's first two works both thematically and in its technical praises of Heraclius. Heraclius's absence in the east was a technical difficulty, but by no means a new one. Since the emperors had ceased serious campaigning more than two hundred years earlier, imperial rhetoric had devised the means to ascribe victory to an absent emperor. The church historians endowed the successors of Theodosius the Great, the last emperor for more than two centuries to campaign with the army, with victories in absentia through their favor with God. Socrates wrote of the palace-bound Theodosius II, "For the God of the universe has afforded this most devout emperor in our times supernatural aid."[30] The same was no less true in panegyric. Corippus, praising the victories of the general John in the *Iohannidos*, ascribed his victories to Justinian, "Justinian, prince, soar to your triumphs, and a joyful victor, deliver the law to broken tyrants."[31] Corippus continued that the war cry of the Roman army did not call on John, but upon Justinian and his divine protector: "Divine Justinian, Christ most powerful will fight for your arms. Best father, preserve the Empire of our ruler."[32] Justinian, Theodosius, and Heraclius shared the traditional claim that victory found its source in their personal favor with God.

In fact the title, *To Bonus,* is rather misleading; there is little about Bonus but a great deal about Heraclius in the poem. George did not praise Bonus for his own deeds, but for his participation in Heraclius's; they were "one soul in two bodies,"[33] and although Heraclius was in Persia, he was "within [Bonus], even if he seems distant."[34] At every turn, George reframed the absence of Heraclius to demonstrate his universal dominion. Even from Persia, "The cosmos sees the sun of Rome [Heraclius] shine."[35]

Unable to return to his city, Heraclius remained its source of security.[36] There could be no substitute for Heraclius, and his own children led the citizens' chorus for his return: "The youthful shoots of your dynasty, lord, the captivating pearls of your life, shedding tears as if they were pearls, will persuade you; for because they are endowed with a mind just like that which sowed them, they hold one consolation of hope, your immediate presence through God's aid."[37] Entirely in the tradition of pagan as well as Christian panegyric, the poem ended with a prayer for divine inspiration and care for the emperor and through him, the city.[38]

George makes clear the true panegyrical object of *Bonus* in the first lines. There, he compares the labors and accomplishments of Heraclius and Heracles. Heraclius, whose labors "no human body might bear,"[39] was far greater because he accomplished cosmic renewal.[40] The character of this renewal is quite specific; it is the restoration of the body politic after the evil rule of Phocas.[41] In the traditional mode, Heraclius would bring "parental" virtue to the work of restoration: "You had pity on us, whom you freed of old, for whose sake you endured such great labor pains when you wished to give birth to the world that had been made sterile by the tyrant [Phocas]. You pitied us as innocent children, yet even children are often insolent in the simplicity of their childish incoherence."[42] Heraclius the parent must discipline and watch over his "innocent children."[43] And George, extending this parental metaphor, goes on to describe how a parent's love might lead him to indulge the child's "slaps."[44] But Heraclius, a more fitting parent, recognized the greater necessity of discipline. "But these [parental] habits are not the same for your power, who raises your fear among us, no, even up to feigning anger."[45] Finally, George concludes his description of Heraclius's restorative powers with a medical metaphor, "But you visit all, as if in a time of universal plague, and yourself a physician, you everywhere confront the universal trauma of the sick."[46]

On Bonus retains the moral causation of the emperor's virtue and vice found in George's first two poems. Nowhere in the poem does George suggest any causal relationship between collective sin and the Avar attack, much less a cycle of sin, repentance, and renewal. Its dominant theme is the praise of the emperor through the same techniques as used by Corippus in the *Iohannidas*.

The *Avaric War,* however, although written only a few months after *Bonus,* was composed in altogether different circumstances: the threat of an Avar siege had been realized and defeated.[47] And it is only in this poem, his fourth dated work, and one written fifteen years into his career, that the restoration themes scholars most identify with George came to dominate his poetry.

The change in emphasis, however, does not mean that George discarded his previous rhetorical and thematic apparatus. The Avars' advance from the Danube was not attributed, initially, to any sinfulness on the part of the Byzantines, but rather to the "uncontrollable and life-devouring dragon," Phocas.[48] Avars did not cease to be mindless, brutal barbarians, posing a threat not to the Romans' religion but to their *kratos,* power.[49] The Persians, remaining mired in their insolence, employed the Avars, "so that they might whet their sharpened sword, the barbarian sword, against us."[50] "Just as fire from fire," barbaric Persian duplicity inflamed barbaric Avar passions.[51] Like the pacific Alexander Severus, Heraclius did not desire war but had been compelled to fight, "for although he had no desire to see the face of war, he had, from necessity, war facing him."[52] Heraclius, the civilized Roman whose first love was peace,[53] first sought peace with the treacherous Khagan.[54]

Barbarian aggression drove Heraclius to war, and for three years he had been absent achieving martial glory.[55] The *Avaric War* shares with *On Bonus* the practical problem of Heraclius's absence, and its rhetorical resolution. The absence of the emperor during the siege was again turned to a demonstration of his universal powers. Even in Persia, his concern for the city never slackened, and his faith in God and tears on their behalf were themselves weapons.[56] The defense of the city was credited to his foresight,[57] his words inspired every Constantinopolitan, both citizen and "foreigner," to stand firm against the enemy.[58] Far away in Persia, Heraclius seemed present to the Constantinopolitans. "Deep within his thoughts, he was very much present, however far the distance between where we were and he stood."[59]

The co-regents of Heraclius, Bonus and the Patriarch Sergius,[60] reflected their master's glory. "For I think it was necessary that such a great Lord necessarily have such great servants."[61] The Patriarch Sergius is especially lauded, for he is the spiritual leader of the Constantinopolitans, and the one who carried the image of the Virgin around the walls.[62] With the inspired power of the Virgin, Sergius, standing in the emperor's stead, becomes a "new" Moses, the Khagan a second Pharaoh, and the Byzantines' sea victory a repeat of the Red Sea miracle.[63]

But despite these similarities with *On Bonus,* the poem's introduction distinguishes the *Avaric War* from George's earlier poems. Instead of praise for Heraclius, George begins, "If some painter desired to make manifest the trophies of battle, he would give primacy to the one who gave birth without the need of seed alone, and paint an icon."[64] But although George includes the conventional clichés of divine intervention in the battle, more mundane causes are given greater weight.[65] Christ hindered the Persians' and Avars' plans to join forces, but the Byzantine blockade of the Persians at Chalcedon was a far more tangible cause.[66] The Avar assault against walls near the Blachernae church inspired George to praise the Virgin's martial might,[67] but rocks and arrows turned back the barbarians.[68] Divine judgment guides the weapons of the defenders,[69] but there is nothing original or even particularly Christian about this.[70] Even in the sea fight by the Virgin's own church at Blachernae, she lent invisible aid but performed no spectacular miracle.[71] Athena at Salamis cut a far more impressive figure.

George does not emphasize divine intervention in battle in the *Avaric War,* because defeat stems from a new source. The sins of the citizens replaced Phocas's vice or barbarian bloodlust as the causal foundation of defeat. Now George maintains, "Barbarian guile did not pursue us, but our in-born sin."[72] This new scheme sets the Virgin in a new light, not as the military patroness of the city but as the agent of catharsis:

> Hail [Virgin], commander of martial tears that burn down the arrogance of the barbarians. . . . For when you saw the flowering filthiness from the sterile villainy of our evil deeds that drove us to the flames and destruction, you rushed forward before the fire, even as it reached toward the kindling . . . and opening the well-springs of your eyes, you watered our barrenness, and cast water on the flame, and raised our barren hearts to bear fruit under a strange rain.[73]

As if this baroque metaphor was not enough, George added another involved nautical metaphor that chastised the Romans for upsetting the ship of state with their sins, and thanked the Virgin for righting the vessel by purifying the citizens' hearts.[74]

A third metaphor illustrates the difficulties that the restoration process of sin and catharsis raised. George compared the citizens' attempts to secure the favor of Christ through the Virgin to suborning a judge. The icon of the Virgin, "not made by human hands," received the citizens' repentant prayers,[75] and interceding with her son, obtained a favorable judgment for her clients.[76] But so rare was the notion that repentance was the source of victory, and so odd the Virgin's intercession in battle through the purification of the citizenry, that George lacked a vocabulary to express it. He thus turned to the Latinism *kompheusos,* from *confessus,* in order to combine both liturgical and judicial senses of confession.[77] Only in this way could he substitute collective repentance and purification in the place of the emperor's personal mediation.

Thus, the Virgin, first in war and first in birth, found a martial context, not of military might but of mediation for the citizens' sins. The victory before the walls was only a reflection of a spiritual victory over sin. "Let us, therefore, sing a new hymn, not on drums, but rather on the instruments that mystically sound the harmony within us."[78] The spiritual renewal of the citizens, played on the instruments of the senses and taught by Christ the pedagogue, had driven away the "childish disorder of the passions."[79] Repentence had became the source of imperial renewal so that "now, leading his shining allies, [Heraclius] could confront the unenlightened barbarians."[80]

It is no coincidence that the theme of collective sin, God's punishment, repentance, and restoration begins with the *Avaric War.* Victory linked Christian triumphalist rhetoric and the rhetoric of restoration; it was pointless to emphasize repentance without victory. Thus, George ended the *Avaric War* with a gloss from Claudian hailing the marriage of victory and Heraclius. But although victory remained the pivot of George's rhetoric, he transcended earlier triumphalist themes so that defeat could be worked into a scheme that promised restoration and protected the emperor's integrity.

There are no further dated poems of George from the Persian War. George reached the climax of his thematic evolution in the *Heraclias,* an epic written after the Persian War. The *Heraclias,* like all George's poetry, glorified the emperor through well-defined court rhetoric and themes. That the *Heraclias* indeed drew from a prescribed thesaurus of stock court formulae can be seen in a comparison of George's epic with the letter of Heraclius in the spring of 628 that announced the victory in the Persian War. Both open with a call to nature, God's creation, to rise and praise God.[81] Both structure this evocation to introduce the dichotomy between the Christians, who worship the creator, and their opponents, who adore the created.[82] Both describe the fall of the "proud" Chosroes into the "depths,"[83] and finally both dwell on the delicious irony of Chosroes' son killing him.[84]

The striking similarity of the letter and the *Heraclias* have led some writers, at least, to suggest George's authorship for both.[85] But there is no reason to believe that George wrote the letter. Rather, their similarity illustrates how the dominant court rhetoric left little room for individual expression. The emphasis on sin and forgiveness tells us little about George's own opinion of his contemporaries' morals, but only that his patron found the citizens' sin an acceptable explanation of imperial disaster. Heraclius may have sincerely felt that sin had brought on disaster; he may have also found this explanation more acceptable than the traditional explanation of the emperor's, his own, vice.

The *Avaric War* introduced the causative role of sin, and the *Heraclias* reiterated that sin, not fate, laid the Romans low.[86] Throughout George's later poetry, God reminds man of his sinfulness through periodic chastisements. God does not always have to apply the rod; sometimes, the threat is sufficient: "And often, although you [God] have stretched your bow, you release the sting, and loose the tension of the string, but you fashion, in appearance, your fear, and you paint the very image of a threat, until the one gazing on the blow, terrified, bends his neck as he goes down to his knees."[87] But when the sin requires, God must adopt drastic measures: "Oh boundless kindness: from one fear, he purifies us of our sickness before the time of judgment, when he applies the purifying fire, and he pricks us with misfortunes that teach, and he contrives a reward for us from sickness, and he accomplishes from the apparent punishment of life, the universal source of salvation."[88] There is nothing new about this idea except its political and collective contexts.[89] Punishment had always turned Christians to repentance, but never before to imperial restoration.

Divine anger initiates an imperial restoration process that creates a political context not only for catharsis, but also for sin itself. George combined the rhetorics of the citizens' sin and the emperor's vice to produce a context for sin that served Heraclius the usurper's political needs. Phocas, "the furious and life-devouring dragon of tyranny," had infected the citizens with sin and wrought harm "even worse than the hydra," for his venom poisoned the commonwealth.[90] But even after Heraclius's accession, "[Phocas's] sickness, taking this starting-point from our deeds, raised many struggles between the factions [*merōn*]."[91] George referred specifically to the struggles of the Blues and Greens, the "circus factions," whose conflict during the civil war between Heraclius and Phocas played a large role in paralyzing imperial responses to the Persians.[92] The *Heraclias* added a lurid description of how the citizens, "who had matured in the drunkenness of [Phocas's] tyranny, endured an internal disorder of the limbs, and the City endured suffering from nearly all its citizens, who roiled about in a frenzy as if a centaur."[93] Thus, George defined sin to serve the political needs of the court; collective sin became political disorder. George's *Life of Anastasius the Persian* explained: "And at that moment when the flood of our sins burst into physical flames in our cities, the new Nebuchadnezzer took Jerusalem and after razing the city with fire, bore away our trophy, the ark of the new covenant."[94] Physical flames are not an abstract metaphor but a reference to deme rioting, which had left a powerful impression on contemporaries. The anti-Jewish dialogue, *Doctrine of Jacob the Newly Baptised*,[95] the *Fall of Jerusalem to Persians* by Antiochus Monachus,[96] and the *Miracles of Saint Demetrius*[97] all judge the conflict of the demes as a form of collective citizen sin.

The citizens' purification, therefore, was not a simple moral issue, but had wide political implications. The emperor assumed a new role as the purifier of the citizens' sins. This association of renewal and purification redefined the imperial office. Heraclius remained the subjects' mediator with God, the possessor of a mystical power that enabled him to beg God's forgiveness, and more importantly, attain it.[98] The conclusion of the *Hexameron* juxtaposes Heraclius's own submission to God and mediation on behalf of his subjects, with the victories that God bestowed on him. "Bending his neck for our sakes to God, all Persia bent in turn at his feet. Inclining his legs for our sakes at the altar, they trampled every barbarian."[99] But Heraclius also assumed the role as the agent of purification: "Since you, just like a father, relieved the swelling of all our innermost places because you leeched the veins within us of passions, and purged us with your blessed purity, you set in bounds our internal contagion of savagery.[100] This medical metaphor is among George's favorites.[101] Both the *Heraclias* and the *Expedition to Persia* include medical metaphors for the restoration of military discipline, and *On Bonus* for the restoration of civil order.[102] In none of these works is sin the main source of the illness. In the *Heraclias,* however, when Heraclius heals the sinful citizens,[103] he is a doctor who "follows the paths of incorruption."[104]

This redefinition of sin as internal political disorder complemented a similar redefinition of war as a struggle against external sin. In *Against Severus,* Chosroes threatened not simply the Romans' cities, but the souls of Christians as well. "It was not for the cursed Chosroes to move simply weapons against our bodies, but he wished more to destroy our hearts, to burn our faith to dust like our cities."[105] Heraclius did not war against Chosroes the barbarian, but against sin's demonic agent.[106] The *Heraclias* called Heraclius a second Noah who set his ark "in martial" to stand fast not only against the military cataclysm of the disastrous first decade of his reign, but against the sinful "flood" of Chosroes in which "all flesh had been drowned in the flood of every sort of sin, until, receiving the branch of the forgotten olive, he saved the remnants of life."[107] The military flood of Chosroes was apposite to the flood of sin, and his defeat, an act of purification that restored God's creation, and transcended the struggle of Roman and barbarian. It is no wonder that George coined a new title for Heraclius, *kosmorystys,* the "savior of the world."[108]

George replaces the traditional bestial barbarian, destructive and stupid with greed, with Chosroes, the personification of the world's sin whose removal restored the creation: "But heaven, earth, fire, water, air, clouds, and all the cosmos of the things above and below acclaims with us the purposes of God, that one [Chosroes] is fallen and everything is saved."[109] The fall of Chosroes invoked the fall of Satan himself. George drew on Isaiah 14:12–13, the "fall of the morning star," Lucifer, for Chosroes' fall. "Now Chosroes understands that his fiery-bright Morning-Star [Lucifer] is darkened."[110] Just as Lucifer the morning star fell, so too did his earthly counterpart: "Let all the chorus of the stars exult, since it displayed the star-slave fallen, even while he was ignorant of his fall."[111] Christ had thrown down the devil from heaven; Heraclius, aided by Christ, "cast down the enemy who was exalted in his evil, from the clouds into Tartarus."[112]

Creation's renewal evoked the mimesis of Christ's creation. Christ had created the world out of chaos, and Heraclius recreated it out of political chaos.[113] The *Heraclias* dubbed Heraclius's six-year campaign in Persia a "hexameron." The last part of George's poem is lost, but the eighth-century chronicler Theophanes preserved George's creation mimesis:[114] "He fulfilled some mystical vision in this way. For God, who created all creation in six days, declared the seventh a day of rest; thus also [Heraclius], who endured many toils for six years, found rest when he returned to the City with peace and joy in the seventh."[115] Heraclius's renewal of the cosmos through victory is one of the dominant themes of the *Heraclias*. Throughout, Heraclius is "the commander of cosmic rebirth,"[116] and from his labors, "a second life has been created, another world, and a new creation."[117]

The imperial metaphor of creation was only one panegyrical springboard for the Christomimetic exaltation of Heraclius.[118] George drew the parallelism of heavenly and earthly emperors in broad strokes: both entered Jerusalem in triumph;[119] both wrote their labors and laws in their own blood, the imperial purple.[120] Most important, however, was the joint imagery of victory through suffering, the crucifixion: both possessed the Cross as their trophy.[121] The *Life of Anastasius the Persian* identified the seemingly miraculous restoration of the Byzantines after the loss of the east with the paradox of the Christ's victory:

> Oh paradoxical wonders beyond all; that Christ seized, was taken to Hades, yet stripped the spoils of death; that the cross of the Lord, a captive, was carried away by the Persians, yet enslaved the Persian creed when it threw down the incarnate Hades, the destroying tyrant, [Chosroes]. For [these events] were an image of that first sack of death.[122]

The symbol of Chosroes' and Satan's victories became the means of their defeat. For George, Heraclius's recovery of the Cross was a demonstration of the symbol's power: "The insolent magoi would have exulted if [Heraclius] had not returned the Cross. But now, I think, they know its power because they have learned by experience how the fire is mystically reduced to ashes when it confronts the glowing wood."[123] The cross transformed the struggle of Roman and barbarian into a struggle of Christian and heathen. Heraclius's victory no longer simply restores the empire, but vindicates Christianity itself.

The sufferings of Christ were the model for one of the great Christian genres of antiquity, martyrdom, and the assimilation of Christ's victory on the cross into the literary iconography of war recast it in a new and unprecedented form.[124] In a lost section of the *Heraclias,* preserved in Theophanes, Heraclius harangued his army that their enemies were not barbarian enemies of the Roman, but heathen persecutors: "Let us stand against the enemies who have performed many horrors against the Christians."[125] The confrontation with persecutors transformed the war literally into martyrdom.[126] "Let not the mass of your enemies terrify you, for when God is willing, one can pursue thousands; let us receive the crown of martyrs."[127] The conflation of martyrial and martial virtue climaxes the transformation of war against heathen into suffering persecution.

This unprecedented assimilation of martyrdom and battlefield death found expression not only in George but also in the *Universal History* of his contemporary Theophylact Simocatta.[128] Written about the late sixth-century emperor Maurice, the work abounds with anachronisms, especially in the speeches. The address to the troops of the general Justinian before battle with the Persians, for example, almost literally echoes the martyrial rhetoric of war in George.[129] Justinian explained that Romans must receive victory because "for [the Romans] there is no lying worship; we have not established false gods who lead us."[130] In the end, God always punished the heathens, and Roman victory was the proof of God's power and the favor to the Romans.[131] But most striking was the insistence that "today angels recruit you, and record the souls of those who are killed, offering to them not their equivalent equal wage, but one that is, in the weight of the donative, exceedingly greater."[132] Later in the *Universal History,* martyrdom is again urged: "Do not avoid being struck lest you fail to be saved."[133]

George and Theophylact did not invent a new rhetoric; they placed an old one in a new context. Martyrs had for a long time emerged victorious against heathen persecutors, but setting martyrdom in a battlefield context was new. Nor should the assimilation of martyrial rhetoric mislead us into thinking that the adoption of this, or other rhetorical elements not normally associated with triumphalist rhetoric represented a rejection of triumphalism. Although his poetry increasingly assimilated restoration themes and rhetoric, even in the *Heraclias,* George still retained many triumphalist *topoi,* especially those that concerned the emperor and dynasty.

Indeed, the conditions under which George wrote required him to preserve these themes and *topoi.* As the thematic uniformity of such different writers as the author of the *Paschal Chronicle,* Theophylact, and George implies, George and the others followed a rhetorical agenda designed at court, and the court never entirely rejected triumphalism, especially its emphasis on the emperor. The need to meet the political needs of the court meant that George could never fully develop the restoration cycle of collective sin and divine forgiveness, or escape the triumphalist tradition that victory was God's gift to the emperor, the mediator between God and the citizens.

But the question remains, why did George, whose early poetry had followed the triumphalist model so closely, incorporate and emphasize previously minor themes and *topoi* in the 620s, and even more exactly, in the summer of 626? This question can only be answered by rejecting the assumptions that scholars have brought to the study of George's poetry: the undue emphasis on the later poetry, the treatment of George's corpus as if it were a unified whole instead of works written over a twenty-year period to meet specific occasions, and a superimposed dialectic between "classical" and "Christian" themes. A chronological study of his poetry reveals that only the later works embrace the thematic complex of collective sin, restoration, and the war of pagan and Christian. The early poetry is thematically far closer to sixth-century literature. Thus, although George's poetry covers a wide thematic and rhetorical range, his choices of themes and *topoi* were dictated by political conditions, especially patronage. George's poetry is not the result of a dialectical process of Christianization. On the contrary, George chose themes and *topoi* that had long been in the Christian Roman rhetorical thesaurus, but had been limited in use.

In his earliest poems, George did his best to avoid any mention whatsoever of defeat. Defeat traditionally conceded moral superiority to the victor, an admission the Christians would not make. The appearance of the Avars before the walls of Constantinople and of the Persians on the eastern shore, however, were evidence of defeat too great for even George to ignore. In order to confront defeat on the scale that the Christians had suffered it, George turned to restoration themes and rhetoric. Further, unable to appeal to the emperor's vice as the cause of defeat, George, like Sozomen, turned to the citizens' sin.

The successful defense of Constantinople offered George an opportunity to relieve Heraclius of the responsibility for defeat and to offer the hope of victory; victory constituted the proof of divine forgiveness and a basis for hope in victories to come. Doubtless, George was devout in his belief in sin's causal role in human affairs and divine forgiveness as the source of restoration, but his panegyrics were dictated by considerations far removed from faith: the changing fortune of war, his patron's dynastic insecurity, the generic traditions of panegyric. Ultimately, George remains a transitional figure in the evolution of seventh-century responses to defeat. He remained bound to triumphal rhetoric because the Romans won; his choices were not as difficult as those of others in the provinces, whose rhetoric was shaped not only by defeat, but also by captivity.

Notes

1. For literary studies, see Theodor Nissen, "Historisches Epos und Panegyrikos in der Spaetantike," *Hermes* 75 (1940): 298–325; H.-G. Beck, *Kirche und theologische Literatur im byzantinischen Reich* (Munich, 1959), 448–49; A. Pertusi,

Giorgio di Pisidia, Poemi: I. Panegirici epici, [*Studia Patristica et Byzantina* 7] (Ettal, 1959) 11–48; Pertusi, "L'encomio di s. Anastasio martire Persiano," *Analecta Bollandiana* 76 (1958): 7–25; J. D. C. Frendo, "The Poetic Achievement of George of Pisidia," *Maistor, Classical, Byzantine and Renaissance Studies for Robert Browning,* ed. A. Moffat, [*Byzantina Australiensia* 5] (Canberra, 1984), 159–87. For historical studies, see Av. Cameron, "Images of Authority: Elites and Icons in Late Sixth-Century Byzantium," *Past and Present* 84 (1979): 3–35, esp. 22–26; P. Speck, *Zufaelliges zum Bellum Avaricum des Georgios Pisides,* [*Miscellanea Byzantina Monacensia* 24] (Munich, 1980); D. Olster, "The Date of George of Pisidia's *Hexaemeron,*" *DOP* 45 (1991): 159–72; C. Ludwig, "Kaiser Herakleios, Georgios Pisides und die Perserkriege," in *Varia III,* [*Poikila Byzantina* 11], ed. P. Speck (Bonn, 1991), 73–128. For art historical studies see J. Trilling, "Myth and Metaphor at the Byzantine Court: A Literary Approach to the David Plates," *Byz* 48 (1978): 249–63. The following abbreviations will be used for George's poetry: from Pertusi's edition, *Poemi, Or Heraclius's Arrival On the Persian Expedition = Per. Exp.; On Bonus the Patrician = Bon.; The Avaric War = Avar.; On the Restoration of the Holy Cross = Rest.; Heraclias = Her.;* from *Patrologia Graeca* 92, *Hexameron = Hex.; Against Severus of Antioch = Sev.*

2. *Sev.,* 695–99.

3. J. D. C. Frendo, "The Significance of Technical Terms in the Poems of George of Pisidia," *Orpheus* 21 (1974): 45–55, has studied the theological *technici termini* of George's work, and concluded that George had no real theological training or special interest.

4. See T. Viljamaa, *Studies in Greek Encomiastic Poetry of the Early Byzantine Period,* [*Commentationes humanarum litterarum* 42, pt. 4] (Helsinki, 1968), 7–29. H. Hunger's advice to the reader of these highly self-conscious rhetorical compositions expresses my own view best: "Die staerkste Stuetze scheint die Rhetorik in Byzanz durch ihre politische Funktion gefunden zu haben," *Die hochsprachliche profane Literatur der Byzantiner,* 2 vols. (Munich, 1978), 1:71; see 1:69–74 for the audience, purpose, and psychology of Byzantine political rhetoric. See also H.-G. Beck, *Res publica romana: Vom Staatsdenken der Byzantiner* (Munich, 1970), 5–11; Beck, *Senat und Volk von Konstantinopel* (Munich, 1966), 51–54.

5. In *Her.,* 21.

6. Ibid., 35–38; see also 39–47.

7. W. Ensslin, *Gottkaiser und Kaiser von Gottesgnaden* [Sitzungsberichte der bayerischen Akademie der Wissenschaften, phil.-hist. abt.] (Munich, 1943), 15–18, 48–53, for the classical precedents, 56–61 for early Christian precedents. S. MacCormack, *Art and Ceremony in Late Antiquity* (Berkeley, 1981): 168–92.

8. See *Per. Exp.* I.5, I.12, I.14–23. Cf. also *Per. Exp.,* I.89, for the extended metaphor on the power and authority of the laws of Rome, "the sting" of the imperial "bee"; yet another classical *topos.*

9. Pliny the Younger, *Panegyricus,* ed. R. A. B. Mynors (Oxford, 1964), 12:4; 81:1–2.

10. *Per. Exp.,* 1.82–88.

11. *Per. Exp.,* 3.48–49; see also George's use of Claudian to praise Heraclius as greater than the Scipiones, *Her.,* 1:97–98, his appeal to Plutarch to praise Heraclius's

military prowess, *Her.,* 1:110–12, and his claim that Heraclius is greater than all the other military leaders of history, *Her.,* 2:1–4.

12. *Per. Exp.,* 2.203; see also the same comparison in *Her.,* 1.22–35.

13. *Per. Exp.,* 2.191–99; *Her.,* 2:83–89.

14. *Per. Exp.,* 3.94–104; *Her.,* 1:103–09; compare with Pliny, *Panegyricus,* 13.1–3.

15. Pliny, *Panegyricus,* 18:1.

16. *Per. Exp.,* 3.296–304.

17. See, for example, the comparison in *Per. Exp.* 3.415–25, between Moses and the "new Moses," Heraclius, whose context is the military aid rendered both by God and by the superiority of Heraclius' knowledge of God. There is no hint in this comparison (which was not original either), of the superiority of Heraclius's god to the Persians' gods.

18. See *Per. Exp.,* 3.437–42, where the error of the Persians' religion is discussed, but only in the context of the victory that it brings to the Byzantines; the moral implications of their inferior religion are manifested in their defeat alone.

19. *Per. Exp.,* 2.24–28; cf. E. Peterson, *Der Monotheismus als politisches Problem: Ein Beitrag zur Geschichte der politischen Theologie in Imperium Romanum* (Leipzig, 1935) for the mimetical relationship of Roman and divine monarchy, especially Peterson's point that the empire's fortunes were focused on the person of the emperor.

20. *Per. Exp.,* 3.409–10; compare with Plutarch, *Life of Alexander,* XXI.4: "Alexander, it seems, thought it more kingly to conquer himself than to conquer his enemies." Both George, *Bon.,* 428–30, and Pliny, *Panegyric,* 94.5, also include in their final prayers the hope that their respective rulers will establish firm dynasties.

21. *Per. Exp.,* 3.428–30.

22. Menander Rhetor, *Menander Rhetor,* "On Panegyric," ed. D. A. Russell and N. G. Wilson (Oxford, 1981), 94–95.

23. *Per. Exp.,* 1.23–24; cf. also 3.1–2, on the Persian reverence of the moon; see Pertusi, *Poemi,* 139.

24. *Per. Exp.,* 2.105–10; cf. Theophanes, *Chronographia,* 2 vols., ed. C. de Boor (Leipzig, 1883), 304.

25. See Chapter 2.

26. *Per. Exp.,* 2.252–53.

27. L. Sternbach, *Georgii Pisidae carmina inedita,* [*Wiener Studien* 13] (Vienna, 1891), 44–48; Pertusi, *Poemi,* 170–71.

28. George clearly drew on the work of Theodore Syncellus (see Chapter 4), as a guide for his own work; see Pertusi, *Poemi,* 215; P. Speck, *Zufaelliges zum Bellum Avaricum des Georgios Pisides,* [*Miscellanea Byzantina Monacensia* 24] (Munich, 1980), 18–19, 24–26, 64, 72–73, whose discourse on the thematic relationship between these works is especially interesting. George's poem and the homily of Theodore Syncellus (see Chapter 4) are our main sources for the siege. For the siege itself, see A. Stratos, *To Byzantion ston Z' Aiōna* (Athens, 1966) 2: 491–542; F. Benešević, "Le siege de Constantinople par les Perses et les Avars en 626," *Byzantion* 24 (1954): 371–95; P. Speck, *Bellum Avaricum,* esp. 30–59.

29. Theophanes, *Chronographia,* 302–03; see also *Her.,* 1:163–64.

30. Socrates Scholasticus, *Ecclesiastical History, PG* 67, VII.42; cf. also, VII.22, "If at any time war was raised, like David, [Theodosius II] had recourse to God, knowing that he is the arbiter of battles."

31. Flavius Cresconius Corippus, *Iohannidos*, ed. J. Diggle and F. Goodyear (Cambridge, 1970), 1.15–16.

32. Ibid., 5.42–44.

33. *Bon.*, 27.

34. Ibid., 47–48.

35. Ibid., 53–54.

36. Ibid., 144–53.

37. Ibid., 116–21.

38. Ibid., 154–69. The ending of the poem partially lost; see Sternbach, *Carmina inedita*, 49–51; Pertusi, *Poemi*, 173–75, for their interpretation. I find Pertusi's usually exact reading of George somewhat less so in this case, since it is hard to accept his Christological reading of the conclusion. It seems to echo not the passion of Christ, but the struggle of Heraclius himself, which has been the main theme of the poem up to this point.

39. *Bon.*, 91–101.

40. Ibid., 1–20. Again, the comparison of Heracles and the emperor is specifically offered as an excellent beginning for a panegyric in Menander Rhetor, "On Panegyric," 80.

41. *Bon.*, 56–59.

42. Ibid., 56–64.

43. Ibid., 60–75. Menander Rhetor, "On Panegyric," 82, 88–92, suggested this very theme, that the emperor's moral excellence could improve the morals of the citizens.

44. *Bon.*, 65–75.

45. Ibid., 76–78.

46. Ibid., 85–88.

47. An analysis of the poem is complicated by its close relationship to a homily on the Avar siege by Theodore Syncellus. It is likely that one used the other or that they both drew on a third source. Compare *Avar.* 204–6, and Theodore Syncellus, *On the Attack of the Avars*, ed. L. Sternbach, *Analecta Avarica* (Cracon, 1900), 304, the metaphor of Scylla and Charybdis, in which Theodore explains that the metaphor was contrived by "a certain poetic individual." See Pertusi, *Poemi*, 215; Speck, *Bellum Avaricum*, 64–65.

48. *Avar.*, 49–66. For George's treatment of Phocas, see Olster, "Usurpation," 3–6.

49. *Avar.*, 16–40, cf. also 63–110.

50. Ibid., 328–32.

51. Ibid., 340–41.

52. Ibid., 278–80.

53. Ibid., 110–11.

54. Ibid., 94–100.

55. Ibid., 250–64. George, ibid., 307–10, promised a future poem dedicated solely to Heraclius's own labors and achievements.

56. See ibid., 237–45.

57. Ibid., 266–77.

58. Ibid., 293–98. The *xenoi* are clearly mercenaries, which sheds some light, perhaps, on the composition of Heraclius' army.

59. Ibid., 248–49.

60. Ibid., 311–27.

61. *Avar.*, 298–99.

62. Ibid., 370–73. For the portrait that adorned this image, see Pertusi, *Poemi*, 220–21; Speck, *Bellum Avaricum*, 54–59.

63. *Avar.*, 495–97. The Patriarch is in fact greater than the mere reflection of Heraclius' glory; see Speck, *Bellum Avaricum*, 15–19, who argues that the poem is a panegyric of Sergius.

64. *Avar.*, 1–3. Perhaps this reference to an icon alludes to that held by Sergius in lines 370–73.

65. So noted A. Frolow, "La dédicasse de Constantinople dans la tradition byzantine," *Revue de l'Histoire des Religions* 127 (1944): 94–95. See also the older but valuable N. Baynes, "The Supernatural Defenders of Constantinople," *AB* 67 (1949): 255–60.

66. *Avar.*, 348–65.

67. Ibid., 403–08.

68. Ibid., 417–30. See Speck, *Bellum Avaricum*, 53–54, 129–30.

69. Ibid., 431–35.

70. At the Frigidus, the pagans' own arrows were turned against them by a divine wind, Theodoret, *Ecclesiastical History,* ed. G. Hansen (Berlin, 1960), V.24. In fact, George uses Homer (*Avar.,* 416) for his description of the fight at the walls.

71. *Avar.*, 440–74. See Averil Cameron, "The Virgin's Robe: an Episode in the History of early Seventh-Century Byzantium," *Byzantion* 49 (1979): 42–56; J. Wortley, "The Oration of Theodore Syncellus (BHG 1058) and the Siege of 860," *Byzantine Studies* 4 (1977): 111–26.

72. *Avar.*, 121–22.

73. Ibid., 141–53.

74. Ibid., 182–89.

75. Ibid., 366–73.

76. Ibid., 374–92.

77. Ibid., 379, and see Pertusi, *Poemi*, 221.

78. *Avar.*, 502–04.

79. Ibid., 522–24.

80. Ibid., 525–26.

81. See *Her.*, 1.1–3 and *Paschal Chronicle*, ed. L. Dindorf (Bonn, 1832), 727.15–16; hereafter, *Pasc. Chron.*

82. See *Her.*, 1.4–8 and *Pasc. Chron.*, 727.17.

83. See *Her.*, 1.9–12 and *Pasc. Chron.*, 728.4–10, and esp. 729.12–14; see also below.

84. See *Her.*, 1.63–64 and *Pasc. Chron.*, 728.13–14 and ff.

85. See Pertusi, *Poemi*, 281–83.

86. *Her.*, 1:148–55.

87. *Hex.*, 453–64; see the similar metaphor in *Bon.*, 76–78.

88. *Hex.*, 501–07.

89. Cf. the note to *Hex.*, 453, col. 1470.

90. *Avar.*, 49–57. The epithet of hydra is used of Chosroes in the *Per. Exp.*, 3:349–59. George made almost no distinction between the Christian "villain" and the pagan.

91. *Avar.*, 58–60; cf. the interpretations of this passage by Speck, *Bellum Avaricum*, 23, 80–81; Pertusi, *Poemi*, 271–72.

92. See D. Olster, *The Politics of Usurpation in the Seventh Century: Rhetoric and Revolution in Byzantium* (Amsterdam, 1993), 101–15.

93. *Her.*, 2.34–38.

94. George of Pisidia(?), *L'encomio di s. Anastasio martire Persiano*, ed. A. Pertusi, *AB* 76 (1958): 35.

95. Anonymous, *Doctrina Jacobi nuper baptizati*, ed. N. Bonwetsch, [*Abhandlungen der koenigen Gesellschaft der Wissenschaften zu Goettingen*, phil.-hist. Klasse, n.s. 13] (Goettingen, 1910), 39, 89.

96. Antiochus Monachus, *La Prise de Jérusalem par les Perses en 614*, trans. G. Garitte, [*Corpus Scriptorum Christianorum Orientalium* 203, *Scriptores Ibirici* 12], (Louvain, 1960), ch. 2.3–8.

97. *Les plus anciens recueils des miracles de saint Démétrius*, ed. P. Lemerle, vol. 1 (Paris, 1979), Miracle 10:81–82.

98. Cf. *Rest.*, 43–46; Heraclius's "mystical power," praised by the City and all creation, follows a description of the "folly of the gentiles," and points to Heraclius's role as mediator.

99. *Hex.*, 1899–1910.

100. *Her.*, 2:66–70. Compare this passage with the more conventional description of Heraclius's purity in *Per. Exp.*, 2:244–48.

101. See J. D. C. Frendo, "Special Aspects of the Use of Medical Vocabulary in the Poems of George of Pisidia," *Orpheus* 22 (1975): 49–56.

102. *Her.*, 1:122–30.; *Per. Exp.*, 2:29–31, 2:191–200; *Bon.*, 84–105. The metaphor that the emperor "healed" or restored the army was practically as old as the panegyrical genre; cf. Pliny, *Panegyric*, 18.1. M. McCormick, *Eternal Victory: Triumphal Rulership in Late Antiquity, Byzantium and the Early Medieval West* (Cambridge, 1986), 64–79, 100–11, 247–51, discusses the purification of the army, an idea as old as Homer, and hardly, as he asserts, Christian, but he ignores the expiatory rites performed *during* such crises as the Avar siege, and their possible relationship to the liturgically influenced "victory" rites performed afterwards.

103. *Her.*, 2:41–54.

104. *Her.*, 2:32–33.

105. *Sev.*, 47–50.

106. See George of Pisidia(?), *L'encomio*, ed. A. Pertusi, 35, for Chosroes' description.

107. *Her.*, 1:84–92.

108. Ibid., 1:65–70; *Sev.*, 452; *Hex.*, 1846.

109. *Her.*, 1:49–53. See also *Hex.*, 418. This idea is echoed by Theophylact Simocatta, who may have possibly taken the expression from George; see Theo-

phylact, *Simocatta, Historiae,* ed. C. de Boor and P. Wirth (Stuttgart, 1972), IV.5.12, "Let the destruction of one man be a teacher of temperance, and let this be a most suitable law, a salvation for those to come."

110. *Her.,* 1:53–54.

111. *Her.,* 1:1–3, also 1.53–55, 1:182–87. See also similar demonic characterizations of Chosroes in the contemporary, and possibly related, *Pasch. Chron.* 728.4–10, and especially 729.12–14, where Chosroes is specifically described as one of Satan's minions.

112. *Her.,* 1:186–87.

113. Cf. G. Bianchi, "Note sulla cultura a Bisanzio all'inizio del VII secolo in rapporto all'*Esamerone* di Giorgio di Pisidia," *Rivista di Studi Bizantini e Neoellenici* 2 (1965): 137–43, esp. 142–43. The mimesis of ruler and diety was old as panegyric, but it is the juxtaposition of purification and creation that make George original; see H. Hunger, *Prooimion: Elemente der byzantinischen Kaiseridee in den Arengen der Urkunden,* [*Wiener byzantinische Studien* 1] (Vienna, 1964), 58–63.

114. Cf. Pertusi, *Poemi,* 25–29, on the lost second and third parts of the *Heraclias;* ibid., 307, for other parallel passages on this theme in George.

115. Theophanes, *Chronographia,* 327–328, which is dependent on the lost third part of George's *Heraclias,* of which a fragment of this passage, *Her.,* fr. 54, remains.

116. *Her.,* 1:201–06.

117. Ibid., 1:82–83, see also 1:82–83, 1:201–06, fr. 54 (Theophanes, *Chronographia,* 327.24–328.2).

118. See, for example, *Rest.,* 21–24, 64–68; *Her.,* 1:1–5; 1:190–91.

119. *Rest.,* 5–8.

120. Compare *Her.,* 1:107–09, for Heraclius; *Hex.,* 450, for Christ.

121. *Rest.,* 30; see also 19–20, 21–24, 64–68, and esp. 43–64, where Satan's lament for his defeat through the crucifixion is a metaphor for Chosroes' defeat and Heraclius's victory.

122. George of Pisidia(?), *L'encomio,* ed. A. Pertusi, 35; see also *Rest.,* 32–34, "The Cross, even in Persia gained converts and punished the enemy, but it did not wish to dwell there."

123. Cf. *Rest.,* 10–14, in which the return of the Cross constitutes the proof that Christianity is true. As V. Grumel pointed out, however, Heraclius's cross fetish appears only *after* the Persian War's conclusion, and must be seen as part of a propaganda campaign; the question to what end has provoked considerable discussion, cf. A. Frolow, "La vraie croix et les expéditions d'Héraclius en Perse," REB 11 (1953): 88–105; V. Grumel, "La reposition de la vraie croix à Jérusalem par Héraclius. Le jour et l'année," *Byzantinische Forschungen* 1 (1966): 139–49; C. Mango, "Deux études sur Byzance et la Perse sassanide," *Travaux et Mémoires* 9 (1985): 105–17; P. Speck, *Das geteilte Dossier,* [*Poikila Byzantina* 9] (Bonn, 1988), 356–72.

124. Cf. George's reference to martyrdom in *Hex.,* 489–99.

125. *Her.,* 3, fr. 3 (Pertusi, 276); cf. Theophanes, *Chronographia,* 307.4–5.

126. Certainly heroic self-sacrifice in deference to a god's command frequently occurs in classical history, but such military martyrdom *on the field of battle* was quite alien to the traditions of Christian military sainthood.

127. *Her.,* fr. 6; cf. Theophanes, *Chronographia,* 310.26–311.2. See also George's contemporary Theophylact Simocatta, *Universal History,* 3.13.20; compare the vocabulary of George's military martyrdom with his description of martyrial victory in *Hex.* 489–99.

128. M. Whitby, *The Emperor Maurice and His Historian* (Oxford, 1988), esp. 28–51; T. Olajos, *Les sources de Théopylact Simocatta historien* (Leiden, 1988), esp. 55–57.

129. The reference to a Persian god "who turns to ashes," if not taken from George, certainly finds its source in court propaganda of the late 620s; see Theophylact, *Universal History,* 3.13.15.

130. Ibid., 3.13.14.

131. Ibid., 4.16.14.

132. Ibid., 3.13.20.

133. Ibid., 5.4.7.

4. A Tale of Two Cities

George of Pisidia illustrates the slow reformulation of the rhetoric of Christian imperialism, war, and history that grew out of the Persian Wars. A rhetoric of restoration gradually began to replace that of triumphalism, permitting the Christians to defend their claim to God's love in the face of defeat. But George, although innovative, neither escaped the limits of his genre nor exploited the full apologetic potential of the Jews. Other authors, uninhibited by George's generic restraints, did exploit the Jews to reshape Roman defeat into Christian victory: Theodore Syncellus in his homily about the defense of Constantinople in 626 against the Avars, and Antiochus Monachus in his *Fall of Jerusalem,* about the Persian sack of Jerusalem in 614. Both confronted the unnerving reality of unprecedented barbarian successes.[1] Theodore had the easier task. He could exult in his city's and religion's victory; Antiochus had to vindicate his religion and polity after a defeat.

Victory at Constantinople and defeat at Jerusalem created distinct social and political backgrounds that defined not only the differences in these authors' apologetics, but also in their rhetorical and thematic use of the Jews. But such differences do not obscure their dependence on the Jews for apologetic effect. Both found in the Jews the means to redefine the Christian Romans, their empire, and their enemies in order to affirm God's love for his errant people. This rhetorical weapon, forged in the heat of battle, remained in the days of peace. In the years after the Persian War, the Christians did not forget their rhetorical enemy, and the anti-Jewish rhetoric generated during the war afterwards inspired political and social policy. Whatever religious motivations led to the unprecedented forced baptism of the Jews after the Persian War, the rhetorical transformation of the Jews in the evolving Christian apologetic was one of the main incitements.

Constantinople as the New Jerusalem

Theodore Syncellus, like Eusebius, identified the Roman Empire with the community of Christians. But while Eusebius had taken advantage of

Roman victory to prove Christianity's material power, Theodore was constrained to use Christianity's prophetic claims to affirm Roman imperialism. The victory at the capital's gates neither ended the Avar or Persian threats, nor compensated for nearly two decades of steady defeat. The Christians had staved off utter defeat, not utterly defeated their enemies. This victory had not restored the empire, but it fit well with Theodore's promise of restoration.

The homily's structure permitted Theodore to elaborate political themes through typological, historical, and eschatological exegeses of 2 Kings 16.1–20, Isaiah 7.1–8.15, Ezekiel 38:1–39:11, and Zachariah 8:18–19.[2] Theodore redefined the Christian Roman Empire as the true Israel, and Constantinople as the true Jerusalem, superior to the old and destined to a better end. Theodore used the narrative from Kings and Isaiah, the Judean king Achaz's defense of Jerusalem against the kings of Samaria and Syria, to establish a historical and typological context of the Avar siege. The prophecies of Ezekiel and Zachariah established an eschatological context for restoration.[3]

Victory inspired Theodore, but years of defeat, not just one moment of victory, formed his homily. Like George of Pisidia, he saw God's forgiveness as the source of Constantinople's survival, but his pride in his city's victory was tempered by the knowledge that "even if we have now received pardon, through the multitude of our sins we could have been the cause of the destruction of this great city"; by their sins, the citizens "could have become unworthy of [Constantinople]."[4] Like George of Pisidia, Theodore blamed sin for previous Christian defeat:[5] "First I say and first I tell about the variety and multitude of our sins, even that we conducted ourselves unworthily of the injunctions of the God who saves us: biting and eating each other up, taking care to make all an image of evil."[6] And like George, Theodore provided sin a well-defined political context: the endemic rioting in the city that had brought down Maurice and Phocas, and had plagued Heraclius.[7] Firm obedience to political (and ecclesiastical) authorities was the best way to demonstrate Christian virtue. Thus, as Christian and imperial victory blended together, so too did Christian and civic virtue.

Although Theodore and George shared broad seventh-century apologetic themes, their treatment of Heraclius was strikingly different. Theodore draped panegyrical *topoi* on Heraclius but modified the place of the emperor's vices and virtues in imperial success or failure. The emperor naturally took his place as a leader of the Christian community, and Theodore credited the emperor with a role in leading the people to repentance and the restoration of God's favor.[8] But he laid special emphasis on ecclesiastical leadership. Rather than present Heraclius as the imperial mediator with God as had George of Pisidia, Theodore placed the patriarch at the head of the chorus of repentance in which all the city took part: "And our archpriest, when he collected together those of every age, from babe to elder, urged them to be hopeful, and not to despair, arming them with his words, 'Come, let us prostrate ourselves and fall on our knees before the only begotten Son of our God and Father.'"[9] The liturgical setting gave the patriarch's call for universal repentance far greater rhetorical weight than the parallel settings for the emperor that George introduced into his poetry.[10]

By deemphasizing the mediative role of the emperor, Theodore laid increasing emphasis on the purification of each individual. Theodore's exegesis of Isaiah 7 and 8, the meeting of Judah's king Achaz and Isaiah at "the field of the fuller," combined the defeat of sin in both the individual and the world: "For I know that the field discussed in the words of training is the cosmos. And what is more, man is a microcosm. And the one in the writings who can cleanse filth is called, figuratively, the fuller."[11] Christ the fuller removed sin at both the imperial macrocosmic, and individual microcosmic levels so that Christian redemption embraced both individual salvation and imperial victory.

Theodore's homily not only redefined the proper response to internal sin, substituting individual catharsis (through ecclesiastical leadership) for the emperor's mediation, but also redefined the divine response to external sin, the demonic enemies of the Christians. Just as George of Pisidia demonized Chosroes, so Theodore characterized the Avar Khagan as an insatiable beast, "for nothing was able or would be able to satisfy that leech."[12] The Khagan "showed himself a child of the devil, not by the will of nature, but by his own will, and all the diabolical evil was incarnate in him."[13] He was "an anti-God"[14] worse than demons, for "even demons have been shamed."[15] Worst of all, he boasted that Christ was powerless before him,[16] a direct challenge to Christ that he would regret. "That insane one has come to appreciate through experience that there is no god more powerful than our God, and the power does not exist that can stand before the Virgin."[17]

Theodore's demonization of the Khagan may seem similar to that of Chosroes by George of Pisidia, but Theodore's description of the divine response to the Khagan's challenge was quite different. Like George, Theodore maintained that "even with unbounded power, the emperor could not be saved, nor the city remain safe, unless the Lord guarded it."[18] Theodore, however, qualified this shibboleth of imperial rhetoric with the promise of direct and personal intervention by Christ and the Virgin. "For the Lord Himself will go to war on our behalf, and the Virgin, the Mother of God, will be the defender of the city if indeed we might run to them with full hearts and willing souls."[19] As we have seen, before the seventh century, divine intervention had been indirect and given to the emperor; the Cross at the Milvian Bridge and the storm at the Frigidus were far from epiphanies. In Theodore's homily, however, the Virgin herself appears on the battlements to defend her city.[20] Even the *Paschal Chronicle* goes in this direction, actually narrating a personal confrontation between the Khagan of the Avars and the Virgin.[21] The Khagan explained that it was not cowardice that compelled him to withdraw from the city, but the Virgin, whom he saw making the circuit of the walls to protect it.[22]

Theodore's eschatology reveals most clearly his interplay of macrocosmic and microcosmic evil, its purification, and epiphanic intervention. He began by identifying the siege of Constantinople as the fulfillment of the Gog prophecy. According to Theodore, Gog referred to a "collection of peoples" from the north who were to attack Jerusalem when it was without its king. Both the absence of Heraclius, fighting Persians in the east, and the march of the Avars from the Danube offered Theodore fulfillment of these criteria. Gog was not an amorphous apocalyptic figure; he was identified with the Avars, the military opponents of new Rome.

Theodore further used eschatology to identify the old Jerusalem and the New Jerusalem, Constantinople, claiming the same spiritual date for the salvation of the one and the sack of the other. Adeptly manipulating Zachariah 8:18 — that fasts in the fourth, the fifth, the tenth months would be times of gladness — he exegetically reconciled the dates of the late winter sack of Jerusalem and the high summer victory of the new Jerusalem.[23] Naturally, this chronological coincidence had been appointed by God in order to single out the new Jerusalem as the recipient of his special mercy.[24]

Constantinople replaced Jerusalem as the spiritual center of Christianity and the geographic center of the true Israel: "But I know that this city is the land of Israel where one glorifies God and the Virgin with holy piety and where the rites of the true worship are celebrated, because the true existence of the genuine Israel means that the Lord is glorified with true heart and devoted soul."[25] More than piety inspired Theodore's translation of Christianity's *locus sanctus*. When Theodore wrote, Jerusalem had been in Persian hands for over a decade, compromising its legitimacy. But Theodore's typological substitution of Constantinople did more than translate Christianity's religious center to a city under imperial control:

> And what other place could be named the "navel of the world" except the city where God has set the imperial residence of the Christians, and that he has created, by its central position, even that it might itself serve as the intermediary between east and west. It is against this city that the kings of the tribes and the peoples assemble. And it is their power that the Lord makes vain, who said to Zion, "Be without fear, Zion! Do not throw up your hands! Behold, your God is in your midst, and it is he who will save you!"[26]

Constantinople bound together the entire world not only in imperial and Christian, but also in apocalyptic, unity. When the Romans besought God to save their city, they asked him to "save the city that possesses your inheritance, and save the people that are called by your name."[27]

Unlike earlier Christians who interpreted prophecy as an allegory of God's rule to come, Theodore combined eschatology and history to create a *Roman* claim to political restoration rather than a Christian claim to spiritual salvation. This eschatological element sets apart Theodore from George of Pisidia. The politicization of sin, the demonization of enemies, and the Old Testament sin-punishment-restoration cycle were all present in George's later poetry. But Theodore went further. Integrating Old Testament prophecies into restoration rhetoric, he made the "new Israel" central to seventh-century imperial apologetic, and the disenfranchisement of the Jews necessary for Christians to secure their own claim. The Jews thus came to occupy a vital place in Christian restoration apologetic. Their competing claim made them a threat, but also the rhetorical foil for Christian claims to be the true Israel, the inheritors of the Old Testament restoration prophecies.

The Jews, therefore, figure prominently in Theodore's apocalyptic interpretation of the siege of Constantinople. Theodore's exegesis is often unwieldy,[28] and he smoothed his way through a contrived debate with Jewish interpreters. More than once, Theodore offers Jewish interpretations of Old Testament prophecies in order to refute them and promote his own exegesis. He defended his rocky exegesis of the Zachariah prophecy by dismissing alternatives: "We know the sons of the Hebrews have interpreted the words of the prophecy otherwise."[29] Elsewhere, Theodore called upon the Jewish authority Josephus to remind his audience that the old Jerusalem had fallen to Nebuchadnezzer and Titus on the same day,[30] and to prepare the ground for his own view that the Khagan of the Avars had been turned away from the new Jerusalem on the same day that the old had been sacked.[31]

The typological transformation of Jerusalem into Constantinople dismissed all Jewish prophetic claims. "It seems clear that the words that Ezekiel spoke were prophecized about the land of the fleshly Israel, but neither the date . . . nor the events of the war against Judah [follow the prophecy]."[32] Nor did the Gog prophecy refer to the Jews; Gog's invasion required a realm to be invaded, and "the fact is that Jews alive today are completely dispersed among all the peoples, and the fleshly Israel does not possess its own land that Gog could invade with the intent of gaining booty."[33] By refuting Jewish prophetic claims, Theodore not only claimed this prophecy of victory for the Christians, but also was able to set it in a contemporary political context.

Theodore's substitution of Christian Romans for Jews in the apocalyptic prophecies shows only one side of the rhetorical use to which he put Jews. The cycle of sin and restoration depended on divine forgiveness of an errant people. From the first, the Jews appear as a foil for Christian claims to God's forgiveness. The mediation of Isaiah had saved Jerusalem in the time of Achaz; faith saved the Romans.[34] Even performed by sinful Christians, Christian rites remained more efficacious for gaining divine aid than anything Jews did. "Our cult is more acceptable, even if we, rather often to be blunt, do not fear to approach the holy sacraments impudently, with a sinful conscience and unclean hands."[35] The proof of Christian claims was victory, all the more convincing when contrasted with Jewish defeat. The Jews, with no kingdom, could not be restored or receive forgiveness.

Theodore not only contrasted Jews and Christians, but also personified and contrasted their moral qualities in their leaders. Despite the salvation of his city, "Achaz remained, nonetheless, the image of disbelief, while the Jews cry even up to our day, 'I will not ask for a sign because I will not tempt the Lord.'"[36] On the other hand, Heraclius personified all the Christian virtues that ultimately saved Constantinople: "But my emperor is faithful, and the sign of faith its steadfastness, since he dedicates his personal life, everything, so to speak, to the care and guard of the divine injunctions, and he leads all his subjects to them."[37] The comparison with Achaz is unusual; for the most part, Theodore compares Heraclius and Sergius to types of virtue, rather than contrast them with types of vice.[38] But it is a seventh-century characteristic to affirm Christian superiority by contrast rather than comparison. Claims of Christian restoration rested on contrast between the reprobate Jews, whose loss of kingdom signaled

God's ultimate condemnation, and the errant but still beloved Christians, whose victory signaled their return to God's favor.

The exegetical foundation of Theodore's claims to restoration rested on the Old Testament prophecies. His eschatological defense of Christian imperialism, for this reason, became inextricably linked to the polemic against the Jews. Theodore was by no means unique. He was only one example of a seventh-century apocalyptic trend whose apologetic agenda, tied to the polemic against the Jews, had few previous parallels in the east.[39]

The *Apocalypse of Pseudo-Methodius,* a Syriac apocalypse whose Greek version dates from the last quarter of the seventh century, was perhaps the most elaborate apocalypse of the century.[40] It includes many standard seventh-century themes: Arab victory as punishment for sin, imperial restoration as the reward for repentance.[41] Writing after the unsuccessful Arab siege of Constantinople in the 670s, the Greek redactor wove this second seventh-century victory at the gates into the restoration cycle as the moment when God relented. Just as the Arabs advance against the city, "the Xylocerus [gate] will scream as it is struck by the Ishmaelites, and a voice will come out of heaven, saying, 'This punishment is sufficient for me.'"[42] Naturally, the siege was the final chastisement of the Byzantines, exemplifying how malleable the historical structure of an apocalypse could be.

Like Theodore, Pseudo-Methodius employed the Jews to defend the promise of Christian imperial restoration. The integrity of the Christian Empire was demonstrated in Pseudo-Methodius through Roman victory over the Jews: "Consider the people of Moses who drowned the Egyptians in the depths of the sea with so many signs and terrors; behold also the case of Jesus, son of Nave, on whose behalf the sun stood. . . . To put it simply, how was all the astounding power of the Jews brought down by the Empire of the Romans?"[43] The Jews' victories had nothing to do with divine favor. God had only used them to prepare the way for the Romans. Indeed, the Jews' victories arose from the same cause as Arab victories:

> The Lord says to Israel through Moses, "Not because the Lord God loves you does he lead you into the promised land to settle it, but on account of the sins of those who dwell there." Likewise for the sons of Ishmael, the Lord God does not give them the power to rule the lands of the Christians because he loves them, but on account of the sinfulness abounding among the Christians.[44]

Pseudo-Methodius put Jews and Arabs on the same level as instruments of God's chastisement. Nor was this comparison accidental; the Jews were the proof that Arab victories would be ephemeral. Pseudo-Methodius enquired, "Did not the Hebrews rule for one thousand years?" The Arabs would not last even that long. Calling upon the authority of Daniel 11:15, Pseudo-Methodius claimed that the Arabs were the "the arms of the south," soon to meet defeat at Roman hands.[45] By contrast with the rise and fall of the Jews and Arabs, the Christian Romans possessed an empire that would last as long as time: "Every realm and every power of this world will be destroyed except this: for it will make war and not be subdued."[46]

The *Daniel Commentary* goes even further; the Jews are not simply a rhetorical foil for the Christian Empire's perpetual rule, they are enemies against whom the Christians contend. "And [the Jews] will come into Jerusalem to their king. And they will persecute the race of the Christians in all the land; and they will pursue the Romans unto death."[47] Indeed, when such historical nuisances as the Arabs are long gone, the anti-Christ will rise from the Jews.[48]

Theodore wrote his homily after a great Christian victory, and victory dominated his rhetoric as he sought to restore the links between God's favor, imperial victory, and Christian legitimacy. Indeed, Theodore strove to reaffirm triumphalism in drastically changed circumstances. Those circumstances required him, however, to integrate restoration into his triumphal framework of victory, and the Jews were a convenient rhetorical device to highlight Christian expectations of restoration. His attacks on Jews did not go beyond theology. Antiochus Monachus and Maximus the Confessor reflected the experience of defeat without the tonic of victory, and they reserved a very different rhetorical and social role for the Jews.

The Old Jerusalem as the New Jerusalem

Antiochus Monachus personally experienced defeat's horror. His *Fall of Jerusalem,* written shortly after Heraclius returned the True Cross from its exile in Persia, is a combination of stylized lament, rhetorical exaltation, statistical enquiry, and historical narrative.[49] Its texture may be confused, but the dominant theme is clear. "Oh my brothers, how was this land of promise made empty; how could destruction have razed the churches of Christ to the ground, and devastation come upon the altars of God?"[50] Antiochus and his audience wrestled with the problem of how heathen Persians could have conquered Jerusalem; Jerusalem was not just another city, its loss not simply another defeat. The fall of the city of Christ to infidels raised doubts about Christ's power. How could he not defend *his* city, "Jerusalem, the city of Jesus Christ, son of David, son of Abraham," where he had walked, taught, and endured the passion?[51]

Antiochus began his lament for Christ's city by claiming it for the Christians. Like Theodore, he used typology to advance his claims: the city belonged to the true sons of Abraham, those who inherited the city through Christ — the Christians.[52] But Jerusalem for Antiochus was not an ideal, but a place where Jews and Christians had played out the history of their religions:

> I do not cry for the temple of the Jews that the prophet Jeremiah mourned. . . .
> Nor do I cry for the priests who murdered the prophets, and the people who
> crucified the Lord, the evil congregation who cried, "Crucify, crucify Jesus
> Christ" . . . I neither cry for them nor lament them because they earned that
> evil that fell upon them through captivity. . . . But I cry and mourn for the holy
> city and the glorious churches, and the sacred altars and the faithful people who
> were murdered without mercy.[53]

Antiochus presents two images of Jerusalem, inhabited by two sets of occupants. The Jews are murderers and persecutors, dispersed throughout the world as a punishment for sins that admit no repentance. The Christians are the persecuted yet faithful people who have suffered but will repent, be restored, and "return sorrowfully to the Lord with tears."[54]

The fall of Jerusalem was the method by which God returned his erring people to himself. The Jerusalemites had destroyed themselves with transgressions of God's laws.[55] Typically, their sins are political: the arrival of the "Blues" and "Greens," the circus factions, with their rioting and uproar, and the presence of the evil Count of the East, Bonosus, the minister of Phocas, bred sinfulness in the Jerusalemites.[56]

The Jerusalemites' sufferings, however, were sent by God to call them to repentance: "Then, the judge of justice, who does not want the perdition of the sinner, but his conversion and salvation, laid upon us the evil race of the Persians, just as if they were a staff of instruction and a remedy for correction."[57] God prescribed sufferings the way a doctor may prescribe an unpleasant medicine.[58] The fall of the city was the salvation of many, "for he led many to repentance, and rescued them from ruin, and those martyred for the sake of his name are numbered among the saints."[59] Defeat was not a sign of God's weakness or hostility, but a visible sign of his care, sent so that "he might teach sinners and purify the poison of their sin through many trials."[60]

Although Theodore and Antiochus shared the scheme of sin and punishment, they described God's chastisement very differently. The Avars were a source of active evil in the world, their Khagan an incarnate Satan who challenged Christ; the Persians were God's passive instrument to punish the Jerusalemites. They possessed no self-will, as had the Khagan, nor was any gauntlet thrown down before Christ, "for their incitement was from God, and by his permission, the devil led that evil people and just as fire, they burned."[61] Antiochus naturally distinguished between God allowing the Persians to take the city, and lending them aid, but at all times he maintained that the fall of the city was entirely due to God's will. In one anecdote a group of monks, asked by the Persians if the city would fall, at first confidently answered that it would not, only tearfully to retract their answer a short time later. When the Persians asked why they had changed their minds, they replied that they had seen a messenger from God order the heavenly guardians of the city to return to heaven and leave the city to its fate.[62] This Persian passivity finds its source in their victory. Had they offered the same challenge to Christ as the Avars, their victory would have compromised Christ's power. Their victory *proved* that they had been sent and directed by God alone, and thus that there had been no challenge.

Lacking a material victory, Antiochus turned to a martyrial one. Whatever peril the Persians posed to the body, they posed no threat other than despair to the soul. On the contrary, martyrdom offered the Christians a victory that transcended their military defeat. On one occasion, a virgin about to be raped by her captor offered to demonstrate the efficacy of a potion that turned aside swords. When her captor stupidly tested the potion on her, he killed her. "And see, my brothers, what this virgin did, for she gave her body to death for the sake of purity, and accepted the crown of victory from the saviour."[63]

Of course the model of martyrial victory was Christ himself, and the narrative abounds with allusions to Christ's passion: on the day of the sack, the sun ceased to shine just as "on that awesome day of the Lord's crucifixion";[64] the captives going into exile left by the same gate as Christ on his way to Calvary.[65] The True Cross, Christ's avatar, stood before the Persian king just as Christ had stood before Pilate.[66] The sufferings of the Patriarch Zacharias personified the city's sufferings and its identification with Christ. "The Cross went forth the first time with Christ, and now the same Cross went forth with the shepherd, the Patriarch Zacharias, into captivity."[67] They were sacrificial lambs. "Christ went forth to suffer for the sake of the salvation of the world, and Zacharias went forth for the salvation of the captives."[68]

All these allusions to the passion climax in the speech of the captive Patriarch Zacharias. Standing beside the True Cross, he explained that the defeat of the Christians was no different from the crucifixion: "The Lord is blessed who brought upon us this castigation. My children, remember the great, lengthy suffering of the Saviour, and how he endured his passion for us. Did not the Lord, on our behalf, change the poverty of captivity into glory at the time of his passion."[69] The sack of the city was no more a defeat than the crucifixion itself; it was a victory of the spirit.[70] Antiochus's typology strongly reinforced this framework of victory. Whereas Theodore Syncellus had favored Old Testament types of victory, like Moses defeating the Amalekites or the royal glory of David, Antiochus favored weak but defiant figures of Jewish history like Daniel or Moses before Pharaoh.

The rhetoric of martyrdom adopted by Antiochus was not new, but the marriage of imperial defeat and martyrdom was. Through martyrdom, Antiochus could reaffirm the sorely tried Christian religious superiority. In order to accomplish this, Antiochus needed a persecutor who could be defeated. He did not use the Persians for this role. Significantly, Persians do not persecute Christians for being Christians; their rapine was generically barbaric. The persecutor Antiochus used was the Jew.

The Christian stood in Christ's place, the Persians played the role of Pilate, and the Jews inherited the mantle of Judas. The Jews were the true villains and persecutors. Heathen agents had killed Christ and Christians, but the traitors who had turned against God and his people with knowing malice were Judas and the Jews. With bitter irony, Antiochus reminded his audience that Judas had received silver from the Jews to betray Christ, but now the Jews spent silver to buy Christian captives from the Persians in order to torture them.[71] They sought to compel Christians to deny Christ, and here lay the true combat of the Christian:

> Oh malignant enemies of God, how greatly you wish to destroy us! But your evil will will not be accomplished! For you became the first traitors to us, and did not remain with us in the fight against the enemies; and now you desire that we become Jews and join in your perdition? Rather now behold! Through you we have become fighters and martyrs of Christ.[72]

Antiochus hinted that the Jews betrayed the Christians in the fight for Jerusalem, but it was little more than innuendo; had there been real treachery, it would have been described at length.[73] Rather, Antiochus telescoped the Jews' persecution of the Christians with betrayal of the Romans. The Jew became, in Antiochus, the true enemy with which both Roman and

Christian did battle, and against whom he could not only win the prize of martyrdom, but win back Jerusalem. Christian Jerusalem was not threatened by the infidel Persians but by the Jews, who, for a time, even received control of the city from Chosroes.[74]

Antiochus shifted his audience's vision from Roman defeat by the Persians to the Christian victory over the Jews. Jews served the Christians as the proper antagonists of a glorious new struggle, one in which the Roman as Christian could carry away the palm. The sting of Persian victory was tempered by the defeat of the treacherous and willfully evil Jews. Even Zacharias in Persian exile had to circumvent the Jews' evil plans against him, and in doing so, convinced Chosroes that he was a prophet.[75]

Antiochus thus transformed Roman military defeat by the Persians into Christian martyrial victory over the Jews. His work climaxed one direction of seventh-century apologetic evolution. George of Pisidia and Theodore Syncellus, who prepared the way, had not jettisoned triumphalism, but in the light of victory and the shadow of the court, had grafted restoration rhetoric onto it. Antiochus firmly rejected the triumphalist rhetoric of victory because he wrote for an audience whose experience of defeat far outweighed the eventual liberation of their city. Antiochus has almost nothing to say about the grandeur of the empire or the promise of its restoration.

This rejection of triumphalism was the consequence of political and social conditions that made it obsolete. It was not enough for Antiochus to graft imperial restoration onto his apologetic, he had to redefine Christian victory.

The role that the Jew plays in these works measures the gap between victory and defeat. Theodore transformed the Christian Empire into the new Israel in order to assimilate Old Testament apocalyptic sources of restoration. Theodore therefore made the Jew an intellectual straw man whose objections he could dismiss, and a typological foil that allowed him to transfer apocalyptic promises of restoration to the Christian Romans. But he retained the rhetoric of victory, for victory was what he celebrated. For Antiochus, the Jew was the bloody murderer and persecutor over whom the Christian could assert his claim as God's beloved through martyrdom. The triumphal rhetoric against barbarians had to be jettisoned; their victory was all too clear. Thus, the Jew moved from the typological sphere in Theodore to the social sphere in Antiochus.

Antiochus gave the anti-Semitic typology of Theodore social definition. The figure of the Jew, the persecutor and Christ-killer, completes the transformation of Roman war against barbarians into a martyrial struggle against Jews. The Jews had long been persecutors and Christ-killers in Christian literature, and Antiochus Monachus was hardly more vehement in his denunciation of Jews than John Chrysostom had been two and a half centuries earlier. The murderous Jews had been long established as a rhetorical cliché. What is new is the social and political context in which the Jews assume this theologically sanctioned role, and even more, its social and political consequences.[76]

The True Enemies of the Christians

This literary transformation of a barbarian war against Rome into a Jewish war against Christians had social and political ramifications far beyond occasional riots in the cities of the Levant.[77] The Christian Empire had for centuries laid legal and social penalties on the Jews, but it had balked at the next step, forced baptism.[78] Only in the charged atmosphere of the early 630s, between the end of the Persian War and the Arab invasions, did Heraclius take the unprecedented step that was the political and social consequence of Christian apologetic in the Levant after the Persian War.

The sources for study of this forced baptism of the Jews are, unfortunately, contradictory and confusing, and it is difficult to discern the actual course of events. The forced baptism is attested by sources of widely varying accuracy, provenance, religion, and language. They range from the eighth-century Latin chronicler Fredegarius, whose value for events in the east is marginal at best; to the eighth-century Pseudo-Dionysius of Tel-Mahre, a Syrian Monophysite, whose chronicle is, for the reign of Heraclius at least, hopelessly confused; to the tenth-century Copt Severus of Aschmainun, whose *History of the Patriarchs of Alexandria* was written in so partisan a spirit that it is difficult to judge its worth. The twelfth-century *Chronicle* of the Jacobite Michael the Syrian is perhaps the most accurate of the later sources, but vague. Fortunately, *The Doctrine of Jacob the Newly Baptised,* an anti-Jewish dialogue that will be analyzed in greater detail in a later chapter, and a letter of Maximus the Confessor, offer at least some contemporary evidence for the forced baptism. The ninth-century Byzantine chronicler Theophanes, the tenth-century Melkite Egyptian Eutychius, the ninth-century Melkite Syrian Agapius, and the eighth-century Armenian Pseudo-Sebeos also mention Heraclius's dealings with the Jews following the Persian War. This collection of widely varying sources leaves a confusing trail to follow, but one that nonetheless illustrates contemporary interest in the Jews. Not even the battle of Yarmuk, which delivered the Levant into the Arabs' hands, is as well documented as this minor event.

The report of Pseudo-Dionysius may be dismissed immediately. He dated the forced baptism to the reign of Phocas, a chronological error of twenty-five years, and his report of the forced baptism simply copied his source, *The Doctrine of Jacob the Newly Baptised*. He even named the source when he dated the forced baptism to the time of "Jacob the Jew," *Doctrine*'s protagonist.[79]

Fredegarius and Severus, despite their temporal and geographic distance from events and each other, have similar narratives. Fredegarius mentioned forced baptism in correspondence between Heraclius and the Frankish King Dagobert. Heraclius asked Dagobert to baptize the Jews because his astrological researches revealed that a circumcised people would overthrow the empire. It is not likely that such a letter was sent,[80] but oddly a similar story appears in the Coptic source Severus. He described how Heraclius dreamed a Semitic people would overthrow the empire, and immediately ordered a forced baptism of the Jews.[81] Severus placed this tale after a Chalcedonian persecution of the Copts, and before the arrival of the Arabs, "a few days" after the dream, using the story to show Heraclius's Chalcedonian foolishness and the punishment he received; he later wrote that Heraclius's heterodoxy was the cause of the Arabs' success.[82] Although it is peculiar that such different sources should recount similar stories, whatever their origin, they are hardly creditable.

The *Doctrine*, which describes a forced baptism of Jews by the eparch of Africa, briefly mentions Heraclius's order.[83] But it also offers convincing evidence that no empire-wide policy of forced baptism was ever implemented. A Constantinopolitan Christian commissioned Jacob as a sales representative, even giving him an exemption from the forced baptism at Carthage; he did not need one in Constantinople.[84] Jacob's opponent, Justus, at first refused to meet Jacob, fearing denunciation, and complained that if he and Jacob were home in Ptolemais or Sykamina, he would not worry.[85] Evidently, there was no forced baptism in these cities either, a point made even clearer when Justus announced that he desired to return to Ptolemais in order to convert his family.[86]

Maximus agrees that the eparch of Africa forcibly baptized the Jews there, and that the eparch was "following the command of our most blessed emperors," when he baptized "all the Jews and Samaritans living throughout all of Africa, both native and foreign, with their wives, children and servants, numbering into many thousands of souls."[87] As for the rest of the empire, Maximus can only say, "I hear that through the whole Roman realm this has happened."[88] But his evidence of an empire-wide forced conversion must be judged in light of the *Doctrine*.[89]

One reliable source witnesses an empire-wide forced-baptism policy, the twelfth-century *Chronicle* of the Jacobite Michael the Syrian. But its report poses as many problems as it solves:

> At this time [632/33], the emperor commanded that all the Jews in the lands of the Empire of the Romans be made Christians. For this reason, the Jews fled from the land of the Romans; they came finally to Edessa. After they were again attacked in this place, they fled into Persia. A great number of them received baptism and became Christians.[90]

Michael next recorded an earthquake and heavenly sign that introduced the Arab invasions beginning with the defeat of the Palestinian Dux Sergius.[91] Theophanes' ninth-century Byzantine *Chronicle* recounted the exact same narrative.[92] But although Theophanes drew on the same sources as Michael, he never mentioned any forced baptism of the Jews.[93]

Michael's report is plagued with problems. If the order to baptize the Jews was empire-wide, why should the Jews flee to Edessa? When the Jews were attacked there, were there imperial orders, or was it a local riot? Michael elsewhere wrote that the large Jewish population at Edessa had nearly been massacred in the retaliations that followed the Persian War.[94] Did Michael confuse or conflate these events? Such difficulties leave his evidence for an empire-wide imperial order for the baptism of the Jews problematic at best.

The confusing and contradictory evidence makes an empire-wide forced baptism doubtful. But oddly, the one particular on which the majority of these diverse sources agreed was not a forced baptism of the Jews, but an imperial pardon for them. Theophanes, Eutychius, Michael the Syrian, and Agapius concurred on this while disagreeing on almost every other detail. Michael reported that the Jews fought with the Persians against Heraclius's brother Theodore at Edessa, when he toured Syria reclaiming cities still held by the Persians after the Persian War. But just before Theodore could slaughter the Jews for their refusal to surrender the city, Heraclius issued the Jews a blanket pardon.[95] Agapius told a similar "Edessene" tale; the Jews were to be massacred for their mistreatment of the Christians. They also received a pardon from the emperor.[96]

Eutychius also reported that Heraclius pardoned the Jews. This time, however, the venue was not Edessa, but Tiberias in Palestine. When Heraclius came to Tiberias with the True Cross, he issued a pardon to the Jews. Only when he reached Jerusalem, and was promised absolution from breaking his oath, did he order a massacre of Jews.[97] Eutychius's story strongly resembles Theophanes'. They shared an outline: pardon at Tiberias, march to Jerusalem, penalties inflicted on Jews there. There they disagreed. Theophanes reported that when Heraclius was in Tiberias, he interrogated Benjamin, the Jewish community leader, about Jewish attacks on Christians during the Persian occupation. Benjamin at once admitted the truth of these accusations, simply declaring, "They were the enemies of my religion." Heraclius thereupon persuaded Benjamin to be baptized.[98] Then, at Jerusalem, Heraclius ordered the Jews expelled.[99]

The evidence for the Jews in the empire, and especially in the Levant, between the end of the Persian War and the beginning of the Arab invasions indicates that Jews were forcibly baptized and persecuted, but it is far from clear that an imperial order commanded an empire-wide baptism. The Edessene reports, whatever the exact events, certainly registered Christian hostility to the Jews after the Persian War, in large part owing to the identification of the Jews as traitors and the allies of the Persians. Theophanes's report of Heraclius's order at Carthage and stay at Tiberias leaves little doubt that Heraclius took a direct interest in the Jews' misdeeds during the Persian occupation and personally participated in some sort of conversion campaign, but does not prove such an order embraced the whole empire.

Thus, while Heraclius clearly took a hand in Benjamin's conversion, extensive imperial participation in forced baptisms is doubtful. Eutychius, Agapius, and Michael agree that Heraclius issued an imperial pardon to the Jews for their conduct during the Persian occupation, and it is likely that Heraclius treated the Jews on a case-by-case basis. But it is equally clear that the victory over the Persians was incomplete without some further demonstration of victory over the true enemies of the Christians.

An Armenian source, the *History of Heraclius* by Pseudo-Sebeos, adds even more confusion to the question of the Jews' status between the Persian War and the Arab invasion. It also related an "Edessene" incident but linked the story directly to Mohammed's rise. As in other sources, Heraclius removed the Jews placed in Edessa by the Persians, although unlike the other sources, there was no fighting or threat of a massacre.[100] Pseudo-Sebeos then continued that the Jews "took the desert road, and arrived in Arabia among the children of Ishmael; they appealed to them for aid, and let them know that they were their parents according to the Bible."[101] The Jews do not succeed in convincing the Arabs of their shared genealogy.

Pseudo-Sebeos immediately follows this narrative with the history of Mohammed, who founds his religion on these same racial as well as religious grounds: "He explained, 'God has promised by an oath to Abraham and his posterity after him unto eternity. Loving only the God of Abraham, go take your land, that God has given to your father Abraham, and no one can resist you in combat for God is with you.'"[102] Pseudo-Sebeos later reports that at first the Jews joined Mohammed since both were the "sons of Abraham," and that they sent an embassy to Heraclius to leave the lands "promised to them through their father Abraham" before he was driven out.[103] Such Jewish inspiration of Mohammed is not unique. Theophanes reported that Mohammed's first followers were ten Jews who supported the prophet even after they realized that he was not the Messiah.[104]

The responsibility of the Jews for the rise of Mohammed fits the pattern that transformed Roman war against barbarians into Christian war against Jewish persecutors. The victory of the Arabs raised once more the need to deflect political disaster through apologetic, and the Jews, defeated in the Persian War, arose to plague Christians once more.

Maximus the Confessor illustrates this apologetic against Islam, and the vital role that the Jews had in it.[105] Mostly he blamed Arab success on the Heraclian dynasty's Monotheletism.[106] But his early letters, from the late 620s after the victory over the Persians, celebrated victory with the same enthusiasm that characterize all Greek sources from this period.[107] Even later, in 632, when Maximus wrote to John the Presbyter about affairs in Africa, he mentioned rumors of Arab incursions but dismissed them with a metaphor:

> I know, and did not arrive at this conclusion randomly, but through anagogical thought, that this flesh, the usurper of divine laws of the spirit in my deepest self, is called Arabia, which is truly, the nourisher of shameless, uncivilized wolves, and which is, in fact, on account of sin's presence, called the west, [cf. Hab. 1:8] where [God] entered, because he was clearly concerned, saw our danger, and on account of this, manifested himself, raised up his own sovereignty, and came in the flesh to save those who were lost.[108]

Like many Byzantine authors, Maximus used a topical reference in a letter whose subject is the conflict of spirit and flesh in the soul. Maximus's interest in the Arabs in 632 was sufficiently superficial that he dismissed them as the "sons of Esau," a mistaken genealogy for the Hagarenes that no one more than tangentially interested in the Arabs would make.[109]

A decade later, however, Maximus had lost his earlier indifference toward the Arabs, who had since conquered Palestine, Syria, and Egypt. In letter fourteen, from the early 640s, Maximus's description of the Arabs has taken on a fearful metamorphosis: "What, as I said, is more terrifying to the eyes or ears of Christians than these events: to see a harsh, monstrous race that connives to reach out its hands against the divine inheritance. But the number of sins we committed made these things come to pass, for we did not worthily order our lives according to the Gospel of Christ."[110] The catastrophe of the Arab invasions had by now become clear to Maximus, and in typical seventh-century fashion, his immediate reaction was to turn to the citizens' sins as the source of disaster. But even in the early 640s, certainly before the *Typos* of Constans II had turned him against the imperial power as the agent of recovery, Maximus still evidently believed that the Arab tide would recede, as had the Persian in the 620s, if the citizens would only repent: "If we pray, we will draw divine grace to our aid, which will be our ally and show us forth victorious against every hostile power."[111]

But whatever abuse Maximus heaped on the Arabs, it was nothing compared with the abuse he heaped on the Jews. Like his contemporaries, Maximus could not conceive that the empire was systemically flawed, and that the Arabs could overpower the empire from the outside. The source of the empire's decline had to have moral causes. And for Maximus, it was the Jews that were the source of the Arab success. Indeed, in letter fourteen, the Arabs served as little more than a distraction from the real problem that faced the Empire, the Jews.

Maximus began his discussion by pointing to the horrors that were now daily occurrences in the east: "For what is more common than the evils now encompassing the world? What is more terrifying to observers than current events? . . . To see a desert, barbarian race march upon our foreign soil as if it were its own; our realm consumed by wild, untamed beasts that have the mere outline of the human form alone."[112] Maximus's description of the Arabs certainly fit the traditional rhetoric of barbarism. The description of the Arabs as animals in human form was a *topos* of classical ethnography,[113] and indeed the threat that the Arabs posed was to the political order of Rome. But Arab barbarism was nothing compared with the evil of the Jews. After describing the attacks of the bestial Arabs, Maximus then turned to the true architects of evil:

> The Jewish people, who have rejoiced in blood from the first, imagining that the murder of the created is alone sufficient for the creator. It is even clearer that the magnitude of their insane rage for the sake of Christian suffering is

greater in the abundance of their immorality than all those who are a by-word for evil, because the single most impious of all races on the face of the earth imagines that God watches over those by whom God is hated; it is the most friendly toward the opposing power, while they lead the parade with every manner and method for that vile advent; even through whom occurs the unveiling of the advent of the Antichrist, since they do not know the advent of the Saviour; and since these things have happened, the hostile and lawless, haters of men and haters of God, are even greater haters of men, because hating God, they have connived to mock him with their insults against his saints. So the moment of vengeance draws near when God will punish them in the end more justly through their deeds after their tyranny and rebellion against God, the foremost race of lies, architect of maniacal murderousness, enemy of truth, bitter persecutor of my faith, through whom the error of polytheism has been released, and the serried ranks of demons have come forth.[114]

In the spirit of the *Miracle of Berytus*, Maximus transferred the assault of the Jews on the Christians' God to the Christians themselves. Maximus expressed little interest in the defeat of such mundane enemies as the Arabs. The war against the Arabs transcended mere material opponents. When Maximus called the Jews "most friendly to the opposing power," he may have meant demons even more than Arabs. Above all the Jews were to blame that "the error of polytheism," an early identification of Islam, had been released.

The Arabs, barbaric and destructive, were not the Christians' true enemies, nor was the Christians' true struggle against them. On the contrary, the truly evil race that afflicted the Christians was the Jews. The Arab invasion was another example of *their* impiety and apostasy. Like Antiochus Monachus, Maximus exploited the parallel of the Jews' murder of Christ, and the Jews' persecution and murder of Christians to redefine Christian victory and, perhaps more importantly, defeat.

On the one hand, Maximus shares the transformation of defeat by barbarians into victory over the Jews; on the other hand, he shares the apocalypticism of Theodore Syncellus and Pseudo-Methodius. He also set the Arab wars in an apocalyptic frame; consequently, ultimate Christian victory would not be against Arabs—although they would eventually be defeated—but over the offending Jews. It was a commonplace in Christian apocalyptic from this period that the Antichrist would arise from, or through the agency of, the Jews. The Arab invasions, inspired by the Jews, were fitted to this pattern, and made the first sign of the Antichrist's arrival. And it would be the Jews, not the Arabs, to whom the Christians' eventual victory would bring vengeance.[115]

The demonic and apocalyptic image of the Jew that Maximus used was not created during the Arab invasions but during the Persian War, and explains one of Maximus's most peculiar remarks. In the conclusion to letter eight, Maximus described how the eparch of Africa, George, "following the command of our most blessed emperors," forcibly baptized all the Jews resident in Africa on Pentecost in 632.[116] But his opinion of the forced baptism of the Jews was not positive. His three reasons expressed different aspects of the image of the Jew that Theodore and Antiochus had created. The first was that the presence of such converts would profane the Christian mysteries. The second was that the assimilation of the Jews would mitigate their crimes, and Maximus was concerned " . . . lest somehow they evade the much-multiplied condemnation that has waxed great in the darkness of their impiety—surely they have cut off the light of grace from themselves because they have the bitter root of their hereditary impiety deeply planted."[117] The Jewish race was unalterably impious and condemned. It was a mistake to permit them to mingle with Christians, and thus permit them opportunities to devise more nefarious plots.

But Maximus's third objection is the most interesting, for it illustrates the apocalyptic mood of the seventh century, and the accepted role that the Jews were to play in the consummation:

> And third, I have reservations about their expected apostasy according to the holy apostle [2 Thess. 2:3], lest, initially, there take place their assimilation with the faithful people, through which they would be able, without raising suspicion among the more naive, to harvest a crop of scandals against our holy faith, and that clear and unambiguous sign be discovered of the disturbances of the final consummation.[118]

Maximus's final objection to the Jews' forced baptism was that it could provoke the end of the world. The assimilation of Jews and Christians was bad enough, but the conversion of the Jews might very well be a sign of the end. Jews by their very nature were incapable of receiving the divine light of Christian truth, and their baptism would only lead to confusion among Christians and apostasy among Jews. Even before the Arab invasions, Maximus set the Jews and their evil into an apocalyptic context. The Jews remained an alien race, irrevocably separated from the Christian race and polity.

Thus, Maximus brought to a climax the evolution of the image of the Jew in the writings of Theodore and Antiochus. Each represented a further step in the assimilation of the Jew into Christian apologetic for defeat.

Christian apologists diverted their audience from Roman reverses by super-imposing an apocalyptic Christian conflict with the Jew upon the historical conflicts with barbarians. In the end, the rhetoric of the true enemy of the Christians led to the forced baptism of the real enemies of Christ.

The role of the Jew in Christian apologetics was malleable and varied widely with the social and political circumstances of the author. Theodore, Antiochus, and Maximus all emphasized different aspects of the Jews to suit their own needs. To differing degrees, they shared the hope of imperial renewal. Antiochus was probably the least overt in his imperialism, but even Maximus, who was eventually hied into court for defeatism, did not despair of imperial renewal, only of imperial renewal under the heretical Heraclian dynasty. But the rhetorical use of the Jew transcended the defense of imperial restoration and came to be an essential element of the defense of Christianity itself. The identification of Roman and Christian as a race whose covenant with God guaranteed its imperial place could also be used to legitimate Christianity after the empire had receded.

Notes

1. Theodore was one of four ambassadors sent to the Khagan during the siege, *Paschal Chronicle,* ed. L. Dindorf (Bonn, 1832), 721 [hereafter, *Pas. Chron.*]; Theodore Syncellus, *On the Attack of the Avars,* ed. L. Sternbach, *Analecta Avarica* (Cracow, 1900), 306; George of Pisidia, *Bellum Avaricum,* ed. A. Pertusi, *Giorgio Pisidia, Poemi: I. Panegyrici epici* (Ettal, 1959), 311–27; see also F. Barišic, "Le Siège de Constantinople par les Avars et les Slaves en 626," *Byz* 24 (1954): 383–84; A. Stratos, *To Byzantion ston Z' Aiōna* (Athens, 1966), 2:517–20; for the date of the homily, see A. Pertusi, ed., *Poemi,* 215; P. Speck, *Zufaelliges zum Bellum Avaricum des Georgios Pisides* (Munich, 1980), 72–73. Much less is known about Antiochus, including his name; it seems likely that the Antiochus Strategius to whom *The Fall of Jerusalem* is attributed is the same as the Antiochus Monachus who wrote the *Epistle to Eustathius,* PG 89, col. 1421–28, which describes not only the advent of the "Chaldean storm," but that of the Ishmaelites as well, see F. Nau, "Note sur les Mss. de Paris qui renferment la notice bibliographique d'Antiochus, moine de S.-Saba," *ROC* 11 (1906): 327–30; P. Peeters, "La Prise de Jérusalem par les Perses," *Mélanges de l'Université Saint Joseph* 9 (1923–24): 3–42.

2. Theodore, 298.35–39.

3. Triumphalism had viewed the Roman Empire a continuation of God's chosen people and polity, but had not invested the capital with the eschatological trappings that Theodore did. See P. Alexander, "Strength of Empire and Capital as Seen through Byzantine Eyes," *Speculum* 37 (1962): 339–57, for Constantinople's place in the political thought of the mature Byzantine Empire; Av. Cameron and J.

Herrin, *Constantinople in the Early Eighth Century: The Parastaseis Syntomoi Chronikai,* (Leiden, 1984), esp. 242–43, G. Dagron, *Constantinople Imaginaire: Études sur le recueil des Patria, [Bibliothèque byzantine, Études* 8] (Paris, 1984), 63–97, 326–28, for the crystallization of Constantinople's Christian origins and its place in the apocalyptic cycles of *Pseudo-Methodius* and the *Daniel-Diegesis;* Dagron, *Naissance d'une capitale, Constantinople et ses institutions de 330 à 451* (Paris, 1974), for the evolution of Constantinople as a capital to the mid-fifth century.

4. Theodore, 319:15–18.

5. See George of Pisidia, *Heraclias,* ed. A. Pertusi, *Georgio Pisidia, Poemi: I. Panegirici epici* (Ettal, 1959), 2.38, and Chapter 3; see also Chapter 2 for the causal role of sin in Eusebius's explanation of the Great Persecution.

6. Theodore, 301.10–13.

7. Riots had brought down Maurice and Phocas in 602 and 610; there had been riots when the corn dole ended in 618–19, riots when Heraclius had left to campaign in the east in 622, and riots against John Seismos, who had charged soldiers for bread.

8. See Theodore, 300.20–23, 302.31–303.04.

9. Ibid., 303.20–24.

10. The better articulated rhetoric of sin and repentance in Theodore supports Speck's view, *Bellum Avaricum,* 26, that George took his lead from Theodore. It is likely, however, that these themes had already become common in Constantinopolitan literary circles.

11. Theodore, 299.35–39.

12. Ibid., 301.13–14.

13. Ibid., 300.37–301.4.

14. Ibid., 301.2.

15. Ibid., 302.17–19.

16. Ibid., 306.34–39.

17. Ibid., 317.15–23.

18. Ibid., 303.25–28.

19. Ibid., 303.28–30.

20. *Pas. Chron.,* 725.9–15.

21. *Pas. Chron.,* 716, explains how Christ saved "his city" through the Virgin. George of Pisidia does not participate in this trend toward epiphany; see Chapter 2.

22. *Pas. Chron.,* 725.

23. Theodore, 309.1–310.36.

24. Ibid., 316.36–40.

25. Ibid., 317.29–34.

26. Ibid., 307.36–38, 23; cf. also *Pas. Chron.,* 727.18, where Heraclius announces his victory over the Persians as the victory of those "who are Christ's people."

27. Theodore, 310.34–36.

28. Typically, he substituted Chalcedon, where the Persians watched the Avar siege, for Tarshish in Ezekiel; see ibid., 315.15–16.

29. Ibid., 309.5–6, see also 316.7–9. The Jews believe that the prophecy refers to their own loss of Jerusalem to the gentiles.

30. Ibid., 310.6–11.

31. Ibid., 310.32–34.

32. Ibid., 314.19–26.

33. Ibid., 316.21–25.

34. Theodore explains that the Jews' faith was "weak with the understanding of the flesh"; see ibid., 304.36–305.2.

35. Ibid., 310.21–24.

36. Ibid., 298.35–37.

37. Ibid., 298.39–299.1. Theodore almost ignores Heraclius's military prowess. More importantly, Heraclius is not a mediator between subjects and deity; that responsibility rested on the patriarch.

38. For typological praise of earlier emperors, see W. Ensslin, *Gottkaiser und Kaiser von Gottesgnaden.* [Sitzungsberichte der bayerischen Akademie der Wessen schafter, phil.-hist. Abt.] (Munich, 1943), 103–04; F. Dvornik, *Early Christian and Byzantine Political Philosophy,* 2 vols. (Washington, D.C., 1966), 2:676–79, 784–86. For typological comparisons by Theodore, see Theodore, 304–05, for Moses; ibid., 305.13–26, that "our Moses," the Patriarch Sergius, was superior to Moses; ibid., 305.6–10, for David; see also 304.21–27, 307.20, 307.33, 308.14, 309.16, and 320.19–29, for other comparisons to the victories of Israel, and the typological claims for the "new" Israel that Theodore makes.

39. Apocalypses primarily respond to events; see G. Podskalsky, *Byzantinische Reichseschatologie. Die Periodisierung der Weltgeschichte in den 4 Grossreichen (Daniel 2 und 7) un dem tausendjaehrigen Friedensreiche (Apok. 20)* (Munich, 1972), 14, who describes the influence of Persian wars on Aphraates' apocalyptic. Aphraates, however, did not write within the empire; Byzantine apocalypses were almost never triumphal; see Podskalsky, *Reichsechatologie,* esp. 8–14, 16–18, 23–32, 51–53; P. Alexander, *The Oracle of Baalbek, The Tibeurtine Sibyl in Greek Dress,* [*Dumbarton Oaks Studies* 10] (Washington, D.C., 1967), esp. 118–21; Alexander, *The Byzantine Apocalyptic Tradition* (Berkeley, 1985), esp. 152–92, although it must be remembered that Alexander deals mostly with apocalypses after the seventh century; K. Berger, *Die griechische Daniel-Diegese. Eine altkirchliche Apokalypse* (Leiden, 1976), esp. 5–7, 39–41, 80–88.

40. The Greek and Syriac versions of *Pseudo-Methodius* reveal how authors incorporated imperial fortunes. The later Greek version also assimilates the siege of Constantinople in the 670s into the apocalyptic scheme. Pseudo-Methodus, *Apokalypse des Ps.-Methodius,* [*Beitraege zur klassischen Philologie* 83], ed. A. Lolos (Meisenheim am Glan), 1976.

41. For the seventh-century apocalyptic tradition see Alexander, *Tradition,* 13–32, 52–60; Podskalsky, *Byzantinische Reichseschatologie,* 53–57. *Pseudo-Methodius* reaffirmed not only the empire's victory over its enemies, but also its duration until the end of time. See P. Alexander, "Byzantium and the Migration of Literary Works and Motifs: The Legend of the Last Roman Emperor," *Medievalia et Humanistica* n.s. 2 (1971): 47–68; Alexander, *Tradition,* 151–92; Podskalsky, ibid., 73–76; even the pessimistic *Daniel-Diegese* does not predict the fall of the empire, only its return to Rome, see Berger, *Daniel-Diegese,* 92–100.

42. *Pseudo-Methodius,* 120–22.

43. Ibid., 92.

44. Ibid., 98.

45. Ibid., 94.

46. Ibid., 90–92.

47. Berger, *Daniel-Diegese,* 15. The *Daniel Commentary* that is today extant is ninth-century, but it is likely to have been a redaction of an early eighth-century apocalypse. Although late, it seems to have thematic roots in the seventh century.

48. Ibid., 136–44. Different as the *Daniel Commentary* and *Pseudo-Methodius* are, they concur in this.

49. For Antiochus Monachus, see n. 1 above; for the fall of Jerusalem in 614, see A. Stratos, *To Byzantion ston z' Aiōna* (Athens, 1965), 1: 261–73; for the return of the cross, see Stratos, *Byzantion,* 2: 671–85; A. Frolow, "La vraie croix et les expéditions d'Héraclius en Perse," *REB* 11 (1953): 88–105; V. Grumel, "La reposition de la vraie croix à Jérusalem par Héraclius. Le jour et l'année," *Byzantinische Forschungen* 1 (1966): 139–49; C. Mango, "Deux études sur Byzance et la Perse Sassanide," *Travaux et Mémoires* 9 (1985): 105–17; P. Speck, *Das geteilte Dossier. Beobachtungen zu den Nachrichten ueber die Regierung des Kaisers Herakleios und seiner Soehne bei Theophanes und Nikephoros,* [*Poikila byzantina* 9] (Bonn, 1988), 68–74, 157–60, 356–78.

50. Antiochus Monachus, *La Prise de Jérusalem par les Perses,* [*Corpus Scriptorum christianorum orientalium,* Scriptores georgi 203], ed. and trans. G. Garitte (Louvain, 1960), I.7.

51. Ibid., I.4.

52. Ibid., I.12–17. Since the fourth century, Christians had identified Jerusalem as a Christian rather than Jewish city; see R. Wilken, "The Restoration of Israel in Biblical Prophecy: Christian and Jewish response in the Early Christian Period," in *"To See Ourselves as Others See Us:" Christians, Jews, "Others" in Late Antiquity,* ed. J. Neusner and E. Frerichs (Chicago, 1985), 337–55. Wilken suggests that Christian claims to Jerusalem were a reaction to Jewish claims; his Jewish evidence is seventh-century.

53. Antiochus Monachus, *La Prise de Jérusalem,* I.13–16.

54. Ibid., I.17.

55. Ibid., I.20, II.7, IV.7.

56. Ibid., II.1–4, IV.7–8; see also A. Cameron, *Circus Factions: Blues and Greens at Rome and Byzantium* (Oxford, 1976), 281–85; D. Olster, *The Politics of Usurpation in the Seventh Century: Rhetoric and Revolution in Byzantium* (Amsterdam, 1993), 112–14, 225–63.

57. Antiochus Monachus, *La Prise de Jérusalem,* II.8.

58. Ibid., V.16.

59. Ibid., XI.14.

60. Ibid., V.16.

61. Ibid., III.4.

62. Ibid., V.1–7, 21–35.

63. Ibid., XII.1–23.

64. Ibid., VIII.10.

65. Ibid., XII.7.

66. Ibid., XIX.4. Antiochus also describes Zacharius brought before Chosroes as Daniel or Moses were brought before foreign kings; see ibid., XIX.5.

67. Ibid., XIII.6. Enchained he was led to Zion through the gate by which Christ had triumphantly entered Jerusalem, ibid., XIII.1.

68. Ibid., XIII.9.

69. Ibid., XIII.22.

70. Ibid., XIII.34.

71. Ibid., X.4.

72. Ibid., X.6–7. See also the description of the Jews' role in *The Martyrdom of Polycarp*, ed. K. Bihlmeyer, Die apostolischen Valtes, t.3 (Tuebingeis, 1970), ch. 17.2.

73. Cf. Antiochus Monachus, *La prise de Jérusalem*, X.6.

74. See Chapter 2, n. 112.

75. Antiochus Monachus, *La prise*, XXI.6–11.

76. R. Reuther, *Faith and Fratricide: The Theological Roots of Anti-Semitism* (Minneapolis, 1974), 124–31; R. Wilken, *John Chrysostom and the Jews: Rhetoric and Reality in the Late Fourth Century* (Berkeley, 1983), 125–27, for the Jews as Christ-killers. M. Simon, *Verus Israel: A Study of the Relations between Christians and Jews in the Roman Empire (135–425)*, trans. H. McKeating (Oxford, 1986), 217–23, and J. Parkes, *The Conflict of the Church and the Synagogue: A Study in the Origins of Anti-Semitism* (New York, 1979 [1934]), 163–66, passed over all mention of Christ-killing in their respective discussions of Chrysostom, perhaps because they did not think anyone capable of taking this accusation seriously.

77. See, for example, John Moschus, *Spiritual Meadow*, PG 87, col. 2861, and especially Chapter 6 below on *Doctrine;* Parkes, *Conflict*, 257–66; M. Avi-Yonah, *The Jews under Roman and Byzantine Rule: A Political History of Palestine from the Bar Kochba War to the Arab Conquest* (New York, 1984), 257–65; Olster, "Usurpation," 240–44.

78. The bibliography on legislation on the Jews is extensive, but often repetitive, and only a few recent works need be mentioned. Scholarship generally divides into two schools, that which blames the church, and that which blames the state for persecuting the Jews. See S. Grayzel, "The Jews and Roman Law," *Jewish Quarterly Review* 59 (1968–69): esp. 95–115; J. Cohen, "Roman Imperial Policy toward the Jews from Constantine to the End of the Palestinian Patriarchate (429)," *Byzantine Studies* 3 (1976): 1–29; K. Reichardt, "Die Judengesetzgebung im Codex Theodosianus," *Kairos* 20 (1978): 16–39; B. Bachrach, "The Jewish Community of the Later Roman Empire as Seen in the *Codex Theodosianus*," in *"To See Ourselves as Others See Us:" Christians, Jews, "Others" in Late Antiquity*, ed. J. Neusner and E. Frerichs (Chicago, 1985), 399–421.

79. Pseudo-Dionysius of Tell-Mahré, *Chronique de Denys de Tell-Mahré, quatrième partie*, trans. J.-B. Chabot (Paris, 1895), 4. Chabot proposes that this is actually Jacob of Edessa (Pseudo-Dionysius, 4 n.2), but the text is clearly a copy of the *Doctrine*.

80. Fredegarius, *Quellen zur Geschichte 7. und 8. Jhr.*, ed. A. Kusternig (Darmstadt, 1982), 230–32; see the comments in Starr, "St. Maximus and the Forced Conversion at Carthage," *Byzantinisch-neugriechisches Jahrbuch* 16 (1940): 195–97, who cast considerable doubt on the letter's authenticity.

81. Severus of Aschmainun, *History of the Patriarchs of the Coptic Church of Alexandra,* ed. and trans. E. Evett, *PO* 5: 491.

82. Ibid., 492.

83. *Doctrine,* 2. It is important to note that this section is not extant in the Greek, but is supplied from the Slavic translation.

84. Ibid., 89. J. Starr, "Byzantine Jewry on the Eve of the Arab Conquest," *Journal of the Palestine Oriental Society* 15 (1935): 289, and A. Sharf, "Byzantine Jewry in the Seventh Century," *BZ* 48 (1955): 110, have noted this passage as well.

85. *Doctrine,* 54.

86. Ibid., 88.

87. R. Devreesse, "La fin de inédite d'une lettre de saint Maxime: un baptème forcé de Juifs et de Samaritains à Carthage en 632," *Revue des sciences religieuses* 17 (1937): 34.

88. *Doctrine,* 35.

89. According to *Doctrine,* only Jewish leaders were baptized. This same pattern is found in Theophanes' description of Heraclius's baptism of the Jew Benjamin at Tiberias, and in the account of the conversion of the Jews of Tomei; see Theophanes, *Chronographia,* 2 vols., ed. C. de Boor (Leipzig, 1883), 328; R. Griveau, "Histoire de la conversion des Juifs habitant la ville de Tomei en Egypte d'aprés d'anciens manuscrits arabes," *ROC* 13 [2ᵈ series, 3] (1908): 309–12. At Carthage, as at Tomei, it seems the families of the community leaders were not baptized, the evidence of Maximus notwithstanding, for when Justus seemed convinced by Jacob's arguments, it is Isaac's wife and mother-in-law who upbraid him, *Doctrine,* 63–64.

90. Michael the Syrian, *Chronique,* 2 vols., trans. J.-B. Chakot (Paris, 1899–1910), 2:414.

91. Ibid., 2:413–414.

92. Theophanes, *Chronique,* 336; see Olster, "Usurpation," 24–27 on the relationship of these two sources.

93. Michael possibly used the *Chronicle* of Jacob of Edessa, whose reference to the Jews under the year 632 is only partially extant. It is not clear what Jacob reported; see Jacob of Edessa, *Chronicon,* trans. E. W. Brooks, *Corpus scriptorum Christianorum orientalium,* Scriptores Syrii, ser. 3, vol. 4 (Paris, 1903), 251.

94. Michael the Syrian, *Chronique,* 2:410.

95. Ibid.

96. Agapius of Menbidj, *Kitab al-'Unvan,* trans. A. A. Vasiliev, *PO* 8 (Paris, 1912), 466. No Greek source mentioned this "Edessene" incident. Theophanes, *Chronique,* 327, reported Theodore's march through Syria and past Edessa without the least trouble with the Jews. Perhaps the oriental and Greek sources relied on different traditions of Heraclius's dealings with the Jews.

97. Eutychius of Alexandria, *Annales, PG* 111, col. 1089–91.

98. Theophanes, *Chronique,* 328. Benjamin's easy admission of wrongdoing is a motif that we will see again in the *Doctrine of Jacob the Newly Baptised.*

99. Theophanes, *Chronique,* 328. Most of Eutychius's tale is invented; the Melkite festival of Heraclius's "oath" is a mythical reworking of the festival of the cross. The anti-Jewish dialogue *Gregentius and Herbanus* corroborates the expulsion

of the Jews from Jerusalem, but not any forced baptism of the Jews there; see Chapter 7.

100. Pseudo-Sebeos, *Histoire d'Heraclius,* trans. F. Macler (Paris, 1904), 94–95.

101. Ibid., 95.

102. Ibid., 95–96.

103. Ibid., 96.

104. Theophanes *Chronique,* 333. See Chapter 5 for the evidence of *Doctrine of Jacob the Newly Baptised* on the Jewish reaction to Mohammed.

105. For Maximus's attitude toward the Jews, see C. Laga, "Maximi confessoris ad Thalassium quastio 64. Essai de lecture," *After Chalcedon: Studies in Theology and Church History,* ed. C. Laga, J. A. Munitiz, and L. van Rompay, [*Orientalia Lovaniensia analecta* 18] (Louvain, 1985), 213–15.

106. See Chapter 2.

107. See *Epistolae, PG* 91: 608c–d, 637c–d; Chapters 2 on George of Pisidia and 4 on Sophronius.

108. Maximus the Confessor, *Epistolae,* 444a.

109. Ibid., 444c.

110. Ibid., 541b.

111. Ibid., 537d–40a.

112. Ibid., 540a.

113. See Chapter 2.

114. *Epistolae,* 540.

115. In fact, in his discussion of Christ's power and authority and restoration of Christian rule, Maximus does not mention the military defeat of the enemies of Christ; see ibid., 540d–41a.

116. Devreese, "La fin inédite," 34.

117. Ibid., 35.

118. Ibid.

5. Christians Without an Empire: The Patriarch Sophronius

In 638 Jerusalem fell to heathen for the second time in a generation. But the Jerusalemites had learned their lesson; this time there was no fight at the walls and no sack with its horrors. The city surrendered on terms, and Christendom's religious center went quietly into captivity. The man who negotiated surrender was the Patriarch Sophronius. A witness of the great drama of the Persian War, he knew the joy of victory and the humiliation of defeat. His writings, covering thirty years, show growing disenchantment with the empire and an intense search for a social and political framework to replace it whose stability could offer security to the individual Christian in the chaos of the Arab wars. Theodore Syncellus, George of Pisidia, and Antiochus Monachus all wrote in the aftermath of imperial victory, and that victory sustained their belief, even when shaken, in the imperial ideal. The man who surrendered Jerusalem did not offer hope in an imperial restoration that he did not have. Instead, he offered hope by disassociating the empire from the Christian community and creating a new Christian identity that was Roman no longer.[1]

Never a strident imperialist, Sophronius displays in his writings ever greater skepticism that imperial success was the barometer of God's favor or forgiveness. As his scepticism grew, imperial restoration themes and *topoi* that his contemporaries used to identify the Romans as God's people disappeared from his works. Like his contemporaries, Sophronius believed that sin plagued the empire, and he was a devout witness to its consequences. But Sophronius suspected that the empire was wounded beyond repair, and not just militarily. His conflict with Patriarch Sergius of Constantinople (who was supported by Heraclius) over the orthodoxy of Monoenergism, and the impotence of imperial arms in Palestine left him increasing frustrated and pessimistic. Nonetheless, despite his theological qualms, he was able to remain silent in the interests of political unity; indeed, his devotion to his episcopal duty even claimed the affections of the Monotheletes in his flock.[2]

Unlike George of Pisidia, Theodore Syncellus, and Antiochus Monachus, Sophronius did not write a particular work dedicated to the empire's wars, but his *Orations* are topical, alive with his efforts to answer his congregation's anxieties and maintain their morale. Throughout his sermons, he responded implicitly, if not explicitly, to the problem, "How was Christ himself, the giver of all good things, and the chorus leader of this, our splendor, blasphemed by gentile mouths?"[3]

In order to answer this question, Sophronius, like his fellow Jerusalemite Antiochus Monachus, transformed Roman defeat into Christian victory; unlike Antiochus, he did not use martyrdom as the rhetorical vehicle. Antiochus externalized Christian victory through martyrdom; Sophronius internalized Christian victory as a psychological, individual conflict with sin without need for an external agent in the ritual of purification.

In a sense, Antiochus had an easier task; there was a historical structure onto which Antiochus grafted his agonistic narrative, and a victory that demonstrated God's forgiveness. But the Arabs had not sacked Jerusalem, and Sophronius himself had negotiated the city's surrender. In fact the Arab invasions, as bloody and destructive as they were, inspired surprisingly few martyriological writings. The *Sixty Martyrs of Gaza* is a rare attempt to follow the martyrial model of Antiochus. But the literary references to martyrdoms in the Persian War are legion. Leaving aside the martyrial narrative of Antiochus Monachus, there are two extensive lives, with martyrdom, of Anastasius the Persian,[4] a *Life* of the Persian martyr Golinduch,[5] and numerous martyrdoms of monastic communities like that at Chobiza.[6] The Jacobites and Copts, hardly pro-imperial sources, echo the Chalcedonian sources: the Coptic *History of the Patriarchs* recorded the advent of the Arabs with near indifference but remembered the Persians with horror,[7] while the Jacobite sources, with no love for the Arabs, nonetheless heaved a literary sigh of relief to be freed from Melkite tyranny.[8]

Sophronius himself had been caught up in the martyrial mood inspired by the Persian War, and his anacreontic poem on the fall of Jerusalem to the Persians echoed Antiochus's martyrial rhetoric and themes. He also drew parallels between the passion of Christ, his city and its dwellers: the crucifixion held the promise of future victory that was realized in the Christians' own sufferings.[9] "Christ, you will subdue the cursed children of the Persian anti-God with the [martyrs'] palms of the Christians."[10]

After the war, Sophronius invested defeat with the same significance as Antiochus or George of Pisidia. His poem celebrating the return of the Cross credited the Byzantines' victory and the recovery of the Cross to

God's forgiveness. "God appeared the one who chastised our evil sins; God appeared a savior, brimming over with his divine mercy."[11] Although somewhat muted, his poems express the same joy, relief, and enthusiasm that one finds in Theodore Syncellus or George of Pisidia. "The time of the heathens is past; the good faith sings."[12] Nor was the emperor forgotten: Heraclius, "the son of Great Rome," took his share of credit as the executor of the divine will.[13]

Sophronius shared another theme with Antiochus; the victory had been not simply against the Persians, but against the Jews. In his poem lamenting the fall of Jerusalem, Sophronius called the Jews friends of the Persians who aided them in their conquest of the city.[14] Sophronius's poem celebrating the return of the True Cross described not only how the Persians had been overcome by its power, but also how the insults of the Jews had been turned to their shame.[15]

Even after the initial incursions of the Arabs, Sophronius did not lose hope of the restoration of God's favor and imperial victory. In one of his earliest works as patriarch, the *Synodal Letter* to the Patriarch Sergius of Constantinople, he requested that Sergius pray for God's forgiveness:

> And I offer you the same wealth of entreaty in order that you might make earnest and unceasing prayer, and beg God on behalf of our Christ-loving and most gentle emperors . . . so that God . . . might be merciful and bountiful to them, appeased by your holy prayers. May he give them great victories and trophies, crown them with grandsons, fortify them with divine peace and provide a strong, powerful sceptre that will scatter the scorn of all the barbarians, especially the Saracens, who have fallen upon us unexpectedly because of our sins. . . . Exceedingly then we beseech your Blessedness to make earnest entreaty with Christ so that He, responding to your prayers, might swiftly throw forth the insolence of their madness, and deliver them to be trodden underfoot, just as he did before.[16]

His audience might well have dictated Sophronius's baroque style, but whether entirely sincere or not, he had not forgotten that God had once forgiven and restored the Christians. At least when he became patriarch, he still followed the seventh-century pattern that God punished sin with defeat and forgave it with victory.

Perhaps Sophronius decided that God's patience had run out; perhaps his Jerusalemite congregation required different handling than Sergius.[17] But whatever the cause, the *Orations*' tone and themes contrast sharply with his earlier writings. They lack any renewal or martyrial rhetoric. Sophronius even reverses the contemporary rhetorical dynamic; rather than use mar-

tyrial or apocalyptic rhetoric to shore up Romanity, he uses imperial rhetoric to define and defend Christianity. Rather than defend an empire in
which he had increasingly less faith, and compelled by necessity to administer a Jerusalem severed from the empire, he fashioned a new apologetic to
bolster his flock's morale in the changed world that the Jerusalemites faced.

One of the most striking literary qualities of the *Orations* is the inversion of the Christomimetic language that George of Pisidia, Theodore
Syncellus, and Antiochus Monacus used to describe the defeat of the
Christian Romans' enemies. By contrast, Sophronius relies on imperial
metaphors to describe the victory of Christ over Satan and his minions:
Christ had freed man from fear of the devil, his hidden plots, and his open
tyrannies;[18] he had chained Satan's "armies" and freed man from the captivity of sin.[19] Christ had "peacefully raised invisible war against those
warring against us, reconciled us with his own father and shown himself to
be our peace."[20] Christ had "opened to us the door of [his] uncircumscribable Empire,"[21] offering his congregation the security of a heavenly rather
than earthly empire. "We would find eternal life and receive, in Christ
himself, an Empire that cannot be destroyed."[22] Christians were "citizens
[*politai*] of the heavenly city, Jerusalem; for where we have our polity, there
we will receive our inheritance, and dwell in eternal abodes."[23] Sophronius
did not offer his congregation the hope that the Empire of Rome would
return, but the hope that "we might become rulers in [Christ's] Empire."[24]

The Jerusalemites were probably used to imperial metaphors of
Christ's victory over sin used for imperial restoration, but Sophronius used
the rhetoric of imperial restoration as a metaphor for the renewal of the
individual soul. Christ's victory in the "invisible war" over sin and demons
freed Christians from their most dangerous enemies,[25] restored their imperial purity, and made them "sharers" of an eternal empire.[26] Man in paradise
had been an emperor; his fall had made him a slave. Christ's victory freed
him from the "barbarian tyranny" of sin and restored him to imperial
dignity.[27]

Sophronius's imperial rhetoric notwithstanding, the institution
through which a Christian participated in Christ's victory, restored his
"imperial" soul, and found peace was not the empire, but the church. "For
he is peace, who brings peaceful concord, unites the heavenly with the
earthly, and constitutes the church with both."[28] Theodore Syncellus and
George of Pisidia used martial victory to define Christian victory and
identity; Antiochus Monachus used martyrdom; Sophronius used "the
sacraments and mysteries of God, their performance earthly, but their

celebration of the one being celebrated heavenly,"[29] where "we properly celebrate [the victory of Christ]."[30] The liturgy was a social ritual that defined an extra-imperial communal social and political identity: "We from the gentiles have become the people of God. . . . We have been given the name of a new people, even Israel, because we look upon the presence of God, and with bent arms submit in our soul to it, and we, since we do not forget it, celebrate it with yearly celebrations."[31] Sophronius's call for unity in the face of the Arab threat was not to join together in resistance, either passive or active, but to express Christian unity through the liturgy: "Let no one be seen to be withdrawn from the celebration; let no one appear to fail to partake of the mysteries."[32]

Using Christ's own victory as the defining ritual of Christian identity separated the imperial imagery of Christian victory from its imperial context. In contrast to contemporaries, Sophronius's "new" Israel had nothing in common with "new" Rome. Even in Antiochus Monachus, martyrdom not only had redeemed the martyrs' souls, but had also been a rite of communal purification whose result was Heraclius's victory over the Persians.

Unlike martial struggle or martyrdom, the mass was a ritual of mystical union, not imitation. The liturgical celebration of Christ's victory united Christ and worshipper; there the Christian "stood to Christ's coming."[33] Sophronius urged his audience to "hurry to possess this union with him, than which nothing is more honorable."[34] *Uiothesia*, adoption, is one of Sophronius's most common metaphors for a mystical union that offered Christians escape from the mundane Arab threat:[35] adoption by Christ released the yoke of slavery,[36] and raised man from slavery to earthly perils to heavenly lordship of all.[37] Not even military defeat can break this bond between man and God, whose very name means "God is with us."[38] Only through liturgical union with Christ could man find peace, "For Christ is truly named heavenly and earthly peace."[39]

Martial and martyrial rituals of imitation of Christ disappear from the *Orations*. Indeed, Sophronius does not mention martyrdom in his patriarchal writings, a striking omission because his writings from the twenty or so years before his patriarchate include an anacreontic poem (XVI) on the martyrs of Egypt, and a good deal about martyrdom in his earlier hagiographic work, "When the faithful people sang the triumphal ode."[40] Yet, as patriarch, his *Orations* are remarkably barren in this regard.[41]

Sophronius's single-minded focus on the liturgy as the mystical bridge between man and God placed the church, the gateway of the bridge to heaven,[42] as the sole necessary Christian social and political institution. It should not be thought remarkable that Sophronius would shape his sermons so that the unity and integrity of the Christian community found its source in the rites of the sole remaining Christian social and political institution. "For to the children of the church and the initiates of the spirit, all the rites of Christ are clear and well-known, and none of the sacraments have been ordained unknowingly."[43]

Sophronius's ecclesiocentric orientation also defined the character and consequences of sin. Where Theodore, George, and Antiochus pronounced political turmoil the sin that laid the Byzantines low; Sophronius ignored politics entirely in his description of the sins that brought the Arabs to Jerusalem:

> For how do we appear before [Christ], when we do not preserve purity of soul or possess chastity of the body? Or how do we draw close to him, not having the sweetness of deeds that are known to please him and give him joy. For the evil of our deeds is exceedingly loathsome to him. And I am given to trembling and I suffer lest we appear as those who do not have and fail to attain the orthodox faith.[44]

Bodily impurity and heresy caused the punishments that God heaped on the Jerusalemites, not political sins.[45]

Sophronius's use of heresy as a causative sin of Christian defeat, moreover, differed from critics of imperial morality like Maximus the Confessor. Maximus had limited heresy to the emperor and his coterie; Sophronius extended the sin of heresy to the Christian community. Only by "holding the true and orthodox faith, would we blunt the Ishmaelite sword, shatter the Hagarene bow."[46] Sophronius placed orthodoxy as the premier Christian virtue because he redefined the community's context. The writers who set Christianity in an imperial context hardly mentioned heresy. But the separation of the Christian community and the empire, and even more, the substitution of the church for the empire as the institutional principle of social order, redefined the moral perspective.

Sophronius's political and social context explains not only his ecclesiology, but also his seeming failure to confront heresy head on as Maximus had. In fact, his ecclesiology was the basis of his attack. He had, at the beginning of his patriarchate, taken an oath to cease attacks on Monoenergists in return for silence on their part. Sophronius the theologian may have been uncomfortable; Sophronius the politician never broke his oath;[47] but Sophronius the patriarch made heresy, above all its threat to the community's ritual of unity, the liturgy, a thematic keystone. Thus, Sophronius

aimed his indirect attacks against Monoenergism at its liturgical consequences.[48] His *Letter to Arcadius,* the archbishop of Cyprus, who was
perhaps tempted to join with the compromisers, attacked the use of the
Trisagion in the liturgy,[49] and in his *Annunciation Oration,* he included a
long digression on the *Trisagion* in a sermon that is devoted to the theme of
heresy and its consequences.[50]

The *Feast of Purification Oration* was his most detailed exposition of the
unity achieved through the liturgy, the problem of heresy, and its social
consequences. Sophronius condemned Nestorius, who "arrogantly divided
the mystery of Christ," and Eutyches, who made "a fantasy" of the mystery
of Christ,[51] for specifically destroying the efficacy of the liturgical rites of
social unity as well as mystical union. "Thus both Eutyches and Nestorius
together have separated from this, our radiant celebration, who are its
enemies and opponents, who vie with each other to corrupt its radiance."
Sophronius called on his congregation to "purify yourselves" and "celebrate
the mysteries as a friend of Christ," rather than exclude themselves from the
celebration.[52] Heretics had to be excluded so that the liturgy might be
without stain, and the community identity without question. He concluded his litany of heresies and heresiarchs in the *Feast of Purification
Oration:* "And let all these be banished from every wonder of Christ,
however many evilly rage like them, or insanely profane like them, in order
that we, who profess the correct doctrine, who today have no stain of any
sort of heresy in celebrating this, greet Christ, God."[53] The sin of heresy
threatened the individual's participation in Christ's victory, and thus his
social participation in the Christian community. The bishop's responsibility
was to defend the community and, above all, its institutional foundation,
the church.

The bishop alone was prepared to engage heretics; only he possessed
the vision to pierce their chameleonlike ability to appear orthodox.[54]
But episcopal responsibility extended beyond doctrinal prerogatives. The
bishop was the guardian of the social and political order as well as doctrinal
purity. Sophronius was intensely aware of his position as the successor of
James,[55] and the vigilant guardian of the apostolic tradition:[56]

> Thus, because he was anxious for our salvation, for the sake of which he had
> descended from heaven to us, he made a selection of fishers, and distributed
> apostolic grace among them which reckoned their number, but did not divide
> their office or confound their order, but which guarded the distinction of the
> order in the union of the apostolic office and grace. For [God] has wonder-
> fully judged that the dignity of the apostle be protected unified, and the

distinction of the order be made known without confusion, so that the order might never pass into disorder, for disorder is the enemy of God.[57]

Just as George of Pisidia and Theodore used Christomimesis to define the emperor as the mediator between heaven and earth, Sophronius used Christomimesis to establish the hierarchy as the link between man and God. "Undivided and unconfused" referred to the activities of Christ's human and divine natures, and defined the hierarchy, like Christ, as the mediator between heaven and earth. Like Christ, the dual natures of the hierarchy were united through its "synergy," another Christological reference.[58] This mediating role of the hierarchy was not simply religious, but included political conotations, as Sophronius also joined the imperial rhetoric of order and disorder to it.[59] And in Jerusalem in the late 630s, social and political disorder was the most concrete disturbance of the congregation's mystical union with Christ: the Arab invasion was itself a "disorder."[60]

Thus, the bishop's sphere of activity was not limited to the divine, but included the social and political as well. Sophronius explained that it was the duty of the bishop to lead his congregation: "[The bishop], the organizer of [the divine] order of combat, will deliver it from the enemies who are hostile to it."[61] The "divine order of combat" was ecclesiastical, but the bishop's responsibility to defend orthodoxy and celebrate the mass incorporated the maintenance of the Christian community's continuing social and political cohesion and identity.

Sophronius's "mystical union" cannot be seen as something distinct from his response to the Arab invasions, as though Sophronius the patriarch and Sophronius the theologian were two distinct authors. Yet, scholarship has resolutely separated these personae. The disappearance in the *Orations* of the Christomimetical and martyrial vocabulary that is so pronounced in his early works appears to be a self-conscious effort to direct his rhetoric into different channels. The themes and rhetoric that dominate his patriarchal "religious" thought are inextricably mixed with his political action and apologetic agenda.

Sophronius's *Christmas Oration,* delivered on Christmas Sunday in 634,[62] shows the apologetic union of religion and politics that characterizes Sophronius's writings. It is an extended exegesis of Luke 2:14, "Glory to God in the highest, peace on earth, goodwill toward men," which echoes through his sermon like an antiphon.[63] He juxtaposed the theme of peace with the recent Arab occupation of Bethlehem in order to respond to Arab victory and reassure his demoralized congregation that neither had Christ deserted them, nor had the Arab victory compromised Christianity's truth. Through his theology of a mystical union that united the earthly and heavenly in Christ, the "double sun" that shed its light on both heaven and earth, Sophronius offered his congregation hope of escape from their fears.[64]

Although the *Christmas Oration* was written more than a year before the decisive Byzantine defeat at the Yarmuk, the Arabs had already seized the hinterland of Palestine and occupied the town of Bethlehem. It was a bleak Christmas when Christians could not go on pilgrimage to Christ's birthplace: "For now, the garrison of the Saracens, as the foreigners [Philistines, cf. 2 Sam. 23:14–17] of old have seized wondrous Bethlehem, and has no mind to furnish us a passage to that city, but rather they raise their destructive sword threateningly if we would go forth to the holy city and dare to travel to the most holy Bethlehem that we desire."[65] The presence of the Arabs so close to Jerusalem, and in the heart of Christ's holy land, certainly raised terrifying memories of the Persian invasion only twenty years earlier. Sophronius's task was not an easy one: he had to raise the hopes of his congregation, even as he prepared them for the worst. That he accomplished these seemingly paradoxical goals is truly one of his finest rhetorical achievements.

Naturally, sin lies at the heart of Sophronius's explanation both of the Arabs' success, and their removal:

> Whence we perform such a celebration in distress, but closeted within the gates . . . I accordingly call, preach and beseech your great longing for Christ himself, that we might amend ourselves, howevermuch we can, and shine with repentance and be pure in our conversion. . . . For this, if we might live a life that is beloved and friendly to God, we would rejoice at the fall of our scourge, the Saracens, and we would shortly observe their destruction, and see their utter devastation. For their bloodthirsty sword would be plunged into their hearts, their bow shivered, and their arrows stuck in them.[66]

Although Sophronius held out the possibility that the cleansing of sin would lead to the removal of the Arab threat, never did he state that imperial power would return.

Sophronius's contemporaries externalized the struggle against sin through the rituals of martyrdom and military victory; Sophronius internalized the Arab invasions as psychological conflict between the Christian desire for mystical union with Christ, and the fear of the Saracens that hindered their union. Sophronius twice contrasted the fear Jerusalemites felt in the face of the Arabs with the steadfast courage of the Magi, who had not let fear hinder their contemplation of Christ's divinity.[67] The Magi had ignored "Herod's infanticide sword," and "neither considering fear a hindrance, or allowing the insanity of Herod to influence them," had not wavered in the contemplation of Christ's divinity. Similarly, Sophronius urged his congregation not to regard the Arabs as a threat, for this would only hinder their own union with Christ:

> But we, on account of innumerable sins and grievous failings, because we are unworthy of the contemplation of the divinity, have been prevented from being there [in Bethlehem] on pilgrimage, and unwilling, not desiring to, we are constrained to remain at home, not bound round with bodily chains, but rather because we are chained by the Saracen fear, and hindered from such heavenly joy, and covered over, finally, by a grief worthy of our most wretched unworthiness of the good things.[68]

The Arabs were less a punishment than an untimely annoyance; the distraction of the faithful from the contemplation of their saviour and his rites of union was the true threat. Christians should be joyful; regardless of the Saracens, they had been saved by Christ and could stand in his presence during the liturgy. If Christians repented and bent their will to honoring God in the liturgy, the Arabs would disappear. Sophronius does not offer an imperial victory to remove the Arabs, but a psychological one between fear of "the beastly, barbaric, Saracen sword, filled truly with every diabolic cruelty, which, radiating fear and flashing murder, sets us apart in exile from [Bethlehem]," and the faith that "if indeed we had desired, today would be joyful, it would even have happened yesterday, if truly we might turn ourselves around, and seek the begotten God with good works; for it will have its flame quenched, if truly we might quench the flames of our sins with repentance and honor the God who was born for us and like us."[69] To recognize that salvation has arrived and to celebrate that victory in the liturgy removes the Arab threat. Sophronius thus transforms the Arab invasions into a mystical struggle in man's own soul. "Even yesterday" the Christians could have found joy had they won this psychological conflict and thereby achieved true participation in Christ's own victory.

The internalization of Christian victory required that the Jerusalemites accept a victory that had no visible signs. Just as the prophets had not seen Christ, yet believed, so too the Christians, prevented from making the pilgrimage to Bethlehem, should still believe in their God, even when heathen victories made it appear he was not present. Citing Matthew 13:17,

"Many prophets and righteous men longed to see what you see and did not," Sophronius assured his audience that they were superior to the prophets; through the incarnation and Eucharist, they had truly seen Christ. Citing 1 Peter 1:8–12, "Though you have not seen him, you love him," Sophronius continued that the Christians, "the partners in the [angels'] blessedness, and the members of the orthodox faith," were even superior to the angels themselves who desired to look upon Christ.[70]

Defeat of the Arabs mattered less than individual Christian salvation; undisturbed Christian contemplation of the divine was far more important than invaders that ranged beyond the walls. The church became the repository of security as the certainty of the Eucharist replaced the uncertainty of imperial power. Sophronius compared the Christians' exile from their holy place to Adam's exile from Paradise, David's exile from the well of Bethlehem, and Moses' prohibition to enter the holy land. Sophronius did not offer the hope of imperial recovery, he offered the solace of the church's sacraments and the ritual participation in Christ's victory: "But what might we, who suffer similar things, do? For we delight in his gifts, are gladdened, rejoice celestially, and possess eternal happiness."[71]

As distinctive as was Sophronius's apologetic response to the Arabs' victories, he, no less than Antiochus Monachus or Theodore Syncellus, required a rhetorical foil to set his apologetic in relief. Like them he turned to the Jews. The separation of the new Israel from the new Rome compelled Sophronius to recast its social and political identity. But the Jews remained the opponent against whom Sophronius's victory by participation was given concrete expression. Man's participation in Christ's victory over death was only half the answer to the question of the Arabs; Sophronius also had to establish Christian claims to participate in the victory of Christ.

Like his contemporaries, Sophronius proclaimed the Christians a race unto themselves, formed by Christ as a new race from all the gentile nations. God had planned from the beginning the conversion of the "faithless gentiles";[72] Christ had come to save them;[73] Christ had been born for them.[74] He had merged all into the "new" Israel. Creating "the new from the old . . ., the new Israel was manifested when it looked upon the radiance of Christ."[75] This new race, chosen by God, supplanted the elder, evil race of the Jews. Christ had given Christians a "gift of victory" over their enemies so that "those who believe in him have clearly overthrown the ancient people of the Jews, and have obtained their former primogeniture."[76]

In Antiochus Monachus, the Jews had given the Christians the opportunity to imitate Christ's victory; in Sophronius, the Jews proved the

Christian claims to participation in Christ's victory. However convincing Sophronius's spiritual victory might have been, it certainly helped to have an enemy that Christians had visibly defeated in order to answer the questions raised by Arab victory: "But we, who have accepted the saviour Christ and shine with faith in Him because we hate and trample on the faithlessness of the Jews, as loathsome and utterly profane in all their lawlessness, we, who honorably desire to run to holy Bethlehem, are unable."[77] The Arabs were undeniably an annoyance for the Christians, but their presence was ultimately irrelevant. The Jews, on the other hand, were the enemy that the Christian had defeated and had to continue to defeat. For it was essential that, whatever the Arabs did, the Christians not fall into the same trap that had led the Jews to destruction. The Jews illustrated how low the Christians could fall if they ever lost their faith in God's power:

> For this reason, let us greet God; let us accuse our thanklessness or fearful contempt for him before him, not shrinking from doing this; and let us hear him saying that which the Jews, truly darkened and unenlightened, heard before, "The light came into the world and man loved the darkness more than the light, for his works were evil." [John 3:19][78]

The Jews' faithlessness had not only lost them their kingdom, but also destroyed them spiritually.[79] As the prophet David had foreseen, "the filthy and lawless Jews would utterly reject the message of Christ to their own destruction and devastation."[80] The Jews' faithlessness served as an object lesson not to lose faith; the Christians stood on the brink, and the Jews were the warning sign that they must not despair. When Sophronius warned Christians against losing faith, he held up the Jews to remind his audience of Christian spiritual victory and the penalty of forgetting it.

Sophronius never moved far from participation in the liturgy as the ritual of Christian victory, and the Jews played an important part in driving this message home. The Jews were shattered because their faithlessness had destroyed their ritual access to God. Sophronius characteristically interpreted Luke 2:34, "This child will be the cause of the fall and rise of many in Israel, and a sign that will be spoken against," to confirm his ecclesiological and liturgical apologetic at the expense of the Jews. The birth of Christ signaled the Jews' utter disenfranchisement. They were "those who do not join his mysteries, who, because they are sharers in unbelief, will suffer a fall.[81] He even used the same term, *metoxoi,* sharers or participants, for the communities both of the unfaithful and of the Christians.

Sophronius not only raised the Christian above the Jew, he used the Jew as a springboard to exalt the Christians even over the Arabs. The Christians were a race "combined from many races into a new Israel and named a new people of God," whose creation had meant the triumph over the "legalistic and fleshly" Jews as well as over "every most impious trace of paganism."[82] In the presence of Christ, participating in Christ's "shining celebration," the Christian triumphed not only over the faithless Jew, but by extension, the pagan, the Arab, as well.

Thus, through the Jews, Sophronius fit his sacramental theology into his apologetic. However much he differed from his contemporaries George of Pisidia or Antiochus Monachus, he shared the Jews as a rhetorical device for advancing his apology for Christianity.

Sophronius's sacramental theology was inextricably linked to his social and political context. But typically, to the extent that scholarship has credited Sophronius with political thought and motivation, it has devoted itself exclusively to his role in the Monothelete controversy. But the Monothelete controversy was a long way from Jerusalem, and the Arabs were a far more pressing problem, and one which, even if Sophronius rarely addressed it directly, most powerfully influenced him. For the first time since Constantine, Sophronius explored the political and social implications of a church without an empire. Theology was as old as Christianity; Sophronius put it to use to reformulate political and institutional definitions. His choices were not accidental. Sophronius the patriarch rejected the Christological analogies of imperial restoration and Christian Roman martyrdom that Sophronius the sophist had employed.

Like his contemporaries, Sophronius defined the field of combat in order to snatch victory from defeat. Arab victory left only one Christian institution standing, the church, and by transforming Roman defeat into Christian internal victory over sin, he not only produced a solid sacramental theology, but also defined Christian victory so that the sole Christian institution that preserved Christian identity was legitimated. When he proclaimed that the true "barbarian tyranny" was not that of the Arabs, but that of sin, and that the victory of Christ on the cross was no metaphor for imperial recovery, the liturgy became the means by which Christian victory was attained: not imitation of Christ, but participation in Christ. The Arabs did not cease to be a divine punishment, but ultimately they were irrelevant. Whatever disasters overtook the empire, the victory of Christ, solemnized in the liturgy, remained.

Notes

1. For Sophronius's literary activity, see Christoph von Schoenborn, *Sophrone de Jérusalem, Vie monastique et confession dogmatique*, [*Théologie historique* 20] (Paris, 1972), 99–114; for his background and patriarchate, see S. Vailhé, "Sophrone le Sophiste et Sophrone le Patriarche," *ROC* 7 (1902): 360–85, 8 (1903): 32–69, 356–87; von Schoenborn, *Sophrone de Jérusalem*, 53–97; H. Chadwick, "John Moschus and his Friend Sophronius," *Journal of Theological Studies* 25 (1975): 41–74. Von Schoenborn in particular draws attention to his increasing pessimism, cf. 89–91.

2. J. L. van Dieten, *Geschichte der Patriarchen von Sergios I. bis Joannes VI. (610–715)* (Amsterdam, 1972), 32–47, for the part played by Sophronius in the Monoenergist controversy. One should not, however, press Sophronius's overt opposition to imperial policy. The Monothelite *Life of Maximus* casts a very different light on Sophronius's attitude; see S. Brock, "An Early Syriac Life of Maximus the Confessor," *AB* 91 (1973): 299–346. Despite the Monothelite biographer's dislike of Maximus, it is clear that he regards Sophronius as orthodox.

3. *Oration on the Holy Baptism*, ed. A. Papadopoulos-Kerameus, *Analecta Ierosolumitikēs Staxuologias*, vol. 5 (Petersburg, 1898), 166.

4. See Chapter 3 on George of Pisidia.

5. See T. Olajos, *Les sources de Théophylacte Simocatta historien* (Leiden, 1988), 67–82.

6. See *Life of George of Chobiza*, ed. C. Houze, *AB* 7 (1888): 133–35. It is possible that Sophronius's anacreontic poem "On the Martyrs of Egypt" was also written to commemorate the Persian persecutions; see Sophronius, *Anacreontica*, ed. M. Gigante, *Sophronii anacreontica*, [*Opuscula. Testi per esercitazioni academiche*, 10–12] (Rome, 1957) 108.

7. Compare the murderous Persians in Severus of Aschmounein, *History of the Patriarchs of the Coptic Church of Alexandra*, ed. and trans. E. Evetts, *PO* 5: 484–86, with the Arabs who leave the Copts in peace, but destroy the tyrannical Romans, ibid.: 493–94; *Life of Pisentios*, ed. and trans. De Lacy O'Leary, *The Arabic Life of S. Pisentios according to the Text of the Two Manuscripts Paris bibl. not. arabe 4785 and arabe 4794*, [*PO22*], 150, who has to flee the Persian invaders; see also the discussion of the Coptic sources in F. Winkelmann, "Aegypten und Byzanz vor der arabischen Eroberung," *Byzsl* 40 (1979): 161–63.

8. See, for example, *Chronicle of 1234*, trans. J.-B. Chabot, *Chronicon ad annum 1234 pertinens, Corpus scriptorum Christianorum orientalium*, Scriptores Syri, ser. 4, vol. 14 (Paris, 1920), 236–37; Michael the Syrian, *Chronique*, trans. J.-B. Chabot, 4 vols. (Paris, 1899–1910), 2:412–13. Naturally, the Jacobites were not overjoyed at Arab rule, and never ceased desiring an orthodox — that is, Jacobite — empire to return; see S. Brock, "Syriac Views of Emergent Islam," *Studies on the First Century of Islamic Society*, ed. G. H. A. Juynboll (Carbondale, Ill., 1982), 9–21, 199–203; J. Morehead, "The Monophysite Response to the Arab Invasions," *Byz* 51 (1981): 579–91; W. Kaegi, "Initial Byzantine Reactions to the Arab Conquests," *Church History* 38 (1969): 139–49.

9. *Anacreontica*, 104.47–50.

10. Ibid., 107.91–92.

11. Ibid., 114.17–19.

12. Ibid., 114.1–2.

13. Ibid., 117.69–80.

14. Ibid., 105.

15. Ibid., 117.

16. *PG* 87, pt. 3, col. 3197c–d.

17. Unfortunately, we cannot date his sermons as patriarch with any degree of historical accuracy, except to note that the *Christmas Oration* was written in 634, before the fall of Jerusalem; see von Schoenborn, *Sophrone de Jérusalem*, 102–4.

18. *Annunciation Oration, PG* 87, 3284b.

19. *Feast of Purification Oration*, 15, col. 2:27–30.

20. *Christmas Oration*, ed. H. Usener, *Weihnachts predigt von Sophronius, Rheinisches Museum* n.f. 41, 9 (1886), 503.31–504.6.

21. Ibid., 510.9.

22. Ibid., 516.15–16.

23. *Annunciation Or.*, 3284b–85a.

24. *Christmas Or.*, 509.28–510.1.

25. Ibid., 504.10–24.

26. Ibid., 516.14–15; the term used is *metoxoi*.

27. *PG* 87, pt. 3:3232b.

28. *Exaltation of the Cross Oration, PG* 87, col. 3308d.

29. *Feast Or.*, 9, col. 1:24–6.

30. Ibid., 9, col. 1:26–7.

31. Ibid., 11, col. 2:27–33.

32. Ibid.: 10, col. 2:34–35.

33. See ibid., 10, col. 2:25–26.

34. *Exaltation of the Cross Or.*, 3309a; see also *Feast Or.*, 10, col. 2:25–26, "Let us all, who blessedly revere his mystery, take our stand to greet him."

35. See also, in addition to below, *John the Baptist Oration, PG* 87, col. 3348a; *Feast Or.*, 15, col. 2:8.

36. *Christmas Or.*, 502.30–503.3.

37. Ibid., 510.16–21.

38. *Annunciation Or.*, 3272d.

39. *Feast Or.*, 14, col. 2:29–30.

40. *Praise of the Saints Cyril and John, PG* 87, col. 3407b–c. Von Schoenborn's analysis of Sophronius's interest in martyrdom and the "imitation of Christ" (237–38), is, significantly, almost exclusively drawn from Sophronius's early works, with the exception of a passage from the *Theophany Oration*, 161.7, whose context is Christ's "dwelling" within the saints, the vocabulary of assimilation, rather than imitation, that one would expect from the patriarchal period.

41. There is, of course, Sophronius's speech to the sixty martyrs of Gaza, yet even if one considers this speech to be literally authentic, Sophronius is still remarkably reticent in his exhortation to martyrdom, see "Sixty Martyrs of Gaza": 301–2.

42. See *Feast Or.*, 9, col. 1:28–col. 2:5.

43. *Feast Or.*, 9, col. 1:30–col. 2:1.

44. *Christmas Or.,* 508.3–10; see also *Feast Or.,* 9, col. 2:21–3.

45. See *Feast Or.,* 9, col. 1:6; *Annunciation Or.,* 3228b. In sharp contrast to contemporaries, the verb *politeuein,* which in George of Pisidia and Theodore Syncellus always carries political connotations, carries none in Sophronius.

46. *Christmas Or.,* 508.22–31.

47. Von Schoenborn, *Sophrone de Jérusalem,* 78–83; van Dieten, *Geschichte der Patriarchen,* 32–34; *Letter to Arcadius,* ed. M. Albert and C. von Schoenborn, *PO* 39: 170–73, is an excellent example of the "economy" practiced by Sophronius in the Monothelite controversy.

48. Sophronius likely thought Monotheletism a form of Monophysitism. He thus held a sour view of the "economy" of doctrinal compromise; see *Letter to Arcadius,* 189, 233. It is worth noting that his attitude did not cause him to attack the compromise.

49. Ibid., 174–76.

50. Cf. *Annunciation Or.,* 3221a, 3223a.

51. Cf. *Feast Or.,* 10.col. 1–2.

52. Cf. ibid., 13, col. 1–2; see also *Christmas Or.,* 509.7–28.

53. *Feast Or.,* 13, col. 2:30–14, col. 1:1.

54. Cf. *Letter to Arcadius,* 207, 215, 223.

55. *Exaltation of the Cross Or.,* 3304c.

56. *Annunciation Or.,* 3225b; see also *Letter to Arcadius,* 223.

57. Apostles *Peter and Paul Oration, PG* 87, col. 3356c–3357a; von Schoenborn, 226–27, says of this passage, "Le intérêt ecclésiologique de ce texte est manifeste."

58. *Peter and Paul Or.,* 3357d; for Christ cf. *Christmas Or.,* 509.197–28; see also von Schoenborn, 225–28.

59. See D. Olster, "Justinian, Imperial Rhetoric and the Church," *Byzsl* 50 (1989): 165–76.

60. *Christmas Or.,* 501.5.

61. *Letter to Arcadius,* 223.

62. See von Schoenborn, 103.

63. *Christmas Or.,* 503.30–31; 504.26–27; 504.30–31; 505.19–20; 505.24–25; 506.18–19; 507.5–6; etc. For a discussion of Sophronius's style, see von Schoenborn, 102.

64. *Christmas Or.,* 501.9–502.1.

65. Ibid. 514.24–28.

66. Ibid. 514.29–515.9.

67. Ibid., 505.25–31; 506.20–21.

68. Ibid., 506.27–507.3.

69. Ibid., 507.22–508.2.

70. Ibid., 512.9–29.

71. Ibid., 510.29–511.11.

72. *Feast Or.,* 8, col. 1:20–23.

73. Ibid., 11, col. 2:19–22.

74. *John the Baptist Oration, PG* 87, col. 3345d.

75. *Feast Or.,* 13, col. 1:10–21.

76. *Annunciation Or.,* 3256b.

77. *Christmas Or.,* 514.10–14.

78. *Feast Or.,* 11, col. 1:30–35.

79. Cf. *Annunciation Or.,* 3228b. One should note that Sophronius described the activity of the Jews' faithlessness as *politeuein,* which has, elsewhere, purely political connotations.

80. *Christmas Or.,* 514.1–9; see also *Feast Or.,* 15, col. 1:22–6.

81. *Feast Or.,* 16, col. 1:33–2:3.

82. Ibid., 14, col. 1:8–1.

6. "We Are Still Better Than You": The Syrian Dialogues

The first decades of the seventh century witnessed increasing exploitation of the traditional Christian rhetorical image of the Jew. Intensifying Christian interest in the Jews was not the result of theological debate, but of a rapidly changing social and political environment. While heathen enemies dismembered the empire, Christian apologists, whose triumphal tradition the presence of the Heraclian dynasty and the magnitude of Roman defeat had made obsolete, turned to alternative rhetorics to sustain Christian morale. Thus, seventh-century Byzantine literature, so strikingly varied in its generic variety, is even more remarkably consistent in its apologetic agenda. From the stylized and often artificial court panegyrics of George of Pisidia, to the lyrical homilies of Sophronius, Christian literature assimilated themes of restoration, whether imperial or ecclesiastical; collective sin; and Christian victory, whether martyrial or liturgical. These themes required a rhetorical anchor: the image of the Jew.

Christians substituted the Jew, the enemy of the Christian, for the Persian or Arab, the enemy of the Roman. The Jews' defeat in the arena of martyrdom, the contrast of the Jews' lost kingdom with the certainty of Christian restoration, and the demonstration of the Jews' blindness and condemnation and the Christians' salvation were apologetic strategies to minimize defeat and restore morale. Whether as social opponent or rhetorical foil, the Jew was used by Christian apologists to transform Roman defeat into Christian victory. With this transformation, imperial history was itself transformed into a cycle of sin, punishment, repentance, and restoration. The Jew became a thematic and rhetorical linchpin of this reformulation of Roman Christian self-definition, whose repercussions extended beyond the literary sphere to the Jews' forced baptism: a social and political expression of the Jews' role as the Christians' foil, inspired by the Persian War.

Not surprisingly, increased production of anti-Jewish works, dialogues in particular, accompanied the widespread expression of anti-Jewish themes in such unrelated literary genres as apocalypses, panegyric, and homilies. If the image of the Jew played so necessary a role in the new apologetic, it was only natural that those genres most directly tied to exploiting this image became popular, but not because they reflected every-day social commerce between Christians and Jews. The dialogues in fact hint at the character of the social dialogues between these groups in the highly charged atmosphere of the seventh century. At one point in *Trophies of Damascus,* Jews and Christians nearly come to blows.[1] The *Doctrine of Jacob the Newly Baptised* limits the ecumenical dialogue to "convert or die."[2]

The dialogues are fictive, their theology derivative. Without this inter-pretive guide, they lose their true significance and recede into the margins of the Christian theology of Judaism. They are dialogues in name only; the Jews hardly defend themselves. Rather, they constantly bemoan their intel-lectual inferiority. The Jew Herbanus complains, "Our fathers did wrong to translate the books of Israel into the Greek tongue so that after you studied them, you might refute us all,"[3] and later praises his Christian opponent, "I am dazzled by the way you make your point, and my mind is divided among your arguments."[4] Even if the Jews do not concede Christian intel-lectual superiority, the Christian protagonist is ready to remind them. As the anonymous monk of *Trophies* explained, it required neither skill nor learning to refute Jews: "Besides, you know that God is a witness that I am not an especially learned Christian; truly, you should not think so. For if some of those whom I know were present, they would crush all your wisdom with one word."[5] Thus the dialogues reassured their audience that any Christian could refute a Jew; no matter how tricky or cunning, the Jews could not stand against Christian truth.

Such techniques established not only Christian intellectual superiority, but moral superiority as well, a fitting context for the apologetic agenda these dialogues pursued. *The Trophies Earned by the Divine and Invincible Church of God and the Truth against the Jews at Damascus* and *The Dispute of the Jews Papiscus and Philo with Some Monk,* illustrate one stream of the seventh-century evolution of the anti-Jewish genre.[6] More than any other dialogues, they sought to defend the integrity of the empire and sustain the hopes of its return.

As anti-Jewish dialogues, they follow a long tradition of asserting the truth of Christianity against the blindness and obstinancy of the Jews. But the seventh-century texts have a far broader range of themes than these, including many that had never appeared in earlier anti-Jewish texts. The generic themes and rhetoric associated with the anti-Jewish dialogues made them perfect literary vehicles for seventh-century authors. The Jews' defeat was a generic *topos,* and the genre's structure permitted the fullest expression of the Christian apologetic that had grown up around the Jews. These texts offer, if not for the first time, at least in the most direct and in detailed fashion, a response to the problem of why, if God so loves the Christians, he allows heathen enemies to defeat them. The anti-Jewish dialogues set this Christian self-doubt in the mouth of the Jewish interlocutors and answered it as part of the inevitable refutation of the Jews' attacks on Christianity. *Trophies* and *Papiscus* constantly revert to this theme, and well they should have, for this was the question that Christians were asking each other.

Before proceeding to the analysis of these dialogues, however, it would be worthwhile to consider their provenance, which has not been established.[7] *Papiscus* and *Trophies* have a number of striking parallels that strongly suggest that they share a common source tradition. They share similar narrative details: in both, the Jews bring books to the debate in order to check references.[8] Common lists of lands and peoples form some of the most distinctive parallels between the dialogues. Both included Britain in their list of far-flung Christian outposts,[9] and mentioned the silent and deserted *manteiai Mempheōs* in their roughly parallel list of deserted pagan *loci sancti.*[10]

An even more significant comparison than the lists is that of the errors both dialogues share in their scriptural citations. Both cite Baruch 3:36–38 as Jeremiah,[11] a not uncommon mistake in early Christian literature, but both also misquote John 11:48, a more unusual scriptural misquotation.[12] The actual passage is a speech by a priest troubled by Christ's miracles, who worries that if Christ continues, "then the Romans will come and take away both our place and our nation." *Papiscus* and *Trophies,* however, cited John 11:48 as a prophecy of Christ: the former wrote, "The Romans will come and take away your kingdom from *you,*" while the latter quoted, "The Romans will come and take away *your* race and *your* city." In both cases, the authors changed John 11:48 to a prophecy of Christ of Jewish destruction. It seems likely, then, that both dialogues shared a source that misquoted John 11:48 in this context, but that each adapted this source in its own way, and according to its own stylistic idiosyncrasies.

The differences make it unlikely that one relied directly on the other, but the similarities make it likely that they shared a third source. This possibility is strengthened by a comparison with *Questions to Antiochus the Duke,* a compendium of varying topics, falsely attributed to the fourth-century Alexandrian Patriarch Athanasius. Although *Questions* is not an overtly anti-Jewish work, it used an anti-Jewish work. The answer to question 137 is directly lifted from a source, likely a dialogue, that began with an address to a Jewish opponent: "That our Christ is true, and not false as you think, oh Jews, we will establish for you not through words, but through deeds."[13] *Questions* certainly relied on some anti-Jewish text, perhaps the same one used by *Trophies,* but certainly the one used by *Papiscus.* Both end with the exact same doxology, and word-for-word boast of their "refutation of Jewish evil-heartedness and insanity."[14] That *Questions, Papiscus,* and *Trophies* are all related is also suggested by their misquotation of John 11:48. *Questions* is the most complete of the three texts, and reads, "[Christ] said, 'The Romans will come and take away your race, city and kingdom.'"[15] Naturally, *Questions'* citation of John was no less an adaptation than the anti-Jewish dialogues, but its format argues that it literally copied some earlier, more schematic, anti-Jewish dialogue, into a composite text with other non-Jewish issues, and that at least *Papiscus,* and possibly also *Trophies,* shared this source.

Whatever the exact relationship of these three texts, they clearly form a sort of Syrian literary circle. Thematically, they are a provincial echo of Constantinopolitan apologetic themes; literarily, they illustrate the assimilation of imperial themes into works whose explicit generic goal had nothing to do with the empire at all. The Syrian case is all the more interesting because other provincial anti-Jewish works did not possess this thematic loyalty.

The Jew in *Trophies* and *Papiscus* personified Judaism, and in his person manifested all the moral failures of a false religion. The Jew's social and political existence was merely the shadow cast by the light of Christianity, but hating the light that defined his existence.[16] The Jew was a social pariah, whose misanthropy was especially directed against the Christian: "The Jews willingly make themselves aliens who right from the womb confirm their error in the circumcision on the eighth day. They speak lies; their actions are marked by an unquenchable hatred against us; they do however much they can against us, just like a snake!"[17] Their religion marked them physically; their hatred separated them from Christian society. Whatever the religions' true social relations, Jewish hatred of Christians was fixed in the popular imagination: the Jew was nothing more than the adversary of the Christians and of their God.[18]

Just as his religion dictated the Jew's social definition, so also, it defined his political status. The Jew was not simply a social alien among Christians, but a political alien, an exile who was dispersed throughout the world without a homeland of his own.[19] "From everywhere God has exiled you, but we dwell there," *Trophies* proudly exulted.[20] This attack on the Jews might seem paradoxical to a modern reader. After all, the Christians claimed universality from their own dispersal across the *oikoumenē*. But there was no paradox for the Roman Christian who easily distinguished Jewish exile from Christian universality by political control of the *loci sancti* of both religions. Both dialogues emphasized that the destruction of the kingdom of the Jews was synonymous with the delegitimization of their religion:

> For what place that God gave you do you hold today? But rather, he wrested all these places from you, and gave them to us. [Sinai, the Jordan, and Jerusalem are ours.] Look to the west, look to the east, seek anywhere under heaven, even the islands of Britain, which are the western end of the world, and you will find the rites of the Jews and the pagans silenced, but the rites of Christ are proclaimed in every place.[21]

Papiscus asserted that without their temple and their rites at Jerusalem, the Jews' religion had lost all legitimacy.[22]

The role that the Jews' loss of their kingdom played in the legitimization of Christianity led both dialogues to offer extensive exegeses of *Genesis* 49:10, "A ruler shall not fail from Judah until the expected one of the gentiles comes." The political implications of this passage are clear; Christ must be the expected one of the gentiles, since the Jews' polity ceased just as Christ came into the world.[23] This citation in anti-Jewish works had a long history back to Justin Martyr, but few works gave such emphasis to the contrast between the Jewish kingdom's end and the Christian Empire's success as *Trophies*.[24]

The Christian claimed prophetic promises of sovereignty because he was an Israelite and the Jews gentiles: "The Christian said, 'Up to this moment I consider myself an Israelite and you a gentile.' The Jew said, '. . . If you are an Israelite, show me your circumcision.' The Christian said, 'If, then, as you say, God loves you, why has he abandoned you to such desolation and dispersion?' "[25] Military defeat and political subordination were the lot of this discredited cult and the unshakable proof of its illegitimacy. To be an Israelite, that is, one who possessed a true covenant with God, one had to receive God's rewards, and such rewards were not spiritual. Both disputants claimed the title of "Israelite"; but only military victory was the proof of God's love.

Jerusalem's loss revealed that Judaism was little more than another discredited pagan religion. Jewish Jerusalem took its place with Memphis,

Delphi, and Heliopolis as deserted sites of dead, idolatrous religions.[26] Pagans and Jews had lost their *loci sancti* to the victorious Christians, and with their cult centers, their religious legitimacy. Thus were the Jews further lowered, from God's people rejected, to merely another dead pagan cult. And Judaism was a dead religion precisely because it lacked the political power to control its religious center or perform its rites there.

Judaism was inferior even to the pagan cults, the Jews mere imitators of the pagans.[27] "When Israel came from Egypt, Israel loved the Egyptians' manners and polytheism."[28] God threw the Mosaic Law as a veil over the eyes of the idolatrous Jews, to whom he revealed no true knowledge. *Trophies* even asserted the Jews' understanding of God was inferior to pagans': "Some of the pagans, especially their philosophers, also knew God, and said much about God. And if you will listen, I will demonstrate to you how some pagans grasped God better than you nit-picking students of the law."[29] *Trophies* never explained how the philosophers were superior to the Jews. But neither dialogue had hesitations about the divine curse that set the Jews below the gentiles, and sealed divine favor for the gentiles.

The Jews' idolatry had resulted in the destruction of the first temple.[30] The destruction of the second temple was a punishment as well, but not for idolatry. "The loss of the first temple was because of the Jews' idolatry, but on what account did the second temple fall, since admittedly, the Jews did not then commit idolatry?"[31] *Papiscus* took its time answering this question, detailing the extent of the Jews' unforgivable sin and irredeemable punishment. The sin was the crucifixion of Christ and the persecution of the Christians; the punishment was exile and the eternal loss of their kingdom.[32]

This sin fit the image of the Jew as persecutor, so integral to seventh-century literature, and led *Trophies* and *Papiscus* to the climax of their polemic against the Jews and the starting point of their imperial apologetic. The crucifixion of Christ and the persecution of the apostles ensured the rejection of the Jews and sealed the covenant between Christ and the gentiles: "When you began to war against the apostles and turn yourselves away from them, and you crucified the one who rose from the dead, then he enjoined his holy apostles, saying, 'Go forth to the world and teach all the nations.'"[33] By Christ's command the gentiles were the object of salvation. The Jews rejected Christ, and in return he rejected them.

The Syrian dialogues did not so much exalt Christianity over Judaism as the gentiles over the Jews. The Christian claimed to be an Israelite, but only figuratively because he possessed a covenant with God.[34] But any covenant between a God and his people was ultimately founded on racial grounds. Thus, the Jews repeatedly insisted that the Christian answer whether he was of the seed of Jacob or Esau (a basic category of racial identity) and liable to the curse laid by God on Esau.[35] This attack on the gentiles' racial descent was one of the Jews' strongest arguments; in *Trophies*, they raise it twice. At first, the Christian refused to answer. "I will avoid the mindless entanglement of this question because I wish to edify the people."[36] The second time, the Christian cited Isaiah 65:15, that the people of God will receive a new name, and asked which was the newest race: "Is it the Jews? This race existed before him. The Samaritans? They too are ancient. The Romans? They are not new. First, therefore, tell me what new name has been given to those who serve God, and I will tell you who I am."[37] When the Jew replied that he did not know God's plans, the Christian responded, "Seek among all the names of the races upon the earth, and you will not find another new name besides that of Christian."[38] Christians are the new, composite, universal race: "Behold, the prophet [Psalm 102:22–23] mentions [that the new race will be assembled from] many races and many kings, not one sole race and king. Therefore, I am a Christian, possessing the name given me by God."[39] Christianity was more than a religion. It was a bond between a race, paradoxically composed of all races, and its God. The Jew's proud boast that his racial purity, his descent from Jacob, guaranteed that the promises of God to Jacob were his alone, was answered in the same vein by the Christian whose race was not descended from a human ancestor, but adopted by God to supersede all earlier races: Jews, Samaritans, Askalonites, Turks, and Romans—the pagan Romans, that is.[40] Christian racialism was the foundation of Christianity's universalism and the means by which the dialogues transferred the universal covenant of God and the Christian race to its empire. The covenant of Christ and his new people guaranteed them ultimate victory. The Christian Roman Empire could not stay defeated because it possessed the eternal bond between the gentiles and Christ.

The Syrian dialogues integrate the bond between Christ and his adopted race into an apologetic of defeat through claims of victory over the Jews. Jews are the first persecutors, but by extension, all infidels hate the Christians.[41] "Therefore, Jews, say right now, why do you hate us? Is it not for the sake of the name of Christ? And all those warring against us, do they hate us for any other reason?"[42] Yet persecution showed Christ's power and Christianity's truth because Christianity not only survived but flourished:

Did you crucify him or not? Speak! . . . He said to his apostles, "They will chase you from their synagogues," [John 16:2] and they will kill you. [cf. Math. 24:9] Say whether you have not stoned Stephen and James the Just? He said, "You will be brought before kings and princes for my sake." [Math. 10:18] Did he lie? Far from it! . . . He ordered us to make a bloodless sacrifice. Has his command been done? Perhaps all the kings of the earth could suppress it? Absolutely not![43]

The author transferred Christian victory against the persecuting Jews, enemies of both God and his people, and for that reason eventually destroyed, to all enemies of the Christians: when *Trophies* and *Papiscus* were written, this meant the Arabs.

The Arabs naturally blend into the dialogues. Present but not obtrusive, they compose part of the audience watching the debate.[44] The Christian even calls on the *barbaroi* in the crowd to witness the truth of his argument against the Jews.[45] But the Arabs are not a mere background detail or topical prop; their victory inspired the Christian authors. In a sense, the Jews are the prop to create a context in which the Arabs, victorious in the arena of battle, could be confronted and defeated.

The dialogues conflate Jew and Arab in ways that range from the mundane to the absurd. Some topics, such as circumcision, were obvious references to the Arabs. The Christian answer to the Jews' citation of Genesis 17:14, that those not circumcised will be destroyed,[46] was clearly addressed not only to the Jews but also to the Arabs, who were also circumcised. Significantly, *Trophies* began its discussion of circumcision by reassuring its readers that it was essential to retain faith in God's promises, despite setbacks.[47]

Arabs had been known to be circumcised since Herodotus, and Christians drew the obvious parallel between Jewish and Arab circumcision throughout their literature on the Arab invasions. Coptic writers even ascribed Heraclius's forced baptism of the Jews to his mistaken interpretation of a dream that predicted a circumcised race would supplant the Romans.[48] *Questions* illustrates how closely seventh-century Christians associated circumcision and the Arabs. The answer to question 38, "Why, when Christ was circumcised, are we not similarly circumcised?" clearly integrated anti-Arab apologetic into anti-Jewish polemic: "Thus, we thereby know clearly that all the circumcised are races that are alien to Christ, whether faithful or unfaithful, Jews or pagans, since they puff themselves up with the Mosaic law, and do not follow Christ."[49] *Questions*' attack on pagans for circumcision was unusual, but insofar as it was not primarily an anti-Jewish work, it could more easily integrate polemic against the Arabs into an anti-Jewish context. *Trophies,* from the same cultural and social milieu as *Questions,* although bound by the more rigid boundaries of the anti-Jewish genre, could still exploit the identification of Jews and Arabs found in *Questions* to transfer its arguments against Jewish circumcision to the Arabs. These authors' primary interest was not the theological implications of circumcision for Jews and Christians, but in the far more important implications that circumcision had for the Arabs, their victories, and the question of God's favor.

The attack on circumcision that linked Jews and Arabs had ethnographic sanction going back to Herodotus. But a charge against the Christians by the Jews can only be explained as a reference to Islam: the accusation that the Christians prayed to the east instead of the south, as the Jews supposedly did. No biblical citations accompanied this accusation, in itself quite unusual. The attack on the direction of Christian worship was rare, the accompanying Jewish assertion that the south was the correct direction to pray unprecedented. Even stranger, *Trophies* attributed the Christians' preference to their worship of the sun. "And also, why do you [Christians] pray to the east if not because you worship the sun?"[50] This attack's artificiality, the absence of a biblical authority, and its almost unprecedented intrusion into the anti-Jewish genre, hints that this section of *Trophies* was likely a seventh-century invention. The reason for its presence had nothing to do with the Jews: it was the Arabs of Syria who prayed to the south.[51]

This odd objection to Christianity is also found in question 37 of *Questions.* But the answer is far more complete and reveals the source of this unusual addition to *Trophies. Questions* lists not one but three responses to this question. "For it is necessary to respond in one way to the Jew, and to explain in another way to the pagan, and again, one must provide wisdom another way to the Christian."[52]

To Jews, one should cite Psalm 131:7 and Zachariah 14:4, which command prayer toward the holy place of God, which, in Zachariah, is said to be the Mount of Olives "to the east of Jerusalem."[53] This is not, however, the answer found in *Trophies.* To pagans, presumably Arabs, one answered, "We do not worship toward the east because God is said to be in the east, but because God is, and is called, the true light of the world."[54] This odd answer could be misinterpreted as sun-worship, and *Questions* was careful to add in its response that Christians worship the creator of light, not the light itself.

Significantly, the Jew of *Trophies* raised the objection that the author of *Questions* had assumed a Moslem would raise, and which he sought to forestall. The Jewish speaker, in effect, has taken the part of an Arab interlocutor. Not surprisingly, the Christian in *Trophies* cited Psalm 112:3 and Zachariah 6:12, that Christ is the light who shines like the sun in the east,[55] biblical citations closely related to those in *Questions*. The author of *Trophies* clearly was acquainted with *Questions* or its sources, and edited its answer to the Arabs to fit a dialogue with Jews.

Questions' answer to the pagans at least possessed biblical authority. The response that *Questions* recommended for Christians was not only unusual, but also showed Moslem influence: "Let the faithful hear and learn that the blessed apostles commanded the Christians' churches to pray to the east in order that we might face toward paradise. Thus, we bow toward our ancient land and homeland, beseeching God that he might return us whence we were exiled."[56] Such an answer makes no sense in a Judeo-Christian context, and indeed such an answer is very unusual, if not altogether unprecedented. On the other hand, the earliest Christian descriptions of Islam, which are partially preserved in Theophanes' *Chronicle,* were almost entirely devoted to a perceived Moslem obsession with paradise, and the fleshly joys that Mohammed promised his followers.[57] The reference to paradise in *Questions* was a response to this perceived Moslem, rather than Christian or Jewish, religious claim. Thus, *Questions* offered to the Christian an answer that responded to perceived Moslem claims so that the Christian might know that he, no less than the Moslem, enjoyed the promise of paradise.

Such responses to the Christians and oblique attacks on the Arabs hint at the ultimate purpose of *Trophies* and *Papiscus.* But another unprecedented series of questions makes the texts' goal explicit. The Persian and Arab invasions had undercut the political and geographic arguments against the Jews rather badly. And the Jewish speaker in *Trophies* responded with the rather unpleasant facts of Christian defeat to the Christian's recitation of the Jews' own: "The Christian said, 'Where do you perform your rituals today? Where do you celebrate Passover when the place in which God commanded you to hold your festival is held by others?' The Jew said, 'If these things are as you say, whence comes the enslavements that have struck you? Whose lands have been laid waste?'"[58]

Trophies never claimed that Christians held Jerusalem, only that the Jews had lost it. But the loss of Jerusalem to the Arabs in fact raised more serious problems for Christians than for Jews. It struck at the foundation of

Christian imperialism. If Christ loved the Christians, contemporary theological logic demanded that his love be shown through victory.

Questions also raised the problem of Christian defeat, but in its proper context. Question forty-four asked how one can convince barbarians of Christianity's superiority. The answer was a demonstration of imperial success. *Questions* explained how the Holy Land remained Christian, belonged to Christians, and was given to them by Christ just as if it were an imperial donation: "And if an opponent [sc. Arabs] says, 'We possess these places by an imperial tyranny,' let such a one learn that even if in fact the barbarians have often taken Palestine, Christ does not permit his own places to be given to heretics. But even if this happens for a short time, swiftly the universal church has again received these places."[59] The truth of Christianity depended on no theological abstraction, but a political and military reality. *Questions'* proof of Christianity had nothing whatsoever to do with Christ, but rather with the political control of the *loci sancti*. We have already seen how Christians used the loss of holy places to discredit paganism and Judaism. *Questions'* contrast of an Arab "imperial tyranny" over Palestine and the church's and Empire's certain recovery of the holy places illustrates how closely Christians associated political integrity and religious legitimacy. This response also fits *Questions'* provenance. It is significant that the author should assert that Christ would not allow the holy places to be given to "heretics"; logically, he should have said "heathens." The reason that he refers to heretics is his Syrian frame of reference. There, following the Arab conquest, Melkite churches were handed over to the Monophysites, so that the author must argue not just on behalf of the empire, but on behalf of a beleaguered minority sect.[60] Hence, these Syrian Melkite authors were concerned over the effect of imperial collapse on Christian morale, but of at least equal concern was the defense of their sect against the majority Monophysites; the empire's success was a guarantee not only of the Melkite's orthodoxy, but also of his security.

The *Trophies'* response to the Jew's use of the Christian's own polemical logic is undoubtedly the weakest link in *Trophies'* apologetic. The three arguments with which *Trophies* rebutted the Jews were clearly improvised, and two of them rested on no biblical authority whatsoever.[61]

The first response is an allegorical interpretation of the peace brought by Christ. Although in other parts of the dialogue the author relied on an imperial definition, that the *pax romana* was a *pax Christi*, he now asserted that the peace brought by Christ meant the cessation of idolatry.[62]

The second response addressed directly, for the only time in the dialogue, the underlying problem that inspired *Trophies'* composition. "Besides, the church has been at peace a long time, and our Empire has enjoyed a deep peace. For the present wars that have arisen have not even lasted fifty years!"[63] Even with this concession that the Arab invasions had occurred, *Trophies* studiously avoided mentioning that the empire had been bested, only that the long-standing Roman peace had been interrupted.

The Christians had not yet lost Jerusalem for as long as the Jews had after the destruction of the first temple; the Jews had been in their second exile almost ten times longer than the first. Herein lay the difference between the temporary chastisement by God of his beloved race, and the permanent punishment of a reprobate race.[64]

It was not very likely that all the hard-pressed Christians of the Levant were convinced that the Arabs were ephemeral by a reminder of centuries of Roman rule. The third response hints that the second response met with at least some skepticism. The world had been turned upside down, and things formerly secure seemed now far less so, even the sacred Scriptures themselves: "Often, God seems to say one thing and do another. See, tell me therefore why do the beasts not now fear us, but rather, we flee them, since in Genesis [9:2] God says of men, 'The fear of you will be upon the beasts and all that creeps on the ground?' "[65]

Not even God's promises of victory, which had been the common assumption of Christian Romans since Eusebius, could be relied on. Paradoxically, much of *Trophies* itself is built on this assumption, although the Jewish antagonist made no use of this extraordinary admission by his opponent. But the desperation of seventh-century Christian apologetics found uneasy expression in the idea that God could say one thing and do another. The Christian's statement was not a defense of allegorical interpretation, but a concession that events had overthrown triumphalist interpretation of Scripture. No amount of interpretation could bring back the claim of Christian invincibility.

The dependence of the empire upon the church in *Trophies, Questions,* and *Papiscus* reversed the dynamic that had, since Eusebius, defined their relationship: that Christianity's truth was proven by imperial victory. They defended the integrity of the empire through the victory of the church. The identification of Jewish persecution with all persecutors, especially the Arabs, permitted these authors to transform the Arab invasions into the Arab persecutions.

The seventh-century Syrian authors transferred the fulfillment of God's promises of peace from the imperial peace and military victory of the empire, into the ecclesiastical peace. The martyrial victory of the church guaranteed eventual imperial recovery. When these authors spoke of the parallel peace enjoyed by church and empire, they revised the Eusebian formulation of this parallelism. For Eusebius, the church enjoyed peace through the agency of the empire, and in turn guaranteed God's protection of the empire's unbroken peace. But in the seventh century, the burden of establishing peace and vanquishing opponents rested on the church. The author of *Trophies* repeatedly transferred the ethos of the church's victory over her enemies to the empire:

> Does not the church stand up to the ends of the earth? Yes or no? Are not the cross and Christ worshipped by every nation? Yes or no? Has tyrant, ruler, emperor or power hindered our faith since the advent of Christ? How many armies have come against us, how many have fought wars, ranged themselves in the battle line? Yet they have disappeared like smoke.[66]

By his linking of references to armies and wars with the traditional *topos* that the church defeated its enemies through the very means, persecution, with which it was attacked, the author was able to transform Arab invasions into an Arab persecution, and thus to create the promise of eventual Roman recovery. Just as *Fall of Jerusalem* transformed Roman defeat into the victory of martyrdom, so *Trophies* transformed on a larger scale Arab conquest into Arab persecution. *Trophies* assured its Christian audience that since the church had undergone such vicissitudes before and had never known defeat, the Christian Empire, linked to the church, could not remain defeated.

The transfer of the church's victory to the empire immediately followed discussion of the Christians' loss of Jerusalem, so that Roman defeat could be transformed into Christian victory: "And this is the most amazing thing: that although war is brought against the church, it remains undefeated and unstoppable, and while all rail against it, its foundation remains firm. For when the head and the Empire stand, the entire body is easily renewed, but a race that is without a head completely dies."[67] The "foundation" of the church was Christ, but the Christian race would find renewal in its "head and Empire."[68] Indeed, the author implied that the empire was already undergoing the process of renewal. Writing about fifty years after the Arab invasions, in the early 680s, the author was likely making an oblique reference to the first Arab siege of the 670s; the "head" of the empire was the imperial city of Constantinople.[69] The psychological impact of the city's defense cannot be measured, but it seems briefly to have inspired hope in the Levant, and especially among the hard-pressed Syrian Melkites, that the empire would soon return victorious.[70]

While *Papiscus* shares many of the same themes and arguments as *Trophies,* it nonetheless differs somewhat in its defense of the empire. Partly this is due to its format, for it is more a monologue than a dialogue. The Jews rarely speak, and when they do, they do little more than ask for clarification. The second reason is its date. Written during the worst of the invasions, it displays a defensiveness that compares poorly with the bravado of *Trophies.*

The author of *Papiscus* approached his defense of the empire in much the same fashion as the *Trophies.* The introduction to his defense is a long description of the sufferings of the Jews: the loss of their temple and kingdom, their diaspora, and their despised condition. Unlike *Trophies,* however, the Christian preempts the Jews' references to Christian defeats: "And do not say to me that today the Christians suffer and are enslaved, for this is our greatness, that by so many races persecuted, hated and combatted, we have our faith still standing, and it is not submerged. And neither is our Empire threatened, nor are our churches closed."[71]

Like *Trophies, Papiscus* defended the empire with the invincibility of the church. Pagan enemies might attack, persecute, and hate the Christians, yet the church, and with it the empire, stood and would continue to stand. The vast expanse of Christian lands from the Britain to the Jordan, "everywhere under the sun,"[72] was coterminous with the Christian Empire's universal sovereignty:

> If, however, the faith is evil, why has not God permitted us to be overwhelmed by so many pagans, Persians and Arabs? For do not tell me that we Christians are punished, but rather explain this to me, why has God entrusted to us, whom you say are sunk in error, the Empire of all the world? Why has no one threatened or been strong enough to rip from our hands the seal of Christ even up to today?[73]

As in *Trophies,* the invincibility of the church was the proof of the empire's invincibility. *Papiscus,* however, went one step further. Where Eusebius had argued that the empire prepared the stage for universal conversion, *Papiscus* argued that the empire was the seal of universal conversion. The apposition of *sphragis* and *basileia,* for example, indicates a new relationship of church and empire. *Sphragis* commonly refers to the sacramental seal of baptism (in contrast to the false seal of circumcision given to the Jews) and the confirmation of the covenant between the Christian and Christ. Its use indicates how vocabulary usually associated with the church was beginning to be used to buttress the imperial image with the institutional covenant of church and Christ.[74]

The author of *Papiscus* carried the identification of the empire as the "seal of Christ" even further when he defined the empire's authority as the obeisance of all to the "sign of Christ":

> Let God show that we Christians might be persecuted, but that we rule over all and are lords over all! For today the sign of Christ is among us and comes from our Empire. Then tell me if the sign were not eternal and invincible and indestructible like the faith and Empire of the Christians, why do you and all our enemies hate and blaspheme the cross, but if you see it on gold [on a coin], do you abhor it, and turn to run? . . . Why do you lust for that which you hate, and marvelously defeated, accept enthusiastically that which you abhor?[75]

At the Milvian Bridge, imperial arms proved the cross's apotropaic power; in *Papiscus,* the cross upheld imperial power. Just as the empire became the "seal" of the church's victory, so the cross, now the symbol of the church's victory, was used to buttress the empire after its defeat.

The audience required not only a promise of future success, but also the assurance of present benefit. The dialogues chose the book of Daniel to make these claims.[76] But unlike most seventh-century authors' use of Daniel, neither dialogue evinced any apocalyptic interest.[77] The dialogues used the weeks of Daniel to lend the incarnation of Christ prophetic sanction,[78] but neither made any effort to predict Christ's return, or to associate imperial recovery with the second coming.

Above all, both dialogues studiously avoided any apocalyptic interpretations of recent history. *Papiscus* interpreted Daniel 9:27, " . . . until the decreed end is poured out upon the desolators," a reference to Christ's return, as a prophecy of the destruction of the Jews' temple and religion.[79] The interpretation of Daniel was directed toward the fallen state of the Jews, and to that alone. And *Papiscus* introduced its exegesis of Daniel by asserting present Christian superiority to the Jews. "Let us block up the Jews' shameful mouths and blasphemies from the great advantage we hold, and these things are necessarily more spoils of victory for us who are saved by Christ."[80] As *Papiscus* made clear, the Christians' "great advantages" were political as well as religious.

Trophies was even more direct in its attempt to steer away from apocalyptic speculation. Its exegesis of Daniel, the author claimed, was to show "how Christ has established a true, eternal, and immutable covenant with us." As the author neatly summed up: "And our discourse is not for Jews alone, but for every sort who does not believe in Christ; since they lack faith in Christ concerning the future, it is necessary to show that the things to

come are fulfilled each day by Christ.'[81] The dialogues avoided the apocalyptic future because it interested neither their authors nor their readers.
The present did. The conclusion of *Trophies* was a last appeal to its demoralized audience that "the things to come are fulfilled each day by Christ,"
and that their enemies, not only Jews, but "every sort that does not believe
in Christ," would concede this.

It is no coincidence that the eighth-century decline of orthodox Christianity in the Levant coincided with the Melkite's final despair of imperial
restoration. *Papiscus* represented an earlier stage in the evolution of seventh-
century imperial apologetic than *Trophies,* but both used the Jews in very
similar ways to demonstrate the integrity not of Christianity alone but of
the empire that, for the Melkites, was indissolubly welded to their religion.
Scholars have not regarded historical context in the closed circle of Jewish–
Christian theological debate, and so have ignored the reason for these
dialogues' composition, and their significance for a Christian audience. On
the contrary, these dialogues show how closely historical context and theology were joined, and how, in a time of crisis, Jewish–Christian theological
debate could be turned to apologetic ends.

Imperial apologetic was not a tangential theme in *Trophies* and *Papiscus:*
it was central. *Trophies* and *Papiscus* transferred the shaken stability of the *pax
romana* to the serene security of the universal church, but thereby placed
Christianity's own prestige in peril. When the empire was not restored,
confidence in Christianity faded as well.

But others were prepared to jettison the empire and accept the new
state of affairs in the Levant. Their task was in some ways more difficult than
the Syrian Melkites'; they had to redeem a religion whose political defeat
they conceded. How they went about that thankless task occupies our next
chapter.

APPENDIX: THE DATES OF *PAPISCUS, TROPHIES,* AND *QUESTIONS*

Although these Syrian texts share many thematic and rhetorical similarities,
they are distinguished nonetheless by certain differences that only their
dates can explain. The date of *Trophies* is reasonably sure; it mentioned the
siege of Constantinople, and its title dated it to the ninth indiction and the
twentieth regnal year of the "the Emperor Constantine after the Emperor
Constantine," 674–75.[82] *Papiscus*'s date is less clear. McGiffert dated it to the

late seventh century, around 700.[83] This derives from the interval that *Papiscus* computed for the lapse of the Jews' rites in the temple, 670 years (which McGiffert reasonably amends to 570 years) from the destruction of Jerusalem by Hadrian around 130 C.E. But *Papiscus* explicitly named Titus and Vespasian as the destroyers of the temple, and the date should be 70 C.E. Secondly, *Papiscus* asserted that the Jews have suffered for 600 years since they crucified Christ, an interval that tallies roughly with the interval of 570 years since the destruction of the temple. Unfortunately, the author also added that Titus and Vespasian sacked the temple 600 years earlier. This conflicts with the agreement of the other two intervals unless it is treated as a general estimate, a round number rather than an attempt to calculate a precise date. On the other hand, 570 is an unusual number, whose calculation was designed to prove that the Jews' punishment had lasted so long that they should despair of God's forgiveness and their own restoration; the Babylonian captivity had after all only lasted 70 years.

The author's temporal frame of reference also indicates an early date for *Papiscus*. If the work had been written after the 670s, it is hardly likely that it would have failed to mention the successful defense of Constantinople like its sister dialogue *Trophies*. On the other hand, *Papiscus* still referred to the Persians as persecutors.[84] *Trophies* in the 670s ignored the Persians; greater disasters had simply driven them from memory.[85] The author of *Papiscus* still lived at a time when the Persian threat was recent enough to compare with the Arabs, yet before the Arabs met their first check at Constantinople.

Finally, *Papiscus* offers numismatic evidence for not only its date, but *Questions'* date as well. *Papiscus* mentioned that the Arabs used Byzantine coins with crosses. In 692, the cross was removed from the coinage and the bust of Christ introduced. This change was revolutionary and led, according to Theophanes' *Chronicle*, to war between the Arabs and Byzantines.[86] Theophanes' version of events should not be accepted at face value, but he gave some indication of the effect this change in Byzantine numismatic iconography had beyond the borders of the empire.[87] Since the author of *Papiscus* obviously knew coin iconographies and began the dialogue with a defense of icons,[88] it is unlikely that he would have overlooked the opportunity to combine these arguments into one with the mention of Christ's appearance on coins. And, as the Arabs copied contemporary Byzantine coin iconography until the 690s, it is possible that *Papiscus* referred not only to the period before the appearance of Christ on Byzantine coinage, but also to the period shortly after the Arab invasions, when Byzantine coinage still remained the dominant currency of the Levant.

The numismatic evidence for an early date for *Papiscus* receives confirmation from *Questions*. The author answered question 42, "How is it certain that the Christians have a better faith than any other faith under heaven; for every faith believes that it is a holier faith than the rest?" with the explanation that Byzantine military prowess demonstrated God's love for the Christians: "No emperor of the Christians has ever been killed by the barbarians, even though so many nations have warred against the Empire. And no one has been able to efface his image with the cross from the nomisma, even though some tyrants have thought about this."[89] Interestingly, the Antiochene church historian Evagrius used this same argument at the end of the sixth century, another possible indication of *Questions'* provenance. Like *Papiscus*, *Questions* added a reference to the nomisma's iconographic power. But the reference to the tyrant is not easily resolved, but it may refer to 'Abd al-Malik's coinage reforms at the end of the seventh century that removed the pseudo-cross from Arab coinage.[90] *Questions'* reference to attempts to remove the cross from the coins may be a later development of the same argument found in *Papiscus*.

It seems likely that *Papiscus* is the earliest of the three texts, from about 640–50, *Trophies* from the mid-670s, and *Questions* from the last quarter of the seventh century.[91]

Notes

1. Anonymous, *Les Trophées de Damas, controverse judeo-chrétienne du VIIe siècle*, ed. G. Bardy, [*PO* 15] (Paris, 1927): 225; hereafter, *Trophies*.

2. See *Doctrine*, 2, for forced baptism of the Jews; ibid., 69, for the forced conversion of a Christian cleric by Jews in Ptolemais.

3. Anonymous, *Disputatio gregentii cum Herbano Judeo*, PG 86: 624c–d; hereafter, *Gregentius*. See also *Trophies*, 215, and *Doctrine*, 5, for their authors' insistence that conversations with Jews be conducted in Greek.

4. *Gregentius*, 664c.

5. *Trophies*, 261.

6. See A. C. McGiffert, *Dialogue between a Christian and a Jew entitled Antibolē Papiskou kai Philōnos Ioudaiōn pros monaxon tina* (New York, 1889), 31–44 for *Papiscus*; Bardy, 184–89 for *Trophies*; A. Lukyn Williams, *Adversus Judaeos: A Bird's Eye View of Christian Apologetics* (Cambridge, 1935), 162–66 for *Trophies*, which he considers historical, 169–74 for *Papiscus*, which surprisingly (in light of his assessment of *Trophies*) he does not; J. Parkes, *The Conflict of the Church and the Synagogue: A Study in the Origins of Anti-Semitism* (New York, 1979 [1934]), 287–89 for *Trophies*; H. Schreckenberg, *Die christliche Adversus-Judaeos-Texte und ihr literarisches und historisches Umfeld (1–11 Jh.)*, (Frankfurt, 1982), 391–92 for *Papiscus*, 449–50 for *Trophies*; M. Waegeman, "Les traités adversus Judaeos: Aspects des relations Judéo-

Chrètiennes dans le monde grec," *Byzantion* 56 (1986): 298–315, for *Trophies.* Schreckenberg attempts to put the best possible face on two rather unpleasant treatments of the Jews and characterizes them both as "freundlich" despite the fact that in *Trophies*, 225, a fight threatens to break out between the Christians and the Jews. In addition, Schreckenberg, 391, further claims that *Papiscus* is related to the anti-Jewish dialogue *Athanasius and Zachaeus,* which is certainly possible, but does not document this claim, and ignores Bardy's suggestion that the text that is most closely related to *Papiscus* is *Trophies.* Certainly the best new work on these dialogues is V. Déroche, "La polémique anti judaique au VIᵉ et au VIIᵉ siècle. Un mémento inédit, les *Képhalaia,*" *Travaux et Mémoires* 11 (1991): 279–83, 288–95.

7. McGiffert, *Dialogue,* 43–44, originally suggested that *Papiscus* had an Egyptian provenance. *Trophies*, 219, n. 1, the editor of *Trophies*, rejected McGiffert's provenance. He proposed that *Papiscus* used *Trophies*, and that since *Trophies* can be reasonably assigned to Syria, it was likely that *Papiscus* should also be assigned there. It was a reasonable suggestion, but was only offered in passing.

8. *Trophies*, 247; *Papiscus*, 56.

9. *Trophies*, 218; *Papiscus*, 60.

10. *Trophies*, 219; *Papiscus*, 74. Bardy drew attention to this in order to refute McGiffert's proposed Egyptian provenance.

11. *Trophies*, 209; *Papiscus*, 57.

12. *Trophies*, 270; *Papiscus*, 59.

13. Pseudo-Athanasius of Alexandria, *Quaestiones ad Antiochem ducem, PG* 28: 685b.

14. *Papiscus*, 82–83; *Quaestiones*, 699b–c.

15. *Quaestiones*, 685b.

16. For pagan accusations of Jewish misanthropy, see L. Feldman, "Anti-Semitism in the Ancient World," in *History and Hate: The Dimensions of Anti-Semitism,* ed. D. Berger (Philadelphia, 1986), 30–32; J. Gager, *The Origins of Anti-Semitism* (New York, 1983), 43–54.

17. *Trophies*, 260.

18. As Parkes, *Conflict,* 185, explained, Christian imperial legislation on the Jews aimed "to shut the Jews within the limits of their own community." As R. Reuther, *Faith and Fratricide: The Theological Roots of Anti-Semitism* (Minneapolis, 1974), 137–41, explains, the social alienation of the Jews originated in early Christianity's racial distinction between Jews and gentiles. Thus were Christian Judaizers judged twice guilty, for they betrayed not only their religion, but also their race. Chrysostom, for example, referred to the Jews as a disease in the midst of the Antiochenes, and those who Judaized betrayed their religion and race by bringing such sickness into the midst of the gentiles; cf. R. Wilken, *John Chrysostom and the Jews: Rhetoric and Reality in the Late Fourth Century* (Berkeley, 1983), 116–27.

19. The Christians did little more than follow the same attacks made by pagans like Manetho, Apion, and Tacitus, see *Greek and Latin Authors on Jews and Judaism,* ed. M. Stern, 3 vols. (Jerusalem, 1976–84), 1: 66–68 for Manetho; ibid., 1:393 for Apion; ibid., 2:17–23 for Tacitus. That the Jews were social aliens had a long history. The effort of the Alexandrians to exclude the Jews from citizenship was such a case of gentile claims that the Jews were merely social aliens dwelling in their midst; see D. Rokeah, *Jews, Pagans and Christians in Conflict,* [*Studia post-biblica* 33] (Jeru-

salem and Leiden, 1982), esp. 40–83; A. Kasher, *The Jews in Hellenistic and Roman Egypt* (Tuebingen, 1985).

20. *Trophies,* 218.

21. *Papiscus,* 60.

22. Cf. *Trophies,* 218–19; *Papiscus,* 78–79. Both dialogues make use of Gen. 49:10 in their argument; see below.

23. See R. Grant, "Eusebius, Josephus, and the Fate of the Jews," *Society of Biblical Literature 1979 Seminar Papers,* ed. P. J. Achtemeier, vol. 2 (Missoula, 1979), 69–86; Wilken, *Chrysostom,* 132–38; Simon, *Verus Israel: A Study of the Relations between Christians and Jews in the Roman Empire (135–425),* trans. H. McKeating (Oxford, 1986), 67–68; Reuther, *Faith and Fratricide,* 144–47. Once again, this is little more than the classical view of the gods' hatred of the Jews, see Cicero in Stern, 1:196–97, who explains that the gods' attitude toward the Jews is shown in their conquest by foreigners.

24. See *Papiscus,* 58; *Trophies,* 240.

25. *Trophies,* 238.

26. *Trophies,* 218–19; see also *Papiscus,* 74 which lists Egypt, Memphis, the worshippers of the Nile, the temple of Artemis, and the temple of Cyzicus.

27. See Simon, *Verus Israel,* 164–65. This attack on Judaism is one of the oldest and dates from the first-century *Epistle of Barnabus.*

28. *Trophies,* 198.

29. *Trophies,* 241, cf. Parkes, *Conflict,* 101–03, for the Christian tradition that the Jews were ignorant of God.

30. See Parkes, *Conflict,* 164–65; Reuther, *Faith and Fratricide,* 124–30, for the Christian attack on Jewish idolotry.

31. *Papiscus,* 78.

32. Ibid., 80.

33. *Trophies,* 244.

34. Here, *Papiscus* parts company with *Trophies,* adding Melchisidek to the argument of the gentiles' covenant with Christ. The gentiles are, for *Papiscus,* a holy race.

35. *Trophies,* 216, 234–35.

36. Ibid., 216.

37. Ibid., 235.

38. Ibid., 235.

39. Ibid., 236. *Genos, ethnos,* and *laos* are used interchangeably.

40. See the list of ancient races, ibid., 235.

41. Ibid., 274.

42. Ibid., 271.

43. Ibid., 271–72.

44. Ibid., 233.

45. Ibid., 267.

46. Ibid., 193.

47. Ibid., 193–96.

48. See Severus of Aschmounein, *History of the Patriarchs of the Coptic Church of Alexandria,* ed. and trans. E. Evetts, *PO,* 5:492.

49. *Quaestiones,* 620.

50. *Trophies,* 250.

51. For the discussion of the Jews' and Christians' direction of prayer, see ibid., 250–54.

52. *Quaestiones,* 617–20.

53. Ibid., 620.

54. Ibid.

55. *Trophies,* 251.

56. *Quaestiones,* 620.

57. Theophanes, *Chronographia,* 2 vols., ed. C. de Boor (Leipzig, 1883), 1:334.

58. *Trophies,* 220.

59. *Quaestiones,* 625c.

60. See the notice in Michael the Syrian, *Chronique,* 4 vols., trans. J.-B. Chabot (Paris, 1899–1910), 4:419, in which the Chalcedonians are said to have abandoned their churches and fled during a Persian attack and then returned after the Arab occupation. The implication is that the Chalcedonians did not receive their churches back. See also D. Olster, "The Politics of Usurpation in the Seventh Century: The Reign of Phocas (602–10)," diss., University of Chicago, 1986, 27–38.

61. Indeed, the author's confusion is evident in the first words with which the monk responds to the Jew's question, *Trophies,* 221, "The Christian [said], "Your question is double, and it is necessary that the answer be double." The Christian, in fact, offers the reader a tripartite answer.

62. Ibid., 221.

63. Ibid.

64. Ibid., 230.

65. Ibid., 221.

66. Ibid., 272–73.

67. Ibid., 222.

68. For renewal as a seventh-century literary *topos,* see D. Olster, "The Date of George of Pisidia's *Hexaemeron,*" *DOP* 45 (1991): 159–72; for the numismatic evidence of imperial renewal themes, see P. Grierson, *Catalogue of the Byzantine Coins in the Dumbarton Oaks Collection and in the Whittemore Collection* (Washington, D.C., 1968), vol. 2, pt. 2: 443ff. and pl. 26.

69. See P. Alexander, "The Strength of Empire and Capital," *Speculum* 37 (1962): 339–57, esp. 341–47. Alexander relies, to a certain extent, on the homily of Theodore Syncellus for the Byzantine identification of the capital as a New Jerusalem.

70. The Arab defeat at Constantinople seems to have had little impact on the Syrian Monophysites; the Monophysite historians, Michael the Syrian, and the *Chronicle of 1254* almost entirely ignore it. Stll, the contemporary Nestorian Bar-Penkayé (*Sources syriaques,* ed. and trans. A. Mingana (Leipzig, 1908), 1:192**– 96**, shows how many in the Levant still expected the Arabs to collapse as late as the end of the seventh century. Theophanes, *Chronographia,* 355–56, describes the reaction of "those in the west," and their rush to conclude treaties with the victorious Byzantines. See also the reactions of the Melkites in Agapius and Eutychius.

71. *Papiscus,* 60–61.

72. Ibid., 60.

73. Ibid., 61.

74. See *Trophies*, 203–04; *Papiscus*, 54–55. *Papiscus* made the sacramental relationship between Christ and the "gentiles" even more explicit, when it called Christ "the priest of the nations." The referrant of both passages was Melchizedek, but *Trophies* simply distinguished the priesthood of Christ from the priesthood of Aaron. *Papiscus* explicitly described the religion of Christ in the same racial context as the imperial.

75. *Papiscus*, 62.

76. *Trophies*, 262–69; *Papiscus*, 80–82. Both dialogues ended with the exegesis of Daniel; it was the topic of the last day's debate in *Trophies,* and the final monologue in *Papiscus.*

77. *Trophies,* 222; *Papiscus,* 56. Their sole apocalyptic claim was that the Jews' Messiah would be the Antichrist.

78. *Trophies,* 267; *Papiscus,* 82.

79. *Papiscus,* 80–81.

80. Ibid., 82; see the similar argument in *Quaestiones,* 685a–d.

81. *Trophies,* 269.

82. This dates the reign of Constantine IV from his coronation by his father in 654; the indictional date is off, but that would more likely be mistaken than would the regnal year. For the reference to the siege, see below.

83. McGiffert, *Dialogue,* 42.

84. *Papiscus,* 61, 62.

85. *Trophies,* 218, does mention that the Persians' *loci sancti* and religion have disappeared, but the Persians are not mentioned as conquerors of the Romans or persecutors of the church.

86. Theophanes, *Chronographia,* 365; for Theophanes, see Olster, "Usurpation," 11–27.

87. J. D. Breckenridge, *The Numismatic Iconography of Justinian II,* [*Numismatic Notes and Monographs* 144] (New York, 1959).

88. *Papiscus,* 51–52.

89. Quaestiones, 624.

90. See P. Grierson, "The Monetary Reforms of Abd al' Malik," *Journal of the Economic and Social History of the Orient* 3 (1960): 241–64. This might also refer to earlier Byzantino-Arabic coinage that simply removed the transverse bar from the reverse cross on their copies of Byzantine coins, but then it is likely that *Papiscus* would have mentioned this too. See in particular the analysis of the numismatic evidence of these texts in W. E. Kaegi, *Byzantium and the Early Islamic Conquests* (Cambridge, 1992), 221–27, 231–35.

91. Kaegi, *Conquests,* 231–35, has convincingly demonstrated that the ninth-century dating of Pseudo-Anastasius the Sinaite's *Disputation against the Jews* must be reconsidered. The evidence for its late date are editorial revisions, but its topical references are clearly seventh-century, and it must be placed with the family of texts that include *Trophies, Papiscus,* and *Questions.* Its chronological place among these works, however, is unclear because of the later editorial revisions. Finally, Kaegi makes the interesting (and entirely admissible) suggestion that the *Disputation* (and by extension this group of texts) might also be related to the *Apocalypse of Pseudo-Methodius.*

7. *Gregentius and Herbanus*: The New Christian *Patria*

The Syrian dialogues, however well they accord with much of the contemporary Constantinopolitan literature, present only one side of the apologetic spectrum. The thematic and theological choices made by the Syrian Melkites were shaped by their own social and political concerns. They assimilated political themes that were largely current in Constantinople and clothed them in the language of a genre that was chosen, quite deliberately, as an appropriate literary medium. In the last few years, scholars have recognized that these provincial echoes cannot be dismissed as merely a ripple of the cultural and literary power of the capital.[1] The Syrian evidence illustrates how complicated were the relations between the capital and the provinces. The Melkites there held on to the imperial ideal, for imperial power was the mainstay of their minority control. But not every provincial was confronted by a large hostile social and religious majority.

Social and political distinctions found expression in literary nuance. The authors of the anti-Jewish dialogues carefully chose the background, characterization, and literary structure for their effects. The Syrian authors set their dialogues in a recognizable Roman urban context with an unnamed monk as protagonist. A very different social context produced a dialogue set at the court of the Ethiopian king at Tephren. Not only the exotic setting, but also the protagonist, distinguished this dialogue. It was no anonymous monk who confronted and confounded the Jew Herbanus, it was the famous St. Gregentius, the fifth-century bishop and apostle to the Arabs himself.[2]

Gregentius differs from *Trophies* and *Papiscus* not only in its setting and characterization, but also in its rhetorical voice, argumentative methods, and themes. The Syrian dialogues' confrontation of the self-confident, at times brash, Christian monk and the confused, often monosyllabic, and self-conscious Jew was highly crafted rhetoric. The Christian's easily won refutation of the Jews permitted the authors to assimilate the apologetics for imperial defeat into a genre that allowed them to mask Roman defeat against the Arabs with Christian victory against the Jews. The monks of *Trophies* and *Papiscus,* armed with the arsenal of Christian truth, overthrew the Jews largely without miraculous aid, simply through the irresistible force of their arguments. The protagonist of *Gregentius,* however, is not an anonymous monk, but a well-known bishop and saint, whose opponent possesses considerable finesse. Gregentius prevails in the end, but not with logic. Only through Christ's own miraculous appearance can he convert the recalcitrant Jews.

The differences in plotting and characterization between the Syrian dialogues *Trophies* and *Papiscus,* and *Gregentius* create narrative structures that support very different allegorical methods and apologetic themes. The Syrian dialogues reshaped the triumphalist identification of church and empire in order to sustain hope in imperial recovery. Through new allegorical choices, or simple reinterpretations of Christian history, they reversed the Eusebian dynamic that relied on imperial success to bolster Christianity's claims: a new rhetoric employed not just by the Syrian dialogues but by a wide range of seventh-century sources.

Gregentius attempted to restore Christian confidence by means that discarded the hope of imperial recovery. The author of *Gregentius* chose to uphold Christian legitimacy by *disassociating* it from past imperial misfortunes, rather than associating it with future imperial revival. The result was a very different perspective of contemporary events, whose subdued tone emphasized the individual's spiritual salvation rather than the collective's political restoration. Thematically, the dialogue most closely approached the social apologetic of Sophronius, and indeed the analysis of *Gregentius* reveals that it is a Jerusalemite product from the generation or so after the Arab conquest, about 650–80.

The characteristic Jerusalemite emphasis on individual salvation in *Gregentius* arises out of a very different view of sin from that found in the Syrian dialogues. Sin in *Trophies* and *Papiscus,* as well as in the Constantinopolitan sources, is invariably communal, and its consequences are political and military; the very logic of imperial recovery depended on linking defeat to sin and imperial recovery to repentance and divine forgiveness.[3] *Gregentius* focused sin, repentance, and salvation in the individual alone. For this reason, *Gregentius* is the least overtly political of the anti-Jewish dialogues. It replaced the restoration cycle with a struggle between demons and Christ for the souls of individual Christians.

The different attitudes toward sin and salvation found in the Syrian dialogues and *Gregentius* had a profound effect on their content. The former studiously avoided any mention of intra-Christian theological is-sues, especially the prickly problem of Christ's natures and wills, the most important intra-Christian theological issue of the seventh century.[4] The author of *Trophies* had composed a separate dialogue devoted exclusively to refuting the Monophysites, but there is no trace of such an interest in his anti-Jewish dialogue. But the author of *Gregentius* incorporated his strongly Dyophysite views directly into the text. The authors of *Trophies* and *Papiscus* shared the doctrinal persuasion of *Gregentius,* but only the author of *Gregentius* included a catechetical recitation of Christ's natures, repeated it so often, or, hardly less significantly, added a proof of Christ's two natures in the dialogue itself.[5]

Gregentius's less overt political rhetoric and theological excursions have misled scholars. They have overlooked *Gregentius*'s indirect references to seventh-century political and military affairs, and have dated *Gregentius* by a comparison with earlier anti-Jewish dialogues like the fifth-century *Timothy and Aquila* or the sixth-century *Athanasius and Zacchaeus.*[6] Despite its differences with the Syrian dialogues, *Gregentius* does not lack detailed and specific references to contemporary events, nor does it fail to respond to the social and political problems they raised. Explicit references to contempo-rary military and political events date the Syrian dialogues, but the most obvious clue to *Gregentius*'s date has been overlooked: the author included two wills in his litany of Christ's natures, the sole reference in any seventh-century anti-Jewish dialogue to Christ's wills.[7] It is ironic that *Gregentius*'s theology should confuse the issue of dating, when actually it provides some of the strongest evidence for the dialogue's seventh-century date.

The difficulty in reconciling the very different styles of the Syrian dialogues and *Gregentius* rests with scholarship's distinction between theol-ogy and politics in Byzantine literature on the one hand, and, on the other, its assumption that the Christian response to the Arab invasion would be monolithic.[8] The Syrian dialogues resemble the contemporary Constan-tinopolitan sources and must therefore represent the normative Byzantine response. But the differences between the Syrian dialogues and *Gregentius* lie not in a distinction between their authors' theologies, but in the distinct social and political conditions under which they wrote.

The overt imperial apologetic of *Trophies* and *Papiscus* was not due to a lack of interest in intra-Christian doctrinal disputes; the existence of an anti-Monophysite dialogue by the author of the *Trophies,* and the combination of overt imperial apologetic and theological exposition in *Questions* show just the opposite. The Syrian Melkites had to confront not only Arab victory and the doubts they raised, but also their own position as a minority sect. A minority long identified with imperial interests, the Melkites did not need a doctrinal refutation of the Jacobites, but proof that the Arabs had not shattered the traditional political and social bond between church and state that had supported them since Chalcedon.[9] The anti-Monophysite dialogue by the author of *Trophies* mentioned neither the Arab invasions nor future imperial recovery; the anonymous Melkite writer, at least, appears to have been quite capable of limiting his topics to suit his needs. And while the evidence is not as clear for the author of *Papiscus,* his striking avoidance of doctrinal issues implies that he shared his contemporary's ability to distinguish between intercommunity doctrinal disputes and intra-community social and political concerns.

Gregentius was not a Syrian Melkite product, and its response to the Arab invasions was dictated by very different social and political needs. The social and political assumptions of *Gregentius*'s Jerusalemite provenance make clear why it departed from the dominant themes of the Constantino-politan and Syrian sources, yet found its inspiration in the same social and political issues.

The author of *Gregentius* was quite aware of the Arab invasions, but his response was indirect: he placed it in the context of the struggle between demons and Christ. Expanding on the benefits that Christ has showered on the faithful, Gregentius explained: "Does not the Lord, therefore, through all the days of this age, protect, watch over and guard those who love him, not only from the fire of evil, that evil connivance of the devil that consumes the souls of men, but also from the invasion, that is, from the demonic south, the remaining tyranny of Satan."[10] The invasion from the south, "the remaining tyranny of Satan," was an oblique reference to the Arab invasion, but its context was very different than in the Syrian dialogues. Gregentius rather than the Jew brought the invasion into the dialogue, and the Jew never referred to the invasion directly. Gregentius mentioned the invasion only to show how God controlled the devil in order to save the souls of men. Indeed, so important was the issue of demons that the author added a section to prove that Christ was the one who dispossessed the demons of their power.[11]

The demonization of the Jews as the murderers of Christ through the instigation of the devil was a commonplace throughout Byzantine litera-ture.[12] Indeed, the transformation of the political enemies of Rome from barbarians to persecutors borrowed much of the rhetoric of demonization that had been used against the Jews.[13] What distinguished *Gregentius* from these Constantinopolitan and Syrian sources, however, was that the former internalizes the struggle between Christ and Satan, while the latter external-ize this conflict. The corollary of this redirection of Christian conflict is the same redefinition of Christian victory that Sophronius used to address Christian defeat. So long as the conflict between Christ and his enemies was external, Roman military victory would be the measure of Christ's victory. When the conflict became internal, any visible standard of Christ's victory, like the greatness of the Christian Empire, disappeared, and with it the need to promise future imperial recovery.

What occurred in *Gregentius* was a curious reshaping of the political theology of the gentiles' inheritance from the Jews. *Gregentius* followed, in part, the same gentile theology as the Syrian dialogues, but ultimately shifted its meaning into a new, nonimperial direction. Like the other anti-Jewish dialogues, *Gregentius* defended the superiority of Christianity by listing its blessings, and linking those blessings to its universalism. "For from the ends of the earth, races, tribes and tongues who believe in the Father, Son and Holy Ghost, have received blessings from the All-ruler on account of their good faith."[14] As in *Trophies* and *Papiscus,* the gentiles were the composite race chosen by God to receive his blessings. But behind this similarity, the dialogues had very different views of the exaltation of the gentiles and the nature of Christian universalism: changes that originated in the internalization of Christ's blessings.

Just as Gregentius shared the theology of gentile universalism with the Syrian dialogues, Herbanus shared their Jews' racial particularism. Indeed, Herbanus, to a far greater extent, made this the basis of his attack on Chris-tianity and defense of Judaism. He returned repeatedly to this point, often brushing aside Gregentius's explanation of properly generic, but clearly secondary, questions, in his eagerness to raise the ethnographic issue. For example, following Gregentius's explanation of the Trinity, Herbanus responded:

> You speak well, and we are not able to offer a refutation on this subject. Except hear what God says when he promises Israel that it is loved by him: "My first-born, my son Israel" [Exod. 4:22], and then, "I have called my son out of Egypt" [Hos. 11:1]. If, therefore, God names Israel his own first-born son, how do you gentiles who are filled with error, and who lack the law, regard Israel itself as something filthy, unclean and impure, when you owe Israel honor rather than dishonor?[15]

Herbanus had no interest in the Trinity or, for that matter, in Mary's virginity or in any generic *topoi* that the Syrian dialogues rehearsed at length. *Gregentius*'s theological interest centers almost entirely on the theology of race and covenant: the classical ethnographic model of the contract between a race and its god. From the very first lines, in which Herbanus and Gregentius trade barbs about whether the "new wine" of the gentiles is sweeter than the "old wine" of the Jews,[16] the dialogue concentrates on the identity of God's people. Throughout the dialogue, Herbanus taunts his opponent as one who lacks the racial seal of approval. "If . . . we who believe in the God of the Law are opposed to [his] light, how much more are you, alien races, who follow practices alien to our God-given and divine Law."[17] Herbanus even lamented the translation of the Old Testament into Greek, for it offered the gentiles the opportunity to claim the heritage of the Jews.[18] None of this is especially original.[19] What distinguished *Gregentius* from the Syrian dialogues was the insistence with which Herbanus pursued this point and the conclusions he drew about Jewish and Roman political renewal. *Trophies* and *Papiscus* used the Jews' objections to introduce a defense of Roman imperialism based on Christian universalism; *Gregentius* followed a very different course.

Gregentius inverted the Syrian dialogues' logic of political and military recovery by making the Jews the proponents and object of such renewal. Herbanus argued that the Jews' repentance would eventually assuage God's anger, at which point they would receive back their kingdom as the proof of His forgiveness. Herbanus's insistence on this point was especially unusual because Gregentius made no similar claims for the empire.[20]

Herbanus thus had no qualms about admitting the sinfulness of the Jews, and that the Jews lost their city and homeland on account of their sins. It was part of his argument for the *Jews*' political renewal that he do so:

> *Gregentius:* For what reason did God throw you to the four winds of heaven?
> *Herbanus:* Clearly on account of our sins.
> *Gregentius:* So I said earlier, that you have been scattered on account of your sins and driven from the promised land.[21]

But conceding this, Herbanus continued that God's punishment was merely to recall the Jews to virtue. When the Jews turned back toward God, he would restore them. To Gregentius's recitation of the punishments that God had and would continue to heap on the Jews in Isaiah 1:8–14, Herbanus countered: "For after he describes the punishments, he adds, 'I will establish your judges as they were before, and your counselors as they were at the beginning, and then you will be called the city of justice, the faithful city of Zion.'" [Isaiah 1.25–26][22]

Herbanus's view of restoration was also explicitly political. The Jews' restoration meant nothing less than the kingdom's renewal. "Does it not seem to you that the Lord God is very shortly again to recall Israel, whom He has banished, and it must necessarily become a strong people and more powerful empire?"[23] Nor did Herbanus neglect the apocalyptic dimension of renewal: "In the consummation of this life, fire will descend from God with a double purpose. The fire will cleanse the Jews, and illuminate God's dwelling-place; but all the remaining races, quick as lightning, will be transformed and pass away throughout the world, consumed, because they are alien and foreign to God's law."[24] Herbanus, like the author of *Pseudo-Methodius,* drew the apocalyptic line between good and evil along racial boundaries. And just as *Pseudo-Methodius* predicted the defeat of the unclean races and the exaltation of the Romans, Herbanus prophecied a similar destruction of the unclean races and exaltation of the Jews.

This is the restoration cycle that informed the Syrian and Constantinopolitan sources, but in a curious reversal of roles, Herbanus is its proponent. He sounded remarkably like the Christian speakers in *Trophies* and *Papiscus,* not only using their logic for Jewish restoration, but also exulting in his opponent's coming humiliation: "Again we Israelites will rise and our city will be occupied, and you crowing Christians will be shamed."[25]

What makes *Gregentius* interesting is not just that the Jew's argument for renewal is based on this cycle, but that the Christian's is not. Gregentius rejected Herbanus's political definition of God's blessings. Far from conferring the gift of military victory or imperial peace on a Christian community identified with New Rome, Gregentius created a context of individual salvation centered on a different center, Jerusalem.

Gregentius turned aside Herbanus's claims for Jewish restoration by readily admitting Christian defeat, and then dismissing it as irrelevant. True Christian victory was the soul's illumination. When Herbanus claimed that Micah's prophecy of the restoration of "the destroyed" and "the rejected" referred to the Jews' return to Jerusalem, Gregentius answered: "Most assuredly, oh Herbanus, you fall when you misapply the prophecy to your own race. For when it says, 'the destroyed,' it refers to the dwellings of the gentiles. And when it says 'the rejected,' it means, I say, the idolotry of those same gentiles that has been rejected."[26] Gregentius willingly conceded Roman defeat because it had little to do with his defense of Christianity. The significant point was the moral interpretation of the passage. Christianity's aim was the spiritual illumination of the gentiles through the true faith.

The crux of *Gregentius*'s defense of Christianity lies here. The author had to demonstrate how Christianity's spiritual illumination outweighed its recent material setbacks. To address this problem, the author had Herbanus interrupt Gregentius as he explained how Old Testament military victories prefigured Christian spiritual victories, and impatiently demand clear evidence of Christianity's material advantages. When Gregentius explained that "wood" in the Old Testament prefigured the saving mission of Christ, Herbanus turned ironical:

> *Herbanus:* You naturally might discover that wood was useful in the Old Testament, now compare it to your cross!
> *Gregentius:* Not only does the wood prefigure the cross, but also the lifting up of the hands, the symbols of battles, and other things similar to these.
> *Herbanus:* Since I anticipated this, I said that you, since you are greatly learned, should directly speak the truth about the benefits you have received.[27]

Herbanus's objection was rather difficult to answer because Gregentius emphatically denied that the Old Testament battles and victories prefigured Christian *military* victory. Whenever Herbanus demanded an explanation of the political and military benefits that Christianity conferred, Gregentius shifted ground to the promises of individual salvation found in allegory and prophecy. Characteristically, he offered Joshua's victory at Gibeon as a prefiguration of Christian victory but insisted that the true victory, far better than mere military victory, was man's salvation:

> And this was a prefiguration of the passion of my glorious Lord, Jesus Christ. For that one was Jesus, and the later one was also Jesus: one was the commander of Israel, the other was emperor and God, not only of Israel, but of all the world: the one defeated the nations, the other, the armies of the demons. . . . The one, by spear and lance destroyed his enemies, the other, by the power of his Godhead, broke the barriers of Hell, and through his honorable Cross, turned the demons to ashes.[28]

Gregentius studiously avoided the typological comparisons between Israelites and Romans that the Syrian dialogues and especially Theodore Syncellus used to foretell the eventual imperial restoration of God's people, the Christian Romans. *Gregentius* did not ignore the Arab invasions, it simply adopted a different apologetic strategy than the Syrian dialogues.

This redefinition of Christian victory took the disenfranchisement of the Jews in a very different direction than did the Syrian dialogues. Naturally, Gregentius did not neglect the geographic dispossession of the Jews, and it was the first point in his refutation of Herbanus's claims for restoration: "In the first place, he took away your kingdom, your law, your rites and your sacrifices; he took the holy city, the mountain of Sinai, the bush, and to put it bluntly, anything that accrued honor to you, he took that away from you, and gave it to us Christians."[29]

As in *Trophies* and *Papiscus,* the political destruction of the Jews was one of the foundations of the Christians' claims that the gentiles had supplanted them. But the Syrian dialogues made the loss of Jerusalem only one facet of the *translatio imperii* from Jews to Christians. In *Gregentius,* Jerusalem assumed a far greater role. The Christian Roman Empire only appeared, for example, as the builder of Jerusalem's many shrines. "And is not the Roman Empire now a great and strong nation? Does it not fill Jerusalem with churches and holy precincts of the crucified Christ?"[30] So great was the author's pride in Jerusalem's monuments that he made the rather unusual assertion that the Holy Resurrection church, built by Helena, the mother of Constantine, was the fulfillment of biblical prophecy foretelling the rebuilding of the temple. Herbanus was not impressed:

> *Gregentius:* "And the house of God will be exalted on the tops of the mountains." [Isa. 2:1] What is this house? Perhaps it is the temple of Solomon? Absolutely not! Come and see that it is razed to the ground! But what building is it? Where the Nazarene was buried and dwelt three days and nights; and he rose again there; and directly above his tomb a church has been built, and the Holy Resurrection is its name. . . .
> *Herbanus:* The prophet makes clear that the nations will come to the house of the Lord! How do you resettle this prophecy in that church that the empress Helena built?[31]

This exchange typifies the central place that Jerusalem and its monuments hold in *Gregentius.* The author's pride in the city itself and its buildings, and his detailed knowledge of them, greatly surpassed anything in *Trophies* or *Papiscus.*

The author's insistence that the Old Testament's prophecies that the gentiles would come to Jerusalem to worship the Lord inspired his belief that the Church of the Holy Resurrection was the rebuilt temple. Elsewhere, this prophecy was interpreted as the continuous flow of pilgrims to Jerusalem: "When you hear the Lord as he speaks through the prophet, 'Behold, I will come to collect all people and tongues,' and, 'Let all flesh come in order to adore me in Jerusalem,' speak no longer, but rather, see that the seventy tongues, continually going up into Jerusalem, adore the God of the Law, the Father of our Lord Jesus Christ."[32] The Syrian dialogues' Christian universalism was generally synonymous with Roman imperialism, but *Gregentius* shaped its narrower Christian universalism around Jerusalem's role as a *locus sanctus* and pilgrimage center. Jerusalem, not Constantinople, was the focal point of Christian unity at whose holy places the nations, the "seventy tongues," joined as one.

The critical role of Jerusalem in *Gregentius* meant that Jerusalem could never leave Christian hands. The Syrian dialogues could concede Jerusalem's loss. When *Trophies* spoke of the "head" of the Christians, it referred to Constantinople. But Gregentius interpreted Ezekiel 36:25, that God would bring his people into the holy land where he would be their God, to mean that not only were the Christians God's people but also that their true inheritance was the holy land and above all Jerusalem: "You say that God selected nations from the nations . . . and that the Lord perhaps settled the nations in the city of Jerusalem as in the land of their fathers. If you have not eyes, it worries me. For look and see, how all Jerusalem is filled with Christians, and of Jews there are none!"[33] Naturally, the Christian possession of Jerusalem had an important place in all the seventh-century anti-Jewish dialogues, but the assertion that Jerusalem constituted a Christian *patria* distinguished *Gregentius:* it contracted the Christian *oikomenē* to a single point, and that point could not be lost.

The concentration on Jerusalem, the detailed discussion of its monuments, and its description as a pilgrimage site imply that the author was a Jerusalemite, or at least Palestinian. For this reason the possession of Jerusalem was so critical to the dialogue's themes of Christian universalism, prophetic fulfillment, and most importantly, the refutation of the Jews' claims of political and spiritual renewal. Of course, it is possible that Jews historically raised these issues,[34] and that the Christian author desired to refute them. But the author did not set these arguments in the mouth of Herbanus merely for the sake of refuting them. He carefully chose this theme to promote a redirection of Christian identity. His rejection of the "imperial" apologetic of *Trophies* and *Papiscus* was made because, as in the case of the Syrian dialogues, the provenance of the work required that certain issues be addressed.

The provenance explains the author's curious reticence to condemn the Jews utterly. Where *Trophies* and *Papiscus* explicitly denied any possibility of salvation to the Jews, and the protagonists even said that they did not desire the Jews to convert, Gregentius repeatedly urged the Jews' conversion. He noted that Christ's saving work was done among both Jews and gentiles, and that the stiff-necked rejection of Christ by the Jews had brought about the fall of Jerusalem to the Romans.[35] Faced with the Arab occupation, he called Christians to recognize that the Jews were not the worst of their enemies. *Gregentius* even went so far as to suggest that "the faithful Jews who lived before the appearance of Christ, and those who lived later, who believed in Christ after he had appeared, and however many from the gentiles who believed . . . have been made brothers." *Gregentius* continued with the rather extraordinary admission that "the Jews who believe in Christ are looked upon more favorably than the gentiles who believe in Christ."[36] This unusual concession did not arise from the author's missionary fervor, but from conditions at Jerusalem. The Jewish–Christian social conflict at Jerusalem was especially heated following the Persian conquest, and later, the Roman reconquest. But the Arab conquest changed Jerusalem's political and social dynamics; the author of *Gregentius* desired social unity in the face of the Arabs, and he urged his audience that Jews and Christians form a *koinōnia* as fellow citizens of Jerusalem.

The "true" Israelites thus also embraced the Jews. The author hoped that the Jewish community at Jerusalem would join its Christian neighbors to create the new Israel: "Indeed, the one who received the converted nations [Christ] will win over the true Israelites, even from Israel, those who observe the law well, who willingly enter into Christianity, that he recalls through faith, that he converts, not only from Jerusalem, but even from all the ends of the earth."[37] The assertion that some Jews would willingly enter Christianity, "not only from Jerusalem," implies that the author was at least acquainted with the Jerusalemite Jewish community. He showed a detailed knowledge of the situation at Jerusalem more clearly when Herbanus rejected Gregentius's appeal to convert. Herbanus accused Gregentius of disingenuousness, exclaiming, "If we come within, you expel us, and if we stay without, you force us in,"[38] a reference to Heraclius's expulsion of the Jews from Jerusalem.[39] An even more explicit reference was Herbanus's claim that the Jews' loss of Jerusalem was temporary: "Since God gave to us the city of Jerusalem, who can speak against [our claim]? Briefly a short time ago, we were expelled, but again, I think, we will receive our own back, and then we will occupy all just as we formerly did."[40] No other source, except Theophanes, mentioned the expulsion of the Jews from Jerusalem.

The Jerusalemite author did not forget events in his city. He could still remember that the Persians had restored Jerusalem to the Jews after the sack of 614, and if the Jewish restoration had been short-lived, its memory was very bitter for the Christians. At one point, Gregentius may have referred to the brief Jewish control of Jerusalem during the Persian War, and the subsequent efforts to convert the Jews: "'Let the islands rejoice,' [Ps. 96:1] it says, when you are called back from them, because they rejoice that they are released from your tyranny when we call you brother believers."[41] The accusation of Jewish tyranny in *Gregentius* was very different than the charge of persecution in *Trophies* and *Papiscus*. The latter dialogues used the charge of persecution to redefine Arab invasions as Arab persecutions, and to transform imperial defeat into Christian victory. Moreover, the vocabulary is quite distinct; a "tyranny" is different from a "persecution."[42] Certainly, as Herbanus's shocked response indicates, he understood not only the difference between persecution and tyranny, but that the issue of Jewish tyranny was linked to their conversion: "Let it not be that we tyrannize anyone! And let it not be that the gentiles rejoice in our conversion. For we do not call you Christians our fellow believers. God speaks entirely about us Jews, who have settled in the islands of our diaspora. For God has no thought for you gentiles."[43] Herbanus's response is another possible reference to the imperial policy of Jewish conversion. His denial that Jews would convert and join the community was itself undercut by the ending; he did convert and met with immediate acceptance. The conversion and assimilation of the Jews at Tephren argued for the unification of all Jerusalemites.[44]

Gregentius argued not only for a new definition of the Jerusalemite community, but also for a reformulation of its social organization. *Gregentius* took the generic *topos* that the law of Christ had come to purify and supersede the old law and invested it with a new social interpretation.[45] *Gregentius*'s treatment of the new law of Christ emphasized that Christianity possessed not simply a law legislating religious practices, but one that regulated and enforced social unity. *Papiscus* conceded that persecution led to the apostasy of some Christians, but *Gregentius* more subtly distinguished the true from the false Christian by his adherence to Christian Law:

> "Cursed be he who does not confirm the words of the law by doing them." [Deut. 27:26] Thus, those not guarding the law are not worthy to be counted with the people that do guard the law, which kind we call Christians, for all Christians are so named. Those who guard the commandments of the Christians are alone Christians, but those who do not keep them do not deserve the name.[46]

Gregentius's vocabulary of Christian Law distinguished it from the Syrian dialogues. While all these dialogues called on Christians to stand by Christianity, *Gregentius* named the church, rather than the empire, the executor of Christian Law.

The Syrian dialogues externalized conflict between Christ and Satan, employing the rhetoric of Jewish or heathen persecution to express the challenge facing each Christian. None of this was in *Gregentius,* which internalized conflict between Satan and Christ, and so minimized external Christian defeat. Instead, the author demonized "all those who did not guard the law of God before Christ, but rather served the devil through their evil works," whether nominally Christian or not.[47] The challenge that faced each Christian was to obey the Christian institutional authority and its law, rather than face persecution.

Christian Law in the Syrian dialogues was often synonymous with imperial authority. But *Gregentius* vested Christian authority *only* in the ecclesiastical hierarchy. Just as the author sought to dismiss the Arab invasions by internalizing Christian conflict, so he placed this conflict not in the imperial sphere, but the ecclesiastical. Christian Law was the expression of the authority of the church hierarchy, and the struggle to enforce Christian law fell to the bishop. It is no surprise that *Gregentius,* a Jerusalemite treatise, set the bishop in this position, for since the fall of Jerusalem to the Persians in 614, episcopal authority had been, excepting the brief moment between the Persian and Arab invasions, the sole Christian authority in the city.[48]

Like the homilies of Sophronius, *Gregentius* argued that the bishop's care for the souls of his congregation was the foundation of not only spiritual but political authority. External dangers such as Persians or Arabs were secondary. As the author explained, citing the allegory of the vineyard in Isaiah 5:

> "For I will remove its hedge and it will be devoured." [Isa. 5:5] What is the hedge? It is clearly the law, which encircled with the hedges of ordinances the vine brought out of Egypt to the promised land. And who are the devourers? Physically, they are the Assyrians, Persians and Romans, but spiritually, they are the demons within the mind, those who create the division of heresy.[49]

Gregentius spoke about the Jews, but his Christian audience would not mistake his meaning. The Persians, for example, were the "devourers" not of the Jews, whom they had actually freed from exile, but of the Christians. Gregentius's anachronism that Moses faced heretics applied to seventh-century Christianity much more than to Mosaic Judaism. "The demons of the mind" were the greater danger that the Christian faced; the threat of heresy a far greater danger than the Persians. Creating a social context for Christian Law, *Gregentius* defined the limits of that law in terms of heresy. Thus was the role of the bishop raised over that of the emperor. Moreover, the orthodoxy of the emperor for most of the seventh century was doubtful, and unlike the situation in Syria, where the Melkites were a minority, the Jerusalemite Christian community, largely orthodox, had, especially under Sophronius, good doctrinal cause to be disenchanted with the emperors.[50]

One of the most striking omissions of *Trophies* and *Papiscus* was their failure to discuss the ecclesiastical hierarchy; neither mentioned the word "bishop." The *ekklēsiai* did not constitute an institution distinct from the empire, but one that was fully integrated. In these dialogues, Christianity was a polity rather than a religious community. It was defined by its political relationship to the empire on the one hand, and to the empire's opponents on the other. Dogmatically vague, its representative was a monk, not a bishop.

By contrast, the main character of *Gregentius* was a bishop. The church was not the polity of Christians whose ecclesiastical institutions had merged with the universal Roman Empire. It was the community of Christians, God's people, led by the bishops, who celebrated and enforced the community's covenant with God. *Gregentius* was explicit about the authority and role of the bishop. The bishop's apostolic succession guaranteed his legitimacy, and more, guaranteed the protection of the community: "And who are those saved from among the nations whom the Lord sends? . . . But of course they are the proclaimers of Christ, the bishops who have been ordained through apostolic succession to shepherd God's universal churches."[51] This legitimation of ecclesiastical authority through apostolic succession has no parallel in the Syrian dialogues. Quite the contrary, for all their claims that Christ was the head and defender of the church, the political and military threats to the church required a more worldly defender, the empire. *Gregentius,* which held a very different view of the threats to the church, could therefore also offer a very different definition of the church itself. By framing the threat to the church differently, the author of *Gregentius* could restructure the church to meet the challenges that the Persian and Arab invasions created.

The ending of the dialogue, whose miraculous denouement contrasts so sharply with *Trophies* and *Papiscus,* was the logical conclusion of a work that placed so heavy an emphasis on the bishop as the community's mediator, not only with Christ, but also with foreign powers. Gregentius was not confronting the Jews in the marketplace, but at the court of a foreign potentate. It is not unreasonable to suppose that the author, for whom Zacharias's trek into exile, Modestus's tenure during the Persian invasion, and Sophronius's negotiated surrender of the city to the Caliph were still fresh memories, might have framed the dialogue's setting with these bishops in mind.

Not only was Gregentius the brilliant dialectician who overwhelmed his opponents' logic and compelled Herbanus's admiration,[52] but well before the intercession of Christ, Herbanus also conceded the bishop's command of potent powers:

> I have heard that nowadays the prophets of the Christians, who have set themselves apart from the world, and gone into the deserts, perform many great signs. Why is this astounding? And since you yourself are one of these, you are not incapable of performing these if you wish to injure me. But rather, persuade me with words, and afterwards, if it seems right to you, do as you wish.[53]

Whoever "the prophets of the Christians" were, monks or stylites, they possessed no greater claim to work miracles than did the bishop. The narrative of the miracle had the goal of reinforcing the authority of the bishop and his claim to authority and power.

The bishop convincingly refuted Herbanus, but neither Herbanus nor the Jews were convinced. Finally, they demanded that Gregentius show them Christ. "Supplicate your Lord, if as you say he is in heaven, to come down so that I might see him."[54] The bishop then called upon Christ to appear miraculously.[55] Naturally, Jesus appeared, struck the Jews blind, and finally restored their sight when they were baptized. But significantly, Jesus attributed his appearance specifically to the prayer of his chosen representative on earth. "On account of the great entreaty of the archbishop, I appear to you [Jews]."[56] This manifestation of the bishop's power awed not only the Jews, but also "the king and his council with him, amazed, displaying great reverence to the archbishop, and revering him in every way with exceedingly great honor, were struck with fear."[57] Thereafter, the king honored the advice of Gregentius in matters of "peace, war and other subjects."[58] *Gregentius* demonstrated for its audience not only the Christian's superiority to the Jew, but also the bishop's superiority to foreign powers; the king of Tephar bowed to the superior wisdom and authority of the bishop.[59] The elevation of the bishop over a foreign king would have certainly pleased a Jerusalemite audience that had had three patriarchs in the last thirty years serve as intermediaries with foreign conquerors.

Given its ecclesiocentric direction, *Gregentius* treated "peace among the nations" very differently than did the Syrian dialogues. When Herbanus asked why Christ had not brought an "abundance of peace" according to Psalm 71:7, Gregentius responded without any hint of imperial renewal. It was the peace of the church to which the Psalm referred:

> The fullness of peace means the great charity of the churches of God that they possess among themselves. And the passage refers to the moon because it means the universal and apostolic church. And until the Lord arrives and the church passes away, until that time the peace of God will be manifested in the midst of the churches. And when the church passes away, then also when the consummation clearly is near, peace will appear from its midst."[60]

The Syrian churches had only spoken of the "peace of the churches" in the traditional triumphalist context. In *Gregentius,* on the other hand, the "peace of the church" was disassociated from imperial peace. It was the church, rather than the empire, that Gregentius welded into an apocalyptic scheme. Apocalypticism was unusual in the anti-Jewish dialogues, and the "passing away of the church" was itself an unusual formula, for it limited the church's venue to the earth. The church that would pass away was no abstract entity, a "city of God," but an earthly institution whose consummation would be the last act of the apocalypse.

This response to the Arab invasions strongly parallels the Palestinian Christian response that characterized Sophronius: an internalization of the conflict between Roman and barbarian and its redefinition as a struggle between demons and Christ in the hearts of the faithful. Equally significant, *Gregentius* and Sophronius defend Christianity by removing its imperial context. By contrast, almost all the non-Palestinian sources identified the Christian community with the imperial polity.[61]

Whether this disinclination to defend the imperial ideal was the consequence of orthodox disenchantment with the perceived heterodoxy of the Heraclian dynasty, the impact of Jerusalem's loss on the Palestinian Christian community, or personal idiosyncrasies of the author, the fact is that the military and political apologetic so assiduously built into the Syrian dialogues does not appear in *Gregentius*. Instead, the author divests Christian identity of its imperial elements, redefining the Christian community around the church. Structurally, bishop replaces monk as the protagonist; thematically, bishop replaces emperor as the personification of Christian authority, while the church replaces the empire as the institution of Christian social order. The enemies of the church also change in the new context of Christian social organization. The Arabs ceased to be the main enemy that the church faced. Heresy, the more properly "ecclesiastical" threat, replaced the "imperial" barbarian threat.

Yet despite the thematic differences between *Gregentius* and the Syrian dialogues, they similarly exploit the anti-Jewish genre for apologetic purposes. Even Herbanus's lively participation in the dialogue, quite different from the monosyllabic utterances of the Jews of *Trophies* and *Papiscus*, ultimately served the same purpose as in the Syrian dialogues. Thematic distinctions notwithstanding, Herbanus was the rhetorical mechanism through which the Christian community's doubts could be assuaged and its legitimacy affirmed. The racial argument of the text, whose vocabulary was not very different from that of *Trophies* and *Papiscus*, established the alien character of the Jew. In his overthrow, both historically at the hands of various conquerors and rhetorically at the hands of Gregentius, Christian superiority could be asserted. *Trophies* and *Papiscus* transfered the image of the Jew as persecutor to the new persecutors, the Arabs, and used the victorious model of martyrdom to defend the fallen empire. *Gregentius* did not choose this path and, rather than concentrate on the Jewish persecution, emphasized the Jew's rejection by God, loss of primogeniture, and the racial succession of the gentiles to God's favor.

The claims and counterclaims of Herbanus and Gregentius to possession of Jerusalem were more than simple anti-Christian or anti-Jewish polemic. Indeed, the dialogue's theology embraced political and social categories that had little to do with an intellectual conflict between Christian and Jew or between Monophysite and Chalcedonian. Orthodoxy in *Gregentius* is not simply theological, it is also a form of social self-definition. No explanation accompanies the catechetical recitation of the Chalcedonian creed. Rather, the Chalcedonian, Jerusalemite author rehearsed the passwords that allowed the community to recognize itself and its members. Theology, indistinguishable from its social and political context, was the basis of a redefinition of the Christian community that had been torn from the imperial orbit. In its effort to confront the changing political and social conditions brought by the Arab conquest, *Gregentius* represented one of the first tentative steps toward Christian reconciliation with imperial defeat.

Notes

1. See P. Brown, "Rise and Function of the Holy Man in Late Antiquity," *Journal of Roman Studies* 61 (1971): 80–101; S. Brock and S. Ashbrook Harvey, *Holy Women of the Syrian Orient* (Berkeley, 1986).

2. For earlier analysis of *Gregentius and Herbanus,* see A. Hulen, "The 'Dialogues with the Jews' as Sources for the Early Jewish Argument against Christianity," *Journal of Biblical Literature* 51 (1932): 65–70; J. Parkes, *The Conflict of the Church and the Synagogue: A Study in the Origins of Anti-Semitism* (New York, 1979 [1934]), 283–85; H. Schreckenberg, *Die Christliche Adversus-Judaeos-Texte und ihr literarisches und historisches Umfeld (1–11 Jh.)* (Frankfurt, 1982), 377–79. Among other anti-Jewish dialogues that have a "foreign" setting there is also the fascinating anti-Jewish dialogue *Das sogennannte Religionsgespraech am Hof der Sassaniden,* [*Texte und Untersuchungen* 4] (Leipzig, 1899), which has been dated to the sixth century, but whose inclusion of a pagan interlocutor makes it somewhat outside the temporal and structural limits of our inquiry.

3. Compare the use of the verb *politeuesthai* in *Disputatio Gregentii cum Herbano Iudaeo,* PG 86: 673a (hereafter, *Gregentius*) with George of Pisidia or Theodore Syncellus above.

4. A. C. McGiffert, *Dialogue between a Christian and a Jew entitled Antibolē Papiskow kai Philōnos Ioudaiōn pros monaxon tina* (New York, 1889), 92, considered this a lapse by the author.

5. *Gregentius,* 645d, 709b–c, 757d.

6. For *Timothy and Aquila* and *Athanasius and Zacchaeus,* [*Analecta Oxoniensia,* I.8], ed. F. C. Conybeare (Oxford, 1898), see *Gregentius,* ix–lvii; Schreckenberg, *Die christliche Adversus-Judaeos-Texte,* 391–92; A. Lukyn Williams, *Adversus Judaeos: A Bird's Eye View of Christian Apologetics* (Cambridge, 1935), 117–23.

7. *Gregentius,* 645d.

8. See Chapter 1.

9. See D. Olster, "Chalcedonian and Monophysite: The Union of 616," *Bulletin d'archeologie Copte* (1985): 93–108.

10. *Gregentius,* 688b–c.

11. Ibid., 641d. Herbanus naturally denies this, and claims instead that the biblical references offered by Gregentius refer to Solomon.

12. See ibid., 717c, that the devil made the Jews kill Christ; also see R. Wilken, *John Chrysostom and the Jews: Rhetoric and Reality in the Late Fourth Century* (Berkeley, 1983), 125–27, for the tradition of the Jews as Christ-killers.

13. See Chapters 2 and 4 for these authors.

14. *Gregentius,* 625a.

15. Ibid., 628c.

16. Ibid., 672b–c.

17. Ibid., 624a.

18. Ibid., 624c–d.

19. See Simon, *Verus Israel: A Study of the Relations between Christians and Jews in the Roman Empire (135–425),* trans. H. McKeating (Oxford, 1986), 186–96, on the Jews' claim that they have sole right to the Scriptures and the Law; Wilken, *Chrysostom,* 79–83, on the Christian Judaizers' implicit recognition of this claim.

20. Cf. A. Hulen "The 'Dialogues with Jews,'" 65–70. Herbanus's forcefulness led Hulen to conclude that the dialogue reflected historical Jewish anti-Christian arguments and was a response to them. Of course, Hulen was not aware that this argument dominated other Christian apologies, and thus Herbanus's argument, even if historical, still reflected the *Christian* author's intra-Christian apologetic.

21. *Gregentius,* 668a–b.

22. Ibid., 728c–d.

23. Ibid., 680c–d.

24. Ibid., 732–33.

25. Ibid., 676a.

26. Ibid., 680c.

27. Ibid., 637b.

28. Ibid., 637c.

29. Ibid., 629b.

30. Ibid., 680d.

31. Ibid., 729–32.

32. Ibid., 700b.

33. Ibid., 700a–b.

34. See R. Wilken, "The Restoration of Israel in Biblical Prophecy: Jewish and Christian response in the Early Byzantine Period," in *"To See Ourselves as Others See Us": Christians, Jews, "Others" in Late Antiquity,* ed. J. Neusner and E. Frerichs (Chicago, 1985), 443–71. Characteristically, Wilken claims that the seventh-century Jewish apocalypses, which we will review in Chapter 8, reflect a fourth-century Jewish claim to the holy land to which Jerome and other fourth-century Christians responded.

35. *Gregentius,* 673d.

36. Ibid., 700c–d.

37. Ibid., 693b.

38. Ibid., 729a.

39. See Chapter 4.

40. *Gregentius,* 701a.

41. Ibid., 757.

42. Ibid., 756–59. Gregentius made the charge of tyranny during a speech about Christ's defeat of the demons.

43. Ibid., 757.

44. *Gregentius'*s tentative offers of unity did not change the Jews' status as "true" gentiles. *Gregentius,* 676b, characteristically reversed the racial categories of Jews and gentiles: "Since you used the law that was given to you wrongly, and mixed with the gentiles and learned their ways, foolish one, God named you gentiles."

45. Ibid., 768d–69c. Christ's Law made Jewish practices obsolete.

46. Ibid.: 693c–d. The author called those Christians who failed to follow Christian Law *achristianos,* a rather rare word, and one that he would later identify with heresy.

47. Ibid., 693–94.

48. See C. von Schoenborn, *Sophrone de Jérusalem: Vie monastique et confession dogmatique,* [*Théologie historique* 20] (Paris, 1972), 83–85, 95–98. One finds a similar assumption of civil authority by Cyrus, the patriarch of Alexandria, during the Arab invasions; Theophanes, *Chronographia,* 2 vols., ed. C. de Boor (Leipzig, 1883), 1: 338.

49. *Gregentius,* 689.

50. The leading role of the bishop in the Jerusalemite community is strikingly

illustrated in a Syriac *Life of Maximus,* ed. and trans. S. P. Brock, "An Early Syriac Life of Maximus the Confessor," *Analecta Bollandiana* 91 (1973): 299–346. Ostensibly written by a member of Sophronius's entourage, who is also a Monothelete, it condemns Maximus as a heretic but defends Sophronius, whose attitude toward Monothelitism, while hardly tolerant, was overshadowed by his social and political role as a community leader and bishop. It is quite possible that the immediate material concerns of even such noted theologians as Sophronius were far more important than the orthodoxy of faraway Constantinople.

51. *Gregentius,* 700b.

52. Ibid., 664c.

53. Ibid., 756b.

54. Ibid., 773c–d.

55. Ibid., 776b–c.

56. Ibid., 777c.

57. Ibid., 777d.

58. Ibid., 781d.

59. See ibid., 781c. Admittedly, the king is Christian, but it is the foreign setting of the dialogue that gives the bishop's victory its significance.

60. Ibid., 641a–d.

61. When Gregentius refers to Christianity, he uses the word *Christianismos,* the only anti-Jewish author to do so; see ibid., 673d, 693b.

8. A Jewish-Christian Dialogue: The Exception to the Rule

The Syrian dialogues *Trophies* and *Papiscus,* and the Palestinian dialogue *Gregentius,* all written after the Arab conquest, differ from each other in a number of significant ways, but all pursue an apologetic agenda that exploits the rhetorical image of the Jew. Generic religious (and racial) stereotypes dominate the dialogues subordinating theological refutation to religio-political apologetic. These texts were meant to answer not the Jews, but the doubts that defeat had raised. These dialogues consistently reaffirm Christianity's integrity and Christian restoration; their goal was not to induce Jews to convert, but to convince Christians not to apostasize.

These structural and thematic similarities of the Syrian and Palestinian dialogues do not extend to the *Doctrine of Jacob the Newly Baptised.* Written before the full disaster of the Arab invasions had been revealed, it differs not only in its temporal frame of reference, but also dramatically in its social perspective, from all other generic representatives.[1] Besides Jewish antagonists, *Doctrine* has a Jewish protagonist, and Jacob's victory is no gentile victory over Jewish unbelief and obscurantism. *Doctrine* in fact almost entirely ignores the apologetic themes that dominate contemporary Christian literature. *Doctrine*'s view of the Roman Empire has no parallel and is by far the most pessimistic seventh-century view of the empire. Indeed, it is the only anti-Jewish dialogue that fails to affirm *any* form of Christian restoration — not simply imperial, like the Syrian dialogues, but even ecclesiastical, like *Gregentius* or Sophronius.

Historical references are rare in the later dialogues, even to the Arab invasions, the event that inspired their composition. This historical vacuum was intentional. The prefaces of *Papiscus* and *Gregentius* offer fifth- or sixth-century dates, a temporal sleight of hand that permitted the authors to avoid mentioning the unpleasant fact of defeat. *Doctrine,* by contrast, overflows with historical detail: the emperors Maurice, Phocas, and Heraclius; the newly arisen prophet Mohammed (in fact, this is one of the first Greek texts to mention Mohammed); the Persian invasion, and the defeat of

Sergius, *dux* of Palestine, by the Arabs. Even more extraordinary is *Doctrine*'s organization of this wealth of historical detail. Unlike the later dialogues, which by and large avoided extensive eschatological speculation, *Doctrine* employed a highly developed eschatological scheme to set these events into a coherent, and unique, apocalyptic scheme. How are we to explain this anomalous work? The explanation is rather surprising. Its unique social and political perspective hints that it is that rarest of anti-Jewish texts, one that is actually intended for the conversion of a Jewish audience.

Unlike the sterile stereotypes of *Papiscus* and *Trophies,* or even the lively but malleable Herbanus, *Doctrine*'s Jews possess a social as well as a religious identity. Jacob's opponent, Justus, has contempt for converted Jews, not only for their weakness, but also for their betrayal of the community. He would not eat with baptized Jews, who evidently did not forsake Jewish dietary restrictions, owing to the attendant social stigma rather than to religious scruple.[2] Even when he finally admits Christianity's truth, he still balks at baptism; his family in Sykamina would reject him as he had others, and he would not be able to convert them.[3]

Justus's contempt for the baptized Jews was also mixed with fear. When asked to speak with Jacob, he suspected that the Jews were setting a trap in order to denounce him to the authorities and curry favor with them. He only agreed to meet with Jacob when he received assurance that Jacob was just as fearful of the Christians. "Do not fear on Jacob's account . . . , nor does Jacob want the Christians to know, for he also fears them greatly and trembles."[4] The same suspicion was awakened when one of the Jews prepared to leave the "safe house" where they had met. Justus immediately assumed that he was going to fetch the Christians, and angrily accused him, "Where are you going so surreptitiously, bastard? Or do you want to betray me to the Christians?"[5]

Throughout the dialogue, Jacob must repeatedly reassure his audience that conversion to Christianity did not compromise the integrity of the Jewish community or leave a social taint. "If therefore one who believes in [Christ] should not be ashamed, we circumcised should believe in Christ and not be ashamed."[6] Neither Jacob nor any other speaker suggested assimilation with the gentiles. Any intercourse with the gentiles horrified the Jews, whatever faith and doctrine they shared. Jacob in particular objected to intermarriage. "For some of the Jews take gentile wives, and I have been much scandalized thereby."[7]

Papiscus, Trophies, and *Gregentius* completely ignored this social dimen-

sion of Judaism; their defense of Christianity in the face of Christian social
and political disaster required that Judaism be defined *only* as a discredited
religion, and that Jews be presented only as the personification of their
rejected faith. Those dialogues limited the social and political context of the
Jews to their persecution of Christ and Christians and their subsequent
punishment by God: the loss of their kingdom, the diaspora, and all the
other social and political phenomena of Judaism that were the consequence
of their failed religion. Similarly, they limited the social and political context of the Christians to the rewards of Christianity's truth: the empire or its
renewal, unbroken occupation of a Christian holy land, and above all, the
end of God's trials for his sinful but beloved people. The misanthropic Jews
in *Papiscus, Trophies,* and to a lesser extent, *Gregentius,* without a community
of their own, were defined by their exclusion. But *Doctrine*'s Jews possess a
social life and community distinct from the gentile world. Where *Papiscus,*
Trophies, and *Gregentius* subordinated the social dimension of the Jews
to the dialogues' apologetic needs, *Doctrine*'s setting and characters were
shaped to fit the social dimensions of Judaism.

Doctrine is alone in recognizing that the Jewish community had leaders
who represented it, and upon whom the burdens imposed by the imperial
authorities fell.[8] *Doctrine* also showed awareness that, in contrast to Christians, Jews did not organize their community around the synagogue.
Priests appear, but they hold no monopoly of religious doctrine, teaching,
or social authority. On the contrary, *Doctrine* shows a lively intellectual life
among the Jewish laity. *Doctrine*'s Jews were literate: Joseph, the author,
secretly recorded the dialogue so that the Carthaginian Jews could later
refer to it.[9] Jewish laymen founded schools: Jacob was himself a student of
Justus's father in Ptolemais.[10] Justus described debates between his father,
priests, and other laymen;[11] had himself written a treatise against conversion;[12] and arrived at the debate with Jacob with written materials.[13] Local
schools had their own exegetical traditions. Jacob amazed Justus not so
much with his memory and argumentation as with his originality. At one
point, Justus exclaimed, "As the Lord lives, that is not the teaching of my
father, [Justus's teacher]!"[14]

Only an author well acquainted with Jews and their social organization could have provided these insights into seventh-century Jewish life;
indeed, *Doctrine* might well be the only anti-Jewish work since Paul's *Epistle
to the Galatians* written by a converted Jew. Authorship is a point to which
we shall return, but it is highly suggestive that the participants' favorite

expletive for cursing each other is not a Greek word at all, but the Hebrew word *mamziros,* bastard, which is still preserved in Yiddish slang.[15]

The author reveals his knowledge of Jewish social life most clearly in his treatment of Jewish–Christian social relations. The protagonist, Jacob, was a merchant who did business with Christians as well as Jews.[16] But his relations with Christians were not always so congenial. As one Jew, who knew him before his conversion, explained: "Do I not know Jacob the son of Thanouma, a most clever and inventive man; the one who occasioned all sorts of evils for the Christians when Phocas was emperor and Bonosus [Phocas's general] was around?"[17] Jacob himself admitted a sanguinary youth, which he spent sailing around the eastern Mediterranean beating Christians wherever and whenever he could. He bashed their heads at Antioch, burned them alive in Constantinople, rioted against them in Ptolemais, and even incited them to kill each other in Rhodes.[18]

The author thus provided Jacob with impeccably violent anti-Christian credentials.[19] Jacob's murderous career against the Christians certainly fit the standard image of the Jew as persecutor. But *Doctrine's* treatment of Christian violence against the Jews hints that the author is not simply following generic stereotypes. Gregory the Eparch's brutal treatment might arouse the modern reader's sympathy for the Jews:

> And when we [Jews] were assembled, [Gregory] said to us, "Are you the servants of the Emperor?" And we answered and said, "Yes, lord, we are the servants of the Emperor." And he said, "His Goodness has ordered that you be baptised." And when we heard this, we were shaken and were filled with great fear, and none of us dared to say what he thought. And when he said, "Do you answer nothing?" one of us, Nonus by name, answered, saying, "We will do nothing right now, for it is not the time for the holy baptism." And angered, the eparch stood before him, and slapped him across the face. . . . And we were baptised whether we willed or no. And we were in great doubt and much sadness.[20]

Jacob himself was not only dragged to the font, but after his discovery and incarceration, was threatened with torture.[21] And while he is grateful that he has come to the true faith, he repeatedly refers to his manner of baptism as violent.[22] Such violence against Jews in Christian literature, especially anti-Jewish literature, is exceedingly rare;[23] Antiochus Monachus, *Papiscus,* *Trophies,* and *Gregentius* used the image of the defeated Jewish persecutor to point to the ultimate defeat of his spiritual successors, the Arabs or Persians. Seventh-century Christians played down Christian retaliation against Jews;

only Syriac and Coptic chronicles recorded Heraclius's forced baptism of the Jews. Theophanes mentioned the edict exiling the Jews from Jerusalem, but his narrative of the baptism of Benjamin of Tiberias scrupulously avoided any hint that Heraclius used force:

> And when Heraclius arrived in Tiberias, the Christians accused one Benjamin by name as one who did evil to them. . . . And the emperor asked him, saying, "Why did you do evil to the Christians?" And he said, "Because they were enemies of my faith," for he was a Jew. And then the emperor, after he had advised and persuaded him, baptised him. . . .[24]

After Benjamin's baptism Heraclius even honored him by staying with him. The entire episode, from the dialogue to the happy ending, strains the reader's credulity, but what Theophanes desired to stress was that no violence was offered to the self-confessed Jewish persecutor of Christians. The conversion of Benjamin was achieved through the emperor's persuasion. Violence and persecution are the allotted methods of Jews and heathens, not of Christians, and it makes *Doctrine* nearly unique that violence is used against, as well as by, Jews.

The forced baptism even made the author uneasy enough to offer a defense for this manner of conversion. But his defense of forced baptism was no defense of Christians. Like Antiochus Monachus, the author attempted to make sense of a recent persecution, yet do so without attributing divine favor (or at least more than his audience possesses) to the agents of persecution. Facing the same problem, it should be no surprise that the author offered nearly the same explanation as Antiochus: "And thus I believe that the merciful God, not wishing utterly to destroy the Jews, who have ever been the most antagonistic to God, commanded that the Jews should come to the light when they had been forcibly baptised."[25]

As Antiochus Monachus had asserted of Christian misfortunes, Jewish misfortunes were God's paradoxical means to save them. *Doctrine* presented the forced baptism as God's backhanded offer of salvation for the Jews. The Persians at Jerusalem and the Christians at Carthage play the same role: "Therefore, let none of us disdain the faith in Christ, lest, when we have fallen into such an indescribably great chaos of destruction, we not be saved, but rather, let us believe in Christ the king of glory, offering thanks to God and to the men through whom God commanded us to be baptised violently."[26] *Doctrine*'s defense of forced baptism explained gentile violence for its audience but did not excuse it. The gentiles, like the Persians, were merely God's brutal instrument, unknowingly opening the door to salvation. Significantly, Jacob offers no defense for the gentiles. They are merely the Jews' "rod of correction," God's unconscious agents of salvation.

Fear of gentiles pervades *Doctrine*. For the Jews to meet Jacob and then hold a debate, a "safe house" must be found that the gentiles do not suspect. Otherwise, the participants would be executed.[27] The audience swore not to take notes of the debate, and Joseph, the author, elaborately explained how and why he broke his oath and recorded this forbidden conversation.[28] At one point, Jacob and Isaac, one of his interlocutors, exchanged threats of denunciation:

> Jacob answered and said [to Isaac], " . . . Perhaps if the Christians heard you, they would not burn you?" Isaac answered and said, "You will not say anything evil to the Christians about me at any time, I think, miserable and evil Jacob. Do I not know what you did to the Christians . . . and how many you killed? And I will speak to them and they will kill you!"[29]

While this exchange might make the Jews look cowardly, it hardly shows the gentiles in the best light. Later, when the Jews asked Jacob to share his teachings with the gentiles, he demurred. On the one hand, he conceded that "when they pronounce that the Son and the Holy Spirit are one substance with the Father, or other mysteries or honored doctrines, they possess [knowledge] that we have still not comprehended." But he continued, "And in no way let them anathematize us as heretics! . . . For the Christians exile and anathematize bishops and Patriarchs for departing in their opinions just a little bit."[30] Jacob's praise of gentile doctrinal monopoly is leavened with a warning that Jews stand in grave danger of denunciation and excommunication. Jacob's amazement that Christians even anathematize each other for minor differences of opinion is another hint that the author was a Jew. Competing schools in Jewish intellectual life had little power to excommunicate opponents, and only a Jew would find such resolutions of doctrinal controversy peculiar.

The treatment of forced baptism, and of the gentile world in general, does not make it likely that *Doctrine* was written to legitimate forced baptism for a gentile audience or persuade them to accept new Jewish converts. Nonetheless, *Doctrine* intended, like many other seventh-century Christian texts, to reassure its audience that "the indescribable chaos of destruction" somehow had meaning. Unlike the other Christian texts, however, *Doctrine* was intended for a Jewish or Jewish–Christian audience. Thus, it is not surprising to find that the author "Judaized" the Christian apologetics to reassure forcibly baptized Jews that their sufferings were part of God's plan. Unlike *Papiscus* or *Trophies, Doctrine* did not try to reassure its audience that the old order would return. Nor like *Gregentius* did it offer an alternative Christian social and political order. For *Doctrine,* the Christian order in inescapable, and it does not so much urge conversion as resignation.

The Syrian dialogues end with the Jews' admission of defeat; *Gregentius* climaxes with Christ's own appearance on behalf of his beleaguered prelate and the baptism of the Jews. But in these dialogues, the Jews' conversion is far less important than their refutation.[31] The authors stressed repeatedly in the prefaces that affirming Christian superiority was their thematic concern, not the Jews' conversion. The narrative structure of these texts further reinforced this thematic design, for whether any Jews convert or not, all concede Christianity's superiority.[32] *Doctrine,* on the other hand, describes not only Justus' refutation, but also his conversion, his baptism, and his Christian education. Nearly half the dialogue takes place after Justus has admitted defeat, and his questions from this point are not objections, but requests for instruction; Jacob teaches Justus not only proofs of the Trinity or Christ's divinity, but the far more prosaic "Our Father" and Nicene Creed.[33] *Doctrine*'s unique narrative structure explains the *process* of Jewish conversion. *Papiscus* and *Trophies* assumed that Jews could not be converted. Their blindness was itself part of their punishment. And if *Gregentius* conceded such a possibility, its admission was hedged about with qualifications and the usual vituperative rhetoric of the anti-Jewish genre. By contrast, *Doctrine*'s structural manipulation implies that its main concern was the conversion of the Jews.

Doctrine's idiosyncratic manipulation of the generic *topoi* extended to generic attacks on Jews and Judaism. It was customary to describe the fall of Jerusalem and the destruction of the Jewish kingdom as a punishment for the crucifixion of Christ. Although *Doctrine* included this charge, it also transformed it. The author made an effort, unique in early Christian literature, to lessen or limit Jewish guilt for the crucifixion. Jacob explained that prophecies of Christ's death referred mostly to the Romans, who were given the greater responsibility for Christ's death. "Thus speaks the Lord, the God of Israel, who redeems you, 'Consecrate the one whose soul is despised, abhorred by the nations, the servants of rulers,' by Pilate and the soldiers."[34]

Doctrine then compared Pilate's command to the Jews, "Take him and crucify him," to the kings who ordered Jeremiah's death; both were guilty with those who advised them falsely.[35]

Naturally, the author did not place all the guilt on Pilate. But *Doctrine* only condemned *some* Jews. Jacob explained that the Jewish crucifiers were the "priests and scribes," the members of the tribes of Levi and Simeon: "Annas and Caiaphas, the miserable crucifiers of Christ, were from the tribe of Levi. And the scribes were from Symeon. Thus, when the blessed Jacob, father of us Jews prophecized, he said, 'Symeon and Levi have deliberately committed injustice; may my soul not enter into their counsel.'"[36]

When *Doctrine* described the punishment that God inflicted on the Jews, he carefully distinguished which Jews were punished. Jacob, asserting that as in the time of the prophets "however many did not believe in Jeremiah were taken into slavery," similarly held that "however many did not receive Christ were taken into slavery among all the nations, and scattered by the Romans."[37] In fact, *Doctrine* asserted that many Jews had believed in Christ, and that God had preserved them from the Roman devastation of Judea:

> But God commanded those Jews who believed in Christ, both before and after the crucifixion, through a divine vision that appeared before them, to leave [Judea], and ordered that they dwell across the Jordan in Pella, as the area was called. Thus, when the Romans conquered all the east, they destroyed the Jews in city and countryside, but they did not approach the Jews who believed in Christ at Pella, for they were guarded by the holy spirit.[38]

Doctrine adapted this story from Eusebius. But Eusebius asserted that the warning came to "the people of the church."[39] *Doctrine* inserted the Jews to change the emphasis from God's love for the gentile church, Eusebius' point, to God's love for the Jews.

Doctrine's argument against Judaizing continues the author's peculiar manipulation of generic *topoi* in order to limit the condemnation of the Jews.[40] Anti-Jewish literature condemned the Mosaic Law as a punishment for idolatry at Sinai.[41] Although *Doctrine* repeatedly admonished its audience not to Judaize,[42] it praised the Mosaic Law. Jacob compared the Mosaic Law to moonlight: weak, but light nonetheless with the sunlight of Christ's Law.[43] What is significant is not the metaphor, but its mild tone. "And I do not say, let it not be, that the moon and the stars are not good," they are simply obscured by darkness.[44]

Unlike the other dialogues, which condemned the law as the punishment of a reprobate and rejected race, *Doctrine* argued that Jews should turn to the "new" law of Christ precisely because it accomplished the ends of the Mosaic Law. The Mosaic Law was not a punishment; its limitations, not its inherent falsehood, disqualified it as the means of salvation. "See, my brothers, that the creation was not saved through the Law of Moses, but rather through another Law, a new Law that appeared."[45] The Mosaic Law had failed even to prevent idolatry among the Jews.[46] On the other hand, Christ was a *nomothetes* like Moses,[47] but one who fulfilled the goal of the Law, the destruction of idolatry.

In an interesting theological twist, *Doctrine* argued that God rejected the Mosaic Law only after the incarnation. "God hates the Judaizers and celebraters of the Sabbath, *since* the coming of Christ."[48] Such a historical distinction is unusual, especially in an author who knew and cited the *Epistle of Barnabus*, which condemned the Mosaic Law as a punishment inflicted on the Jews for their idolatry at Sinai.[49] It was this historical process, not divine punishment from Sinai, that compelled the Jews to leave "the evils of their fathers" and convert to the "new" Law of Christ.[50]

What is unusual about this formulation of Christ's mission is the assumption that the Jews did in fact have the knowledge of God; they were simply unable to apply it or to share it with the gentiles. Other anti-Jewish works asserted that Christ had come to save the gentiles and condemn the Jews. But *Doctrine* maintained that Christ, "the one who freed the cosmos from the error of idolatry," had come to admit "all the gentiles into the knowledge of God, as the prophets foretold; for the prophets said that the gentiles would be saved by Christ."[51] *Doctrine* interpreted Christ's epiphany as an expansion of the knowledge of God from the Jews to the gentiles, and through this, the removal of idolatry. Thus, the *topos* that the gentiles were a "new people," on which so much of the apologetic of *Papiscus, Trophies,* and *Gregentius* was based, was another reason for Jewish conversion: "If therefore, the exalted God of Abraham bears witness that this new people of the Christians worships the true God and possesses the correct faith, why then would we wish to Judaize and hold the Sabbath and revolt against God?"[52] As the true inheritors of the "Christian" revelation, the Jews should assume their birthright, not leave it to the gentiles. They had voluntarily surrendered their link with God, but if they converted, they would certainly be received back. While *Papiscus* and *Trophies* condemned the Jews as irretrievably cursed, and *Gregentius* held out hardly more hope for them, *Doctrine* sweetened the blow of their forced baptism with the restoration of their position as God's people.

In even sharper contrast to the traditions of anti-Jewish theology, *Doctrine* asserted that the Jews as well as the gentiles were the object of Christ's mission. Perhaps even more striking, *Doctrine* held that the Jews would preserve their identity even after their conversion. *Doctrine* interpreted Christ's kingship of the Jews literally; he was "our king," who took up his rule of the *believing* Jews when the foreigner Herod usurped the throne of David.[53] The Jews will share the glory of the kingdom of Christ, as an individual nation among the other nations who worship Christ; they will in no way be submerged in the mass of gentile worshippers. Jacob explained that the Jewish kingdom still, in theory, existed under the aegis of Christ, "For Judah and Israel and the nations that believe in Christ have one rule and one king, Christ."[54] The gentiles were not God's chosen people from the beginning but were permitted the privilege of participating in the covenant of the Jews: "For the worthy Jews, a large group, received Christ with the gentiles, and God spoke the truth, saying, 'I will establish a covenant for them with the beasts,' [Hosea 2:18] that is, with the gentiles. For those from the Jews and gentiles who believe in Christ have and possess one faith."[55] Both the characterization of the gentiles as beasts before Christ and the assertion that they were grafted onto the Jewish covenant were Pauline. What is surprising is that they are found six centuries later, in a genre that had long labeled the gentiles God's chosen people.

Doctrine claimed not only that Christ had come for the Jews, but also that the punishments they had received for killing Christ, their loss of a kingdom and despised condition, were reversible through conversion. The persistence of Jews in unbelief was the cause of their troubles. "For if we are unfaithful to him, all of the evils in Scripture will overtake us, both now and in the future."[56] But conversion made possible the restoration of the Jews as God's own people, and their return to the status of God's most favored race:

> "For all places will be filled with the knowledge of the Lord, as the breadth of water covers the sea. And in that day, the seed of Jesse will rise to rule the nations; the nations shall find hope in him." And Hosea says, "The children of Israel will seek the Lord their God and David their king, and will come terrified to the Lord and his goodness at the end of days." And the prophet says these things about us, the baptised Jews who have turned to God through Christ.[57]

The promise of Christ's return in glory and the restoration of his people is apocalyptic. For this reason, and once again in sharp contrast to *Papiscus, Trophies,* and *Gregentius,* the temporal dynamic of *Doctrine* is decidedly apocalyptic.

The first reaction of the Jewish leaders and Jacob, when they were ordered to submit to baptism, and Justus, when he was first told of the forced baptism, was that the time had not yet arrived.[58] Evidently, the author took it for granted that at least some Jews were prepared to be baptized when the Messiah arrived. His argument that the right time had arrived was the most important weapon in Jacob's missionary armory. His eschatological imperative led him to incorporate historical material that *Papiscus, Trophies,* and *Gregentius* ignored. His apocalyptic source, Daniel's prophecy of the four empires — Chaldean, Persian, "Greek" or Macedonian, and Roman — was commonplace.[59] But *Doctrine*'s assertion that the fourth empire, the Roman, was in decline and that its fall was imminent was unique in seventh-century literature. No other text from this period argued that the Roman Empire was about to fall; they asserted, in fact, just the opposite, that the Roman Empire, after severe trials, would emerge victorious, and that its victory would announce the apocalypse. Other apocalyptic works, like the *Apocalypse of Pseudo-Methodius* and the *Daniel Commentary,* incorporated contemporary events into their apocalyptic schemes, but also maintained that the Roman Empire was predestined to defeat the Arabs; Christ himself would save the empire from its heathen foes. But *Doctrine* held the overthrow of the emperor Maurice and the accession of Phocas in 602 to be the first sign of the empire's end:

> In Sykamina, we were standing near the house of Marianos after the killing of the emperor Maurice, and the leader of us Jews began to speak, saying, "Why are the Jews pleased that Maurice was killed and Phocas reigns through the shedding of blood? In fact, we have witnessed the lessening of the empire of the Romans. And if the fourth empire, that is, the Roman Empire, is shriveled, destroyed and overthrown, Daniel states exactly that there will verily be no other . . . , and immediately [will occur] the consummation of the world and the rising of the dead. And if this is so, we have erred in not accepting the Christ who has come, for the expected one who comes from the seed of Jesse in the name of the Lord, the Lord God, will come before the destruction and shriveling of the fourth beast, and of the ten horns.[60]

The consummation's imminent approach formed Jacob's most powerful argument for conversion. Yet it is an argument that opposed the entire thrust of seventh-century apologetic. Ironically, it was *Doctrine*'s Jews who insisted that the empire would yet be restored:

> Jacob said, "How does the Roman Empire seem to you? Does it stand as it has from its beginning, or has it declined?" Justus answered, "Even if it has somewhat declined, we hope that it will rise again, because Christ must first come during the time that the fourth beast, that is, the Roman Empire, has stood."[61]

Justus, Judaism's defender, asserted that the empire would be restored; Jacob, Christianity's defender, that the empire would shortly fall. *Doctrine* broke the apocalyptic link with imperial restoration that *Pseudo-Methodius* had so assiduously built.

Jacob's temporal and geographic perspective is wide. His analysis of the empire's fall includes not only the Persian War or early Arab successes, but also the empire's centuries-long decline:

> For from the ocean, that is, from Scotland and Britain, and from France, Spain, Italy, Greece and Thrace, and up to Antioch, Syria, Persia and all the east and south, and Egypt, Africa, and beyond Africa, the borders of the Romans and the boundary-posts of their emperors seemed composed of brass and ivory until today. For all the nations were subjected to the Roman Empire by the command of God, but today we see the Roman Empire humbled.[62]

In the sixth century, Agathias or Menander Protector could describe imperial reverses without admitting imperial decline. Agathias had ridiculed those who interpreted disasters in an apocalyptic framework. The Heraclian court, in quite different circumstances, had supported the restoration cycle of sin, repentance, and victory with its patronage. But *Doctrine* made no effort to equate imperial defeat with divine punishment, because there was no future for the empire. Since imperial collapse had nothing to do with Roman sins, repentance could not halt imperial decline. Imperial collapse was merely an inescapable step in an apocalyptic process inexorably set in motion: "For the flood of the peoples and the humbling of the Empire of the Romans signifies nothing else than that the ten horns, and ultimately the small horn, the devil, and the consummation of the universe are about to occur."[63] *Doctrine* made no effort to restore Christian confidence through the promise of imperial recovery. Jacob saw Rome entirely within the prophetic context of its fall; the mighty machine of Daniel's prophecy of the four empires would crush the Roman Empire.

This indifference (or even hostility) toward the empire is reflected in two related corollaries of Jacob's interpretation of Daniel: that the empire is *not* the only truly Christian nation, and that the empire does not uniquely possess the true church.[64] The identification of Christianity, both as a religion and as an institution, with the empire was a necessary corollary of imperial restoration: God's love for the Romans meant they monopolized God's religion. But *Doctrine,* far from identifying the empire as the agent of Christianization, asserted that Christian universality, another step in the apocalyptic process, depended on the empire's fall: "And we see the nations believing in Christ, and the fourth beast fallen and dismembered by the nations in order that the ten horns might rule, and Hermolaos, the little horn, Satan, might appear."[65] The nations' conversion as well as their conquest of the empire signaled the apocalypse. The Jews' salvation was linked to the nations' progress because it was their conversion (as we saw above) that would shame the Jews into following their example.

Christ's universal rule also underwent a transformation in *Doctrine*. He was the ruler of all nations, but he did not exercise his rule through the empire. Every nation was set under his sceptre, including the Jews. *Doctrine* discarded the imperial universalism that had dominated Christian Roman literature since Eusebius. Instead, the church was the universal divine institution because the Roman Empire no longer extended to the four points of the compass, but the church, by contrast, "is great because it rules from east to west and north to south," a church in which God had given his peoples "rulers in peace, and leaders in justice."[66] The term for leaders here is *episkopous*.

In some ways, this imperialization of the church approaches the presentation of the church in Sophronius or *Gregentius*. Certainly to the extent that restoration rhetoric appears in *Doctrine,* it applies to the church. On one occasion, a Jewish leader has a dream in which he sees "that the churches that the Jews had burned were built with gold and pearls, and shone like a light, and our synagogue, by the harbor, was destroyed."[67]

Gregentius used a similar image of the church to promote the continuity of Christianity as an institution, but never asserted its immediate apocalyptic consummation. *Trophies* used the universality of the church to support the empire's claims; wherever the church spread, the empire would conquer or reconquer. *Doctrine*'s imperialization of the church was quite different: *Doctrine* treated the Jews as an integral element of the church. The Roman Empire brought Jews and gentiles under one government, but the church united them under one faith.[68] The imperialized church was as necessary a part of the prophetic tradition as the Incarnation itself. "It is a great wonder that the prophets announced both Christ and the priests of the new covenant."[69] With the fall of the empire, the church inherited its mantle: "And God speaks about the bishops of the churches through Jeremiah, 'I will give you shepherds according to my heart, and they will watch over you, shepherding you with understanding.'"[70] As the empire receded, the knowledge of God brought by the church united man in the far more important struggle against the demons who promoted the sin of idolatry.[71] The final salvation of the gentiles, now accomplished through the church, marked the moment of the apocalypse to the Jews, and therefore the moment of their baptism and conversion. The "right time" had arrived.

Doctrine completed its apocalyptic analysis and its argument for the Jews' conversion by identifying not only the first sign of the apocalypse, Maurice's fall in 602, but also the last sign of the apocalypse, the recent arrival of a prophet from Arabia. Justus's brother Abraham wrote him: "For when Sergius the *Candidatus* was put to the sword by the Saracens, I was in Caesarea, and I went by ship to Sykamina. And they said, 'The *Candidatus* has been killed,' and we Jews were very joyful. And they said that a prophet had appeared, coming with the Saracens, and he proclaimed the arrival of the one to come, the expected one, Christ."[72]

Doctrine hinted that the Jews initially greeted Mohammed's arrival with high hopes that he was a prophet. When Justus is ready to return to Sykamina, Jacob upbraids him for a faint-hearted belief in Christianity and asks him what would happen if he were tortured by "the Jews who mix with the Saracens," evidently referring to Jewish followers of Mohammed.[73] *Doctrine,* however, takes some care to refute the claims of these "Islamicizing" Jews. Justus's brother Abraham asked an old and learned man if Mohammed was truly a prophet: "And he said to me, 'He is false. For the prophets did not come with sword and chariot! In fact, the events of today are the works of confusion, and I fear lest the first Christ who came, the one that the Christians worship, was himself the one sent by God and that we have received Hermolaos [the Antichrist] instead of him.'"[74] *Doctrine's* apocalyptic interpretation of contemporary history led back to the argument for the conversion of the Jews: the fall of the empire and the imminent appearance of the Antichrist proved that the first Christ is the true Christ.

This apocalypticism could only have been meant for a Jewish audience, its later appeal to Christians notwithstanding. The point of the apocalyptic discussion is to convince Jews that the apocalypse is imminent and that they must immediately convert. Jacob must overcome their expectations of Roman recovery in order to convince them that the apocalypse is near: "And we see all these events, and finally nothing else is left, except the flood of the nations, and I fear that the prophecy of Jeremiah [of desolation] is meant for the Jews who do not believe in Christ."[75] The defense of the empire by the Jews and the insistence on its collapse by the Christian protagonist is one of the most peculiar aspects of an altogether unusual text. It constitutes, with *Doctrine's* extraordinary promise of ultimate salvation and restoration for the Jews, themes that stand in opposition to the entire seventh-century anti-Jewish corpus, and indeed to the thematic thrust of seventh-century Byzantine literature in general. But the fall of Rome and the redemption of the Jews also link *Doctrine* to contemporary Jewish apocalypses, and suggest a source for its idiosyncratic apocalyptic bent.

The social and political turbulence of the seventh century shattered the accustomed social order for the Jews as well as for the Christians, and it is not surprising that Jewish eschatological interest intensified.[76] The so-called *Apocalypse of Zerubabel* is perhaps the best known of these, but *Signs of the Messiah* and other anonymous works offer important insights into the turmoil of the Jewish communities of the east. These texts, no less than the contemporary Christian sources, expressed the same dread and uncertainty, and also the same desire to set the confusion of their time within a comprehensible historical context.

Just as the same historical causes gave rise to both sets of texts, so also the soteriological scheme chosen by the Jewish apocalypses differed very little from contemporary Christian ones. Both found sin the source of their community's calamities, and repentance the only remedy. Zerubabel explained, "If you wish to be saved, pray and repent and the Messiah will arrive."[77] *Signs of the Messiah* was even more explicit, describing how repentance would bring the intercession of the archangel Michael: "Master of the universe, remember what you promised their ancestors; remember for their sake what you said to your faithful servant Moses (as it is written), 'I have pardoned you according to my word.' "[78] Nor did these texts fail to describe the Jews' restoration. The Jews would once more regain their kingdom and land and again sacrifice at Jerusalem.[79] What is odd is the literal echo of this idea in *Doctrine*. There, the conversion of the Jews was an opportunity for pardon, and Jacob implies that Jewish acceptance of Christ would restore the Jewish kingdom: "For if Christ, the one born of Mary, was not the elect of God, the one proclaimed by the Law, our race of the Jews would have been glorified and raised to imperial rule for killing and crucifying an antigod and sinner."[80]

The other anti-Jewish dialogues naturally used this argument against the Jews, but there is no hint in those texts that the Jews could ever possibly be rewarded. For *Doctrine,* the issue is not whether the Jews will be rewarded for their repentance, but when. *Doctrine* defends the Jews' forced baptism for precisely this reason: God has chosen to forgive his erring people, and now, "when we have fallen into such an indescribably great chaos of destruction,"[81] is the time that he has chosen to exercise his prerogative to forgive.

The most significant parallels between the Jewish apocalypses and *Doctrine*, however, lay in their characterizations of the Messiah and the Antichrist themselves. *Trophies, Papiscus,* and *Gregentius* all asserted that the Jews' expected Messiah would be the Antichrist. Their rather sketchy outline of the Jews' messianic expectations, furthermore, was built around the mistaken idea that the Jews expected only one Messiah, for whom they would mistake the Antichrist. The Jewish apocalypses differ completely from this "Jewish eschatology." They expected not one but two Messiahs, who are named, respectively, Nehemiah, son of Housieh, and Menachem, son of Ammiel.[82] Perhaps the best hint of *Doctrine*'s authorship and intended audience is its assimilation of this distinctive contemporary Jewish apocalyptic scheme. When Jacob asks Justus when the Messiah is due to arrive, Justus answers: "After sixty-nine weeks [of Daniel] and the cessation of all prophecy, then, after a time, will be the appearance of Hermolaos, the evil devil, and then will occur the great and shining day, the glory of Christ, the son of man of whom Daniel speaks."[83] When Jacob continues, "What then, do you say that there are two appearances [of the Messiahs]?" Justus answers, "Yes, as the Lord lives," and proceeds to prove their appearance from Scripture. While it should not seem surprising to anyone acquainted with the Jewish materials that the Jews should expect two Messiahs, such a notion is entirely alien to the Christian tradition of misrepresenting Jewish apocalypticism.

The Jewish apocalyptic scheme of two Messiahs brings the Jewish background of *Doctrine* into higher relief. Although the apocalypses express hostility to both Persia and Rome,[84] it is Rome that is portrayed as the greater enemy of the Jews. The Antichrist, Armilus, will arise from Rome.[85] According to Zerubabel, the Romans exile the Jews from Jerusalem just before the apocalypse. In this way, he incorporated Heraclius's expulsion of the Jews from Jerusalem into his apocalyptic framework.[86]

Armilus, the Antichrist, is the most obvious clue to *Doctrine*'s reliance on Jewish sources for its unique Christian apocalyptic perspective. Armilus, the "little horn" of Daniel, follows the royal "horns" of the prophecy.[87] Zerubabel explained the etymology of Armilus as "the destroyer of peoples," which derives from the Greek name Hermolaos.[88] In fact, an Armaleus turns up in Christian apocalypses, not as Antichrist, but as the king of Rome who received the promise of Rome's eternal rule.[89] Hermolaos also appears in *Doctrine,* but as the Antichrist: "For when the ten horns arise, and Hermolaos the evil one comes, there will be great confusion among the peoples."[90] The character of Armilus cannot be simply identified as a historical figure, but the Jewish authors may very well have used Heraclius to frame this apocalyptic metaphor of Rome. Zerubabel explained that Armilus's victories would cause the gentiles to believe in him, a possible reference to Heraclius's Persian victories.[91] The evolution of Armilus's genealogy also hints that the Jewish authors referred to Heraclius. Zerubabel, who followed an older Jewish tradition, referred to Armilus as the "Son of Satan, born of a stone."[92] "Signs," however, changed the parentage of Armilus to the "Son of the Cross," a redaction explained by Heraclius's return of the cross to Jerusalem.[93]

Not only do the messianic schemes of *Doctrine* and the Jewish apocalypses correspond. All emphasized the restoration of the Jews' kingdom. Of course, almost every Jewish apocalypse includes the restoration of the Jews' kingdom, and "Signs" and "Zerubabel" are no different.[94] But the more heavily reworked "Signs" set the restoration in a clearer seventh-century historical context. Initially, the king of Edom (that is, Rome) will fight a great battle against the Saracens, be defeated, and be pursued beyond Jerusalem, another assimilation of contemporary events.[95] The author, however, was not skillful at integrating contemporary events into a literary pattern. After the Romans' defeat, he simply announced the withdrawal of the Arabs so that he could return to his source's apocalyptic model.[96]

"Signs'" apocalyptic pattern, however, raises questions about its author's sources. In "Zerubabel," the Messiah, with angelic aid, kills Armilus, who is the companion of Gog, and immediately restores the kingdom of Israel:[97] an apocalyptic scheme with scant historical references. "Signs," which integrated contemporary events to a far greater degree, has the Messiah destroy not the Antichrist Armilus, but the "king of Edom," while Armilus appears later.[98] The author of "Signs" clearly reworked the chronology of "Zerubabel." Not only did "Signs" change the character and role of Armilus to fit contemporary events better, but it added an odd passage that is not borrowed from a Jewish source at all. Before the king of Edom is destroyed, he performs an interesting ceremony at the sanctuary in Jerusalem: "When Manzur [the Saracen king] retreats, the king of Edom will return [to Jerusalem]. . . . He will take the crown which is on his head, and depositing it on the stone, he will say, 'I return to you that which my ancestors have taken.'"[99] This ceremony of the Edomite king has no other Jewish parallels; its only parallel is the *Apocalypse of Pseudo-Methodius* and its associated texts. Thus, the author of "Signs" assimilated not only contemporary events into his apocalypse, but also contemporary Christian apocalyptic schemes.[100]

The Arab invasions inspired the Christians to write anti-Jewish texts; they inspired the Jews to write anti-Christian texts. The anti-Jewish writings identified the Jew with all the doubts that Christians themselves might have felt in the face of political and military disaster; the *Doctrine* and the Jewish apocalypses hint at a similar crisis that the Persian War, Heraclian persecution, and Arab invasions provoked among the Jews. Not only were Jewish and Christian apocalyptics thematically related, but also they seem to have drawn on each other for material. The author of "Signs" does not seem to have had any qualms about using Christian apocalyptic sources; a similar interpenetration of Christian and Jewish historical and apocalyptic schemes and visions explains the strange hybrid text, *Doctrine*. *Doctrine* represents a second step from the assimilation of Christian literary themes and *topoi* to actual conversion with the consequent assimilation of traditional Jewish apocalyptic elements in Christian literature.

Doctrine is the exception that proves the rule. An anti-Jewish work that is addressed to Jews, it departs structurally, thematically, and theologically from *Trophies, Papiscus,* and *Gregentius*. More importantly, however, it shares the same desire to make sense of the disasters that have struck the community. Its eschatology, drawn at least in part from Jewish sources; its partial defense of Jews against the charge of killing Christ; and its bifurcated view of Jewish-Christian and gentile-Christian salvation, depart strikingly from common Christian theology. It is the only seventh-century anti-Jewish dialogue whose theology is more than another recital of plodding clichés. But whatever interest the theology of *Doctrine* might hold for the historian of dogma, its unusual theology reveals to the historian how theology also expressed social and political apologetic. One could not identify its audience or author, or recognize its distinctive theology, without also realizing how the effects of the Persian and Arab Wars, the forced conversion of the Jews, and their social position within Christian society framed its composition.

Notes

1. For the date and character of the dialogue, see J. Parkes, *The Conflict of the Church and the Synagogue: A Study of the Origins of Anti-Semitism* (New York, 1979 [1934]), 285–87; H. Schreckenberg, *Die christliche Adversus-Judaeos-Texte und ihr literarisches und historisches Umfeld (1–11 Jh.),* (Frankfurt, 1982), 347; P. Crone, *Hagarism* (Cambridge, 1977), 4; and W. E. Kaegi, Jr., "Initial Byzantine Reactions to the Arab Invasions," *Church History* 10 (1969): 141–42, 147; G. Dagron and V.

Déroche, "Juifs et Chrétiens dans l'Orient du VIIᵉ siècle," *Travaux et Mémoires* 11 (1991): 246–47. Of these, only Kaegi and Dagron make any effort to relate the *Doctrine* to contemporary events.

2. *Doctrine:* 62, and see below. *Doctrine's* description of the forced baptism differs from that of Maximus (see Chapter 3) because only the Jewish leaders are baptized, not their families.

3. Ibid., 88.

4. Ibid., 53.

5. Ibid., 54.

6. Ibid., 38.

7. Ibid., 41.

8. See Chapter 4 on the forced baptism of the Jews.

9. *Doctrine,* 42–43.

10. Ibid., 63.

11. Ibid., 63.

12. Ibid., 53.

13. Ibid., 53.

14. Ibid., 62–63. Of course, the author could have purposely minimized the synagogue's role in Jewish life. But there is no compelling evidence in *Doctrine* to suppose that the synagogue played the same role in the Jewish community that the church did in the Christian.

15. Ibid., 39, 54.

16. Ibid., 2, 90–91. One of his Christian business partners even provided him with a "safe conduct" that was to exempt Jacob from the forced baptism at Carthage.

17. Ibid., 17.

18. Ibid., 89.

19. This evidence does not prove that before the Persian occupation Jewish–Christian relations had degenerated into chronic armed violence. Doubtless there was an atmosphere of hatred between Jews and Christians, as between Monophysites and Chalcedonians, but except during the Persian occupation, when Jews in Ptolemais burned the church, *Doctrine,* 69, all Jacob's attacks on Christians took place as a member of a circus faction, or as a supporter of Heraclius or Phocas during the civil war of 608–10; see D. Olster, "The Politics of Usurpation in the Seventh Century: The Reign of Phocas (602–10)," diss., University of Chicago, 1986, 225–62, for the social and political tensions and urban violence in the cities of the Levant before the Persian War; A. Cameron, *Circus Factions: Blues and Greens at Rome and Byzantium* (Oxford, 1976), 149–52, 281–85, 290–93, for the role of religion in urban violence in late antiquity. The Persian occupation ignited Jewish attacks on Christians and Christian retaliation against the Jews, because it unleashed social tensions and loosened the social fabric (which heightened individual identification with a religious group).

20. *Doctrine,* 1–2.

21. Ibid., 2.

22. Ibid., 39, 54.

23. For example, the Jews at Tomei voluntarily convert after being bested in a

debate with a local monk, see Anon., "Histoire de la conversion de Juifs habitant la ville de Tomei en Egypte d'aprés d'ancíens manuscrits arabes," trans. R. Griveau, *Revue de l'orient chrétien* 13 [ser. 2, 3] (1908): 306.

24. Theophanes, *Chronographia,* ed. C. de Boor, 2 vols. (Leipzig, 1883), 328.

25. *Doctrine,* 68.

26. Ibid., 79.

27. Ibid., 3.

28. Ibid., 42–43.

29. Ibid., 39–40.

30. Ibid., 48.

31. Cf. Schreckenberg's discussion of the role that the Jews' admission of defeat plays in the structure of the anti-Jewish dialogues, *Adversus-Judaeos-Texte,* 26–27.

32. The "Conversion of the Jews of Tomei" is an exception that described the process of Jewish conversion and assimilation. But see, on the other hand, the seventh-century *Historia conversionis Abramii Judei, Acta sanctorum* 12, (Oct. 28): 762–69, which has far less to do with the Jews than with imperial military palladia.

33. *Doctrine,* 88.

34. Ibid., 50.

35. Ibid., 84.

36. Ibid., 24.

37. Ibid., 84.

38. Ibid., 21.

39. Eusebius, *Ecclesiastical History,* ed. E. Schwartz, 3 vols. (Leipzig, 1903–09), III.5.

40. See Simon, *Verus Israel: A Study of the Relations between Christians and Jews in the Roman Empire (135–425),* trans. H. McKeating (Oxford, 1986), 306–38; R. Wilken, *John Chrysostom and the Jews: Rhetoric and Reality in the Late Fourth Century* (Berkeley, 1983), 158–60, for a discussion of the themes of Judaizing and Sabbatizing in anti-Jewish literature. Both authors naturally concentrate on the Christian worry about Judaizing within the Christian community.

41. See Simon, *Verus Israel,* 163–73; Parkes, *Conflict,* 95–97; R. Reuther, *Faith and Fratricide* (Minneapolis, 1974), 149–65, on Mosaic Law. The Law as a punishment is a literary tradition that goes back to *The Epistle of Barnabas.* Significantly, the author twice cites *The Epistle of Barnabas* and thus must have been acquainted with the generic attacks on the origins and purpose of the Mosaic Law. His rejection of this tradition, therefore, must be considered yet further evidence of his effort to ameliorate the more extreme attacks on the Jews in order to promote his own prosletyzing efforts; see *Doctrine,* 6, 35.

42. See *Doctrine,* 9, 15–16, 27, 31, 49, 72–74; the other dialogues, whose audience was Christian, largely ignored this issue.

43. Ibid., 10–11.

44. Ibid., 11.

45. Ibid., 9.

46. See ibid., 8, 19, 29, 83; ibid., 71 discusses the Mosaic Law in the context of the prophecy of Daniel.

47. Ibid., 8.

48. Ibid., 16.

49. See ibid., 6, 35.

50. Ibid., 37.

51. Ibid., 19; cf. also 8, 14.

52. Ibid., 15.

53. Cf. ibid., 19–20.

54. Ibid., 56.

55. Ibid., 66.

56. Ibid., 18.

57. Ibid., 57.

58. Ibid., 52–53; see also the Jews' objections at their forced baptism, 1–2.

59. Ibid. 59–60. On the political agenda of Byzantine eschatology, see G. Podskalsky, *Byzantinische Reichseschatologie, Die Periodisierung der Weltgeschichte in den 4 Grossreichen (Daniel 2 und 7) un dem tausendjaehrigen Friedensreiche (Apok. 20.)* (Munich, 1972), esp. 71–74, 43–47 for the anti-Jewish dialogues; Klaus, *Die Daniel-Diegesis,* esp. 32–39; P. Alexander, *The Byzantine Apocalyptic Tradition* (Berkeley, 1985), esp. 180–84. See also the discussion of Pseudo-Methodius above.

60. *Doctrine,* 63, cf. also 59.

61. Ibid., 60.

62. Ibid., 62.

63. Ibid., 88.

64. See Alexander, *Tradition,* 52–60, on the evolution of *Pseudo-Methodius*'s views of the relationship of church and empire, and the characterization of the Romans as a Christian nation.

65. *Doctrine,* 60.

66. Ibid., 71.

67. Ibid., 69. *Doctrine* explained away the visible evidence of the church's defeat, through its visible restoration after Heraclius's victory.

68. See ibid., 56, 66.

69. Ibid., 72.

70. Ibid., 72.

71. See ibid., 13, 14, 19.

72. Ibid., 86.

73. See ibid., 87–88.

74. Ibid., 86.

75. Ibid., 72.

76. See A. Sharf, "Byzantine Jewry in the Seventh Century," *BZ* 48 (1955): 109–12. At least three seventh- or early eighth-century Jewish apocalypses survive; L. Marmorstein, "Les signes du Messie," *Revue des Études Juives* 52 (1906): 176–86; I. Lévy, "Une apocalypse Judéo-arabe," *Revue des Études Juives* 67 (1914): 178–82; Lévy, "L'Apocalypse de Zerubabel," *Revue des Études Juives* 68 (1914): 131–60. See also, for the Jewish interpretation of the "weeks of Daniel," I. Lévy, "Les soixante-dix semaines de Daniel dans la chronologie juive," *Revue des Études juives* 51 (1906): 161–90, esp. 173–75.

77. "Zerubabel," 157; see also Zerubabel's own repentance, ibid., 145, and the cries of Israel to the Lord, ibid., 153.

78. "Signes," 186.

79. See "Zerubabel," 150, 151; "Signes," 185; "Apocalypse Judéo-Arabe," 179. The victory of Nehemiah ben Housiel over the king of Edom does not explicitly state that sacrifices will be renewed, but the orders of Armilius imply that it had. The "Judeo-Arab" text, dating from the eighth century, states that "Moawia," an Arab ruler, would "rebuild the walls of the temple."

80. *Doctrine,* 58.

81. Ibid., 79.

82. See "Zerubabel," 151; "Signes," 185, for Nehemiah; see "Zerubabel," 154; "Signes," 186, for Menachem.

83. *Doctrine,* 59.

84. See "Zerubabel," 146, for Rome; ibid., 151, for Persia.

85. See ibid., 147, 152, 153, 159; "Signes," 185.

86. "Zerubabel," 153.

87. See ibid., 149–50, 153 n. 1.

88. See ibid., 152, esp. 152 n. 6.

89. Pseudo-Methodius, *Apocalypse des Ps.-Methodios* [*Bertraege zur Klassischen Philologie* 83], ed. A. Lolos (Meisenheim am Glan, 1976), 86; see Alexander, *Tradition,* 57–59.

90. *Doctrine,* 74, see also 59, 70–71, 76.

91. "Zerubabel," 153, see also 152, on how Armilus is a mighty warrior.

92. Ibid., 147.

93. "Signes," 185.

94. See "Zerubabel," 155; "Signes," 185.

95. "Signes," 185.

96. Ibid.

97. "Zerubabel," 154–55, 160.

98. "Signes," 185.

99. Ibid.

100. Marmorstein's suggestion, "Signes," 179–80, that "Signes" had a Palestinian provenance was based, in part, on "Signes"'s interest in the king of Edom's presence at Jerusalem, the sanctuaries at Jerusalem where the king's ceremonies were performed, and on the invasions of Palestine by the Arabs. He would hesitantly suggest a Syrian connection by which the author would have become acquainted with the Pseudo-Methodius apocalyptic tradition. Similarly, the Judeo-Christian apocalyptic scheme of "Signes" hints that the work might have shared the Syrian provenance of *Doctrine.*

Conclusion

Seventh-century literature reveals the Christian preoccupation with the collapse of the imperial world-order in the wake of the Arab, Persian, and Slav invasions. But their preoccupation with defeat did not find primary expression through the historical genres. Classical biography disappears entirely. Theophylact Simocatta is not only the sole extant historian from the seventh century, but the sole known historian, and he chose to narrate the victories that closed the sixth century, not the defeats that opened the seventh. From the *Paschal Chronicle* at the end of the 620s to Theophanes' *Chronicle* at the beginning of the ninth century, there is no extant chronicle, and Theophanes' narrative poverty testifies to the Christians' reluctance to face defeat. Christians may have been preoccupied with defeat, but they had no interest in recording it. They had far less interest in what had happened than in how the past would be restored.

A sudden rejection of classical rhetoric and genres does not explain the disappearance of historical writing from Byzantium. The explanation lies in the Christian Roman rejection of history itself. Acutely aware of the disaster around them, they sought refuge in the glories of their past and the hope of their return. Seventh-century disasters firmly fixed the return of the imperial world-order in the Christian Roman psyche, and there it remained until the empire's end. The need to redefine the chaos around them inspired an apologetic of restoration, and they chose literary vehicles with this purpose in mind.

This reordering of Christian Roman historical priorities explains the prominence of previously unexploited genres. Apocalyptic was the history of the imperial restoration to come; martyrology achieved the fusion of imperial with Christian victory. And throughout all seventh-century Christian Roman literature, the Christian Romans' sins explained defeat without sacrificing God's love or limiting God's power: a necessary apologetic for Christianity itself. Christians did not turn to such literary themes and genres simply for solace, but for self-justification and future hope.

Nonetheless, despite the appropriation of similar themes, seventh-century literature expresses an exceptionally wide range of reactions to events. The apologetic responses are so varied precisely because their social and political contexts defined them. In Syria, the collapse of the God-guarded empire removed the Melkite's greatest support of their orthodoxy, the power to impose their opinions, and challenged them with this apparent proof of their heterodoxy. Jacobites and Copts, by contrast, found proof of their orthodoxy in imperial collapse. Indeed, of the three competing Syrian Christian sects, Jacobites, Melkites, and Nestorians, it was the Nestorians — who had long experienced Persian rule, and for whom the Arab conquest was merely a change of heathen masters — who most successfully accommodated themselves to their new conditions. Not surprisingly, the Melkites were the least successful.

The orthodox communities themselves, Constantinopolitan, Syrian, and Palestinian, were as different from each other as they were from their Christian competitors. Their responses were dictated not by the Christianity they confessed, but by the divergent social and political problems that the invasions raised within each community. In Constantinople, writers dominated by the court continued to play on triumphal themes in deference to the needs of their patrons, Heraclius and Sergius. In Palestine, the profound impact of Jerusalem's double loss within a single generation led to a radical revision of the traditional identification of Christian and Roman to produce a new definition of the Christian community that could survive the loss of its empire in a way that the Syrian Melkites, faced by the Jacobites, could not. The insecure and despairing Jerusalemite congregation inspired Sophronius's ecclesiastical redefinition of Christian victory and renewal, just as much as the political needs of a usurper and seemingly defeated emperor inspired George of Pisidia.

Seventh-century Christian Roman literature did not directly address the social and political dimensions of defeat; the vocabulary did not exist. What seventh-century authors possessed were rhetorical traditions that supplied the form, and in many ways determined the substance, of their works. The rhetorical tradition found causation in the moral sphere, and restoration, both imperial and ecclesiastical, consequently claimed a moral source. This obviously religious context in which the causative role of God's anger is set, however, should not mislead us into thinking that religion was not intimately tied to its social and political context. Even more should we avoid the conclusion that any sort of religious "intensification" took place. People felt fear and looked to God to free them from it. But the consequences of God's anger may have been less conducive to

Christian belief than those of God's favor. For while imperial success argued that Christianity was the religion favored by God, imperial defeat was just as convincing that Christianity was not God's favored faith. The conversion of Christian Syria, Palestine, and Egypt to Islam had many causes, but not the least was the Christians' final resignation (or despair), by the end of the eighth century, that the empire was not returning, and that Allah, not Christ, might be, after all, the one true God.

The anti-Jewish texts reinforce and extend the conclusions that we have drawn from seventh-century Byzantine literature as a whole, and show how artificial is the supposed thematic divide between "classical" and "Christian" genres. Few seventh-century texts more brazenly claimed Christianity's imperial superiority; fewer still so directly confronted the fragility of that claim. The apologetic rhetoric of restoration, which some-times appeared ungainly in other generic settings, fit the anti-Jewish genre perfectly. Unlike the other genres of the seventh century, the anti-Jewish dialogues did not compel the Christians to argue their case from their strengths. They could instead, and far more successfully, argue their case from their opponents' weakness. The Christian Romans' racial superiority, continuing possession of empire or cult center, and intellectual command over the Jews permitted these authors to set Christian disaster against a very different background: one that softened the shock of defeat with the cushion of others' misfortunes.

The Jews were the nominal target of Christian polemic, but they did far better service as a rhetorical device for Christian apologetic: not only as a well-defined enemy in whom the Christians' self-doubt could be person-ified and exorcised, but as a substitute for the Arabs. Scholars have noticed the curious hesitancy with which Christians took up the pen against Islam. Not until the mid-eighth century did John of Damascus compose the first anti-Islamic treatise, and not until the end of the eighth century and into the ninth century did authors within the political boundaries of Byzantium begin to write against Islam. *Trophies, Papiscus,* and *Gregentius,* in different ways, illustrate how Christians confronted victorious Islam through victory over the Jews, and thereby legitimated Christianity and promised restora-tion. Nor were Christians alone in exploiting racial claims to divine favor for apologetic ends. The *Doctrine of Jacob the Newly Baptized,* different in many ways from its gentile counterparts, still shares their same fears of chaos and destruction, and offers the same responses based on cultural assumptions about race, religion, and divine favor.

Students of Christian Roman history are tempted to believe in a past spirituality unsullied by such mundane concerns as victory or defeat. But it is we moderns, who, with our science, separate spirit and matter, losing ourselves in mystification. The realm of the spirit was far closer to the flesh in the seventh century than most moderns might wish to believe, and religion far better integrated into the political culture than many might expect.

In the end, the study of these works reveals to us a cultural ambience not so different from our own: a period of decline and instability in which contemporaries searched intently for an explanation of why things had gone wrong. Perhaps most similar to our own time, they found the same answers in moral causation: that moral failure was the cause, and moral regeneration the panacea. And perhaps all too human, the Christian Romans discovered all too much of their virtue by examining the failings of others.

Bibliography

ORIGINAL SOURCES

Agapius of Menbidj. *Kitab al-'Unvan.* Trans. A. A. Vasiliev. *PO* 8. Paris, 1912.

Agathias. *Historiarum libri quinque.* Ed. R. Keydell. Berlin, 1967.

Ammianus Marcellinus. *Res Gestae.* Ed. C. V. Clark. 2 vols., Berlin, 1910–15.

Anastasius Apocrisarius. *Relatio motionis inter Maximum et principes. PG* 90: 109–29.

Anastasius Sinaites. *Sermo iii in imaginem dei. PG* 89: 1152–80.

Anonymous. *Acta sancti Anastasii Persae.* Ed. H. Usener. *Prgramm,* Bonn, 1894.

Anonymous. *Dialogue between a Christian and a Jew entitled Antibolē Papiskou kai Philōnos Ioudaiōn pros monaxon tina.* Ed. A. C. McGiffert. New York, 1889.

Anonymous. *The Dialogues of Athanasius and Zacchaeus and of Timothy and Aquila,* [*Analecta Oxoniensia,* I.8]. Ed. F. C. Conybeare. Oxford, 1898.

Anonymous. *Disputatio Gregentii cum Herbano Iudaeo. PG* 86.

Anonymous. *Die griechische Daniel-Diegēsis.* Ed. K. Berger. Leiden, 1976.

Anonymous. *Doctrina Jacobi nuper baptizati* [*The Doctrine of Jacob the Newly Baptised*]. Ed. N. Bonwetsch. [Abhandlungen der Koenigen Gesellschaft der Wissenschaften zu Goettingen, phil.-hist. Klass, n.s. 13] Goettingen, 1910.

Anonymous. "Histoire de la conversion des Juifs habitant la ville de Tomei en Egypte d'après d'anciens manuscrits arabes." Trans. R. Griveau. *ROC* 13 [ser. 2, 3] (1908): 298–313.

Anonymous. *Historia conversionis Abramii Judei. Acta sanctorum* 12 (Oct. 28): 762–69.

Anonymous. *Das sogennannte Religionsgespraech am Hof der Sassaniden.* Ed. E. Bratke. [*Texte und Untersuchungen* 4]. Leipzig, 1899.

Anonymous. *Sermo de Miraculo Beryti. PG* 28: 797–805.

Anonymous. *Les Trophées de Damas, controverse judéo-chrétienne du VIIᵉ siècle.* Ed. G. Bardy. [*PO* 15]. Paris, 1927.

Antiochus Monachus. *Epistle to Eustathius. PG* 89: col. 1421–28.

Antiochus Monachus. *La Prise de Jerusalem par les Perses,* [*Corpus scriptorum christianorum orientalium,* scriptores georgi 203]. Ed. and trans. G. Garitte. Louvain, 1960.

"L'Apocalypse de Zerubabel." Ed. and trans. I. Levi. *Revue des Études Juives* 68 (1914): 131–60.

"Une apocalypse Judéo-arabe." Ed. and trans. I. Levi. *Revue des Études Juives* 67 (1914): 178–82.

Pseudo-Athanasius of Alexandria. *Quaestiones ad Antiochum ducem. PG* 28: 597–709.

Bar-Penkayē (*Sources syriaques,* vol. 1). Ed. and trans. A. Mingana. Leipzig, 1908.

Bar-Penkayē. Trans. S. P. Brock. "North Mesopotamia in the Late Seventh Century: Book XV of John Bar Penkayē." *Jerusalem Studies in Arabic and Islam* 9 (1987): 51–75.

The Chronicle of 1234. Trans. J.-B. Chabot. *Chronicon ad annum 1234 pertinens, Corpus scriptorum Christianorum orientalium*, scriptores Syri, ser. 4, vol. 14. Paris, 1920.

Dio Chrysostom. *First Discourse on Kingship.* Ed. G. de Budé. Leipzig, 1916, 1919.

———. *Third Discourse on Kingship.* Ed. G. de Budé. Leipzig, 1916, 1919.

Flavius Cresconius Corippus. *In laudem Iustini Augusti minoris libri iv.* Ed. and trans. Av. Cameron. London, 1976.

———. *Iohannidos.* Ed. and trans. J. Diggle and F. Goodyear. Cambridge, 1970.

Pseudo-Dionysius of Tell-Mahré. *Chronique de Denys de Tell-Mahré, quatrième partie.* Trans. J.-B. Chabot. Paris, 1895.

Eusebius. *Church History.* Ed. E. Schwartz, 3 vols. Leipzig, 1903–09.

———. *Tricennalia Oration.* Ed. I. A. Heikel. Leipzig, 1902.

———. *Vita Constantini.* Ed. I. A. Heikel. Leipzig, 1904.

Eutychius of Alexandria. *Annales.* PG 111.

Evagrius Scholasticus. *Ecclesiastical History.* Ed. J. Bidez and L. Parmentier. London, 1898.

Fredegarius. *Quellen zur Geschichte 7. und 8. Jhr.* Ed. A. Kusternig. Darmstadt, 1982.

George the Monk. *Chronicon.* Ed. C. de Boor, 2 vols. Leipzig, 1904.

George of Pisidia. *Bellum Avaricum.* Ed. A. Pertusi. *Giorgio di Pisidia, Poemi: I. Panegirici epici.* Ettal, 1959.

———. *Carmina inedita.* Ed. L. Sternbach. *Georgii Pisidae carmina inedita, Wiener Studien* 13 (1891): 1–62.

———. *Contra Severum.* PG 92:1621–1675.

———. *Expeditio Persica.* Ed. A. Pertusi. *Giorgio di Pisidia, Poemi: I. Panegirici epici.* Ettal, 1959.

———. *Heraclias.* Ed. A. Pertusi. *Giorgio di Pisidia, Poemi: I. Panegirici epici.* Ettal, 1959.

———. *Hexameron.* PG 92:1125–1578.

———. *In Bonum patricium.* Ed. A. Pertusi. *Giorgio di Pisidia, Poemi: I. Panegirici epici.* Ettal, 1959.

———. *In Heraclium ex Africa redeuntum.* Ed. A. Pertusi. *Giorgio di Pisidia, Poemi: I. Panegirici epici.* Ettal, 1959.

———. *In restitutionem S. Crucis.* Ed. A. Pertusi. *Giorgio di Pisidia, Poemi: I. Panegirici epici.* Ettal, 1959.

George of Pisidia (?). *L'encomio di s. Anastasio Martire Persiano. AB* 76 (1958): 5–63.

Greek and Latin Authors on Jews and Judaism. Ed. M. Stern, 3 vols. Jerusalem, 1976–84.

Herrdian. *Historiae ab excessu divi Marci libri octo.* Ed. C. Stavenhagen. Stuttgart, 1967.

Isocrates. *Panegyricus.* Vol. 1. Ed. G. Benseler and F. Blass. Leipzig, 1913.

Jacob of Edessa. *Chronicon.* Trans. E. W. Brooks. *Corpus scriptorum Christianorum orientalium*, scriptores Syri, ser. 3, vol. 4. Paris, 1903.

Justin Martyr. *Dialogue with Trypho.* Ed. G. Archambault. Paris, 1909.

Life of George of Choziba. Ed. C. Houze. *AB* 7 (1888): 97–144, 336–59.

Life of Golinduch. Ed. G. Garitte. "La Passion Georgienne de St. Golinduch." *AB* 74 (1956): 405–40.

Life of Maximus. Ed. and trans. S. Brock. "An Early Syriac Life of Maximus the Confessor." *Analecta Bollandiana* 91 (1973): 299–346.

Life of Pisentios. Ed. and trans. De Lacy O'Leary. *The Arabic Life of S. Pisentios according to the Text of the Two Manuscripts Paris bibl. nat. arabe 4785 and arabe 4794,* [*PO* 22]. Paris, 1930.

Vie de Théodore Sykéôn, [*Subsidia hagiographica* 48]. Ed. A.-J. Festugière, 2 vols. Brussels, 1970.

Life of St. Theognis, "Theognis, Bishop of Betelia (+522)." Ed. I. van den Gheyn. *AB* 10 (1891): 78–113.

John Lydus. *De magistratibus populi romani libri tres.* Ed. R. Wuensch. Leipzig, 1903.

John Moschus. *Spiritual Meadow, PG* 87: 2852–3112.

John of Thessalonica et al. *Les plus anciens recueils des Miracles de Saint Démétrius.* Ed. P. Lemerle, 2 vols. Paris, 1979–81.

Justinian, *Corpus iuris civilis.* Ed. P. Krueger and T. Mommsen, 3 vols. [Berlin, 1893–1912], Dublin/Zurich, 1972.

Claudius Mamertinus. *Gratiarum actio, XII panegyrici latini.* Ed. R. Mynors. Oxford, 1964.

Martyrdom of Polycarp. Ed. K. Bihlmeyer. *Die apostolischen vaeter,* t. 3. Tuebingen, 1970.

Martyrdom of the 60 Martyrs of Gaza. Ed. H. Delehaye. *Passio sanctorum sexaginta martyrum, AB* 23 (1904): 289–307.

Maximus the Confessor. *Epistolae. PG* 91: 364–649.

——. *Opuscula polemica et theologica. PG* 91: 1–285.

——. *Relatio motionis. PG* 90: 109–29.

Menander Protector. *Historia. FHG* 4.

Menander Rhetor. *Menander Rhetor "On Panegyric."* Ed. D. A. Russell and N. G. Wilson. Oxford, 1981.

Pseudo-Methodius. *Apokalypse des Ps.-Methodios,* [*Beitraege zur klassischen Philologie* 83]. Ed. A. Lolos. Meisenheim am Glan, 1976.

Michael the Syrian. *Chronique.* Trans. J.-B. Chabot, 4 vols. Paris, 1899–1910.

Nicephorus the Patriarch. *Breviarium.* Ed. C. de Boor. Leipzig, 1880.

Paschal Chronicle. Ed. L. Dindorf. Bonn, 1832.

Pliny the Younger. *Panegyricus.* In *XII Panegyrici Latini.* Ed. R. A. B. Mynors. Oxford, 1964.

Plutarch. *The Fortune or the Future of Alexander.* Ed. and trans. F. Babbitt. Cambridge, Mass., 1957.

Procopius of Caesarea. *Wars.* Ed. J. Haury and G. Wirth. *Opera Omnia.* Leipzig, 1962.

Romanus Melodus. *Sancti Romani melodi cantica: Cantica genuina.* Oxford, 1963.

Pseudo-Sebeos. *Histoire d'Héraclius.* Trans. F. Macler. Paris, 1904.

——. *Sebeos' History.* Trans. R. Bedrosian. New York, 1985.

Severus of Aschmounein. *History of the Patriarchs of the Coptic Church of Alexandria.* Ed. and trans. E. Evetts. *PO* 5.

"Les signes du Messie." Ed. and trans. L. Marmorstein. *Revue des Études Juives* 52 (1906): 176–86.

Socrates Scholasticus. *Ecclesiastical History. PG* 67.

Sophronius the Patriarch. *Anacreontica.* Ed. M. Gigante. *Sophronii anacreontica,* [*Opuscula. Testi per esercitazioni academiche,* 10–12]. Rome, 1957.

——. *Praise of Saints Cyrus and John. PG* 87: 3380–3421.

——. *Annunciation Oration. PG* 87: col. 3217–88.

——. *Apostles Peter and Paul Oration. PG* 87: 3356–64.

——. *Christmas Oration.* Ed. H. Usener. *Weihnachtspredigt von Sophronius, Rheinisches Museum* n.f. 41 9 (1886): 500–16.

——. *Exaltation of the Cross Oration. PG* 87: 3301–09.

——. *Feast of Purification Oration.* Ed. H. Usener. *Sophronii de praesentatione Domini sermo, Progr. Univ. Bonn,* 8–18. Bonn, 1889.

——. *John the Baptist Oration. PG* 87: 3321–53.

——. *Letter to Arcadius.* Ed. and trans. M. Albert and C. von Schoenborn. *Lettre de Sophrone de Jérusalem à Arcadius de Chypre. Version syriaque inédite du texte grec perdu. Introduction et traduction française. PO* 39.

——. *Synodal Epistle to Sergius. PG* 87: 3148–3200.

——. *Theophany Oration.* Ed. A. Papadopoulos-Kerameus. *Analecta Ierosolumitikēs Staxuologias,* vol. 5, 166. Petersburg, 1898.

Sozomen, *Ecclesiastical History.* Ed. G. Hansen. Berlin, 1960.

Strabo. *Geographica.* Vol. 1. Ed. A. Meineke. [Graz, 1969], Leipzig, 1877.

Theodore Syncellus. *On the Attack of the Avars.* Ed. L. Sternbach. *Analecta Avarica.* Cracow, 1900: 298–320.

Theodoret of Cyrus. *Ecclesiastical History.* Ed. L. Parmentier and F. Schweidweiler. 2d ed. Berlin, 1954.

Theophanes. *Chronographia.* Ed. C. de Boor, 2 vols. Leipzig, 1883.

Theophylact Simocatta. *Historiae.* Ed. C. de Boor and P. Wirth. Stuttgart, 1972.

——. *On the Predestined Terms of Life,* [*Arethusa Monographs* 6]. Ed. and trans. C. Garton and L. G. Westerink. Buffalo, 1978.

Velleius Paterculus. *History.* Ed. K. Halm. Leipzig, 1863, 1875.

Zosimus. *New History.* Ed. L. Mendelssohn. [Leipzig, 1887], Hildesheim, 1963.

MODERN SOURCES

Adshead, K. "Thucydides and Agathias." In *History and Historians in Late Antiquity.* Ed. B. Croke and A. Emmett, Sydney, 1983, 82–87.

Alexander, P. *The Byzantine Apocalyptic Tradition.* Berkeley, 1985.

——. "Byzantium and the Migration of Literary Works and Motifs: The Legend of the Last Roman Emperor." *Medievalia et Humanistica* n.s. 2 (1971): 47–68.

——. *The Oracle of Baalbek, The Tiburtine Sibyl in Greek Dress,* [*Dumbarton Oaks Studies* 10]. Washington, D.C., 1967.

———. "The Strength of Empire and Capital as Seen through Byzantine Eyes." *Speculum* 37 (1962): 339–57.

Alfoeldi, A. *Insignien und Tracht der roemischen Kaiser. Mitteilungen der Deutschen Archaeologischen Instituts* 50 (1935): 3–158.

Alvarez, J. "Apostolic Writings and the Roots of Anti-Semitism." *Studia Patristica* 13.2 (1975): 68–76.

Anastos, M. "The Ancient Greek Sources of Byzantine Absolutism." *Harry Austryn Wolfson Jubilee Volume*, 89–109. Jerusalem, 1965.

———. "Nestorius was Orthodox!" *DOP* 16 (1962): 119–40.

Avi-Yonah, M. *The Jews under Roman and Byzantine Rule: A Political History of Palestine from the Bar Kokhba War to the Arab Conquest.* New York, 1984.

Bachrach, B. "The Jewish Community of the Later Roman Empire as Seen in the *Codex Theodosianus.*" In *"To See Ourselves as Others See Us:" Christians, Jews, "Others" in Late Antiquity*, ed. J. Neusner and E. Frerichs, 399–421. Chicago, 1985.

Balsdon, J. P. V. D. *Romans and Aliens.* Chapel Hill, 1979.

Barišić, F. "Le siège de Constantinople par les Avars et les Slaves en 626." *Byz* 24 (1954): 371–95.

Baynes, N. H. "Eusebius and the Christian Empire." *Annuaire de l'institut de philologie et d'histoire orientales* 2 (1933): 13–18.

———. "The Supernatural Defenders of Constantinople." *AB* 67 (1949): 255–60.

Beck, H.-G. *Kirche und theologische Literatur im byzantinischen Reich.* Munich, 1959.

———. *Res publica romana. Vom Staatsdenken der Byzantiner.* Sitzungsberichte der bayerischen Akademie der Wissenschaften, phil.-hist. Abt. Munich, 1970.

———. *Senat und Volk von Konstantinopel. Probleme der byzantinischen Verfassungsgeschichte.* Sitzungsberichte der bayerischen Akademie der Wissenschaften, phil.-hist. Abt. Munich, 1966.

Benešević, F. "Le siège de Constantinople par les Perses et les Avars en 626." *Byz* 24 (1954): 371–95.

Bianchi, G. "Note sulla cultura a Bisanzio all 'inizio del VII secolo in rapporto all 'Esamerone di Giorgio di Pisidia." *Rivista di Studi Bizantini e Neoellenici* 2 (1965): 137–43.

Bonnicc, L. "Aspects religieux de la guerre à Rome." *Problèmes de la guerre à Rome.* [*Civilisations et Sociétés* 12], 101–15. Paris, 1969.

Breckenridge, J. D. *The Numismatic Iconography of Justinian II*, [*Numismatic Notes and Monographs* 144]. New York, 1959.

Brock, S. "Syriac Views of Emergent Islam." In *Studies on the First Century of Islamic Society.* Ed. G. H. A. Juynboll, 9–21, 199–203. Carbondale, Ill., 1982.

Brock, S., and Harvey, S. A. *Holy Women of the Syrian Orient.* Berkeley, 1986.

Brown, P. "A Dark Age Crisis: Aspects of the Iconoclast Controversy." *Society and the Holy in Late Antiquity*, 251–301. Berkeley, 1982.

———. *The Making of Late Antiquity.* Cambridge, 1978.

———. "The Rise and Function of the Holy Man in Late Antiquity." *Society and the Holy in Late Antiquity*, 103–52. Berkeley, 1982.

Cameron, A. *Circus Factions: Blues and Greens at Rome and Byzantium.* Oxford, 1976.

Cameron, Av. "Corippus' Poem on Justin II: a Terminus of Antique Art." *Annali della Scuola Normale Superiore di Pisa* 5, t. 3 (1975): 129–65.

———. "Images of Authority: Elites and Icons in Late Sixth-Century Byzantium." *Past and Present* 84 (1979): 3–35.

———. *In laudem Iustini Augusti minoris.* London, 1976.

———. "New and Old in Christian Literature." *The Seventeenth International Byzantine Congress: Major Papers,* 45–588. New Rochelle, 1986.

———. *Procopius and the Sixth Century.* London, 1985.

———. "The Virgin's Robe: An Episode in the History of Early Seventh-Century Byzantium." *Byz* 49 (1979): 42–56.

Cameron, Av. and Herrin, J. *Constantinople in the Early Eighth Century: The Parastasis Syntomoi Chronikai.* Leiden, 1984.

Chadwick, H. "John Moschus and his Friend Sophronius the Sophist." *Journal of Theological Studies* n.s. 25 (1974): 41–74.

———. "The Relativity of Moral Codes: Rome and Persia in Late Antiquity." In *Early Christian Literature and the Classical Intellectual Tradition: In honorem Robert M. Grant.* Ed. E. Schoedel and R. Wilken. Paris, 1979, 135–53.

Chesnut, G. F. *The First Christian Historians: Eusebius, Socrates, Sozomen, Theodoret and Evagrius,* [*Théologie historique* 46]. Paris, 1977.

Chrysos, E. "The Title *Basileus* in Early Byzantine International Relations." *DOP* 32 (1978): 29–75.

———. "Der Kaiser und die Koenige." In *Die Voelker an der mittleren und unteren Donau im fuenften und sechsten Jahrhundert,* ed. H. Wolfram and F. Daim, 143–48. Vienna, 1980.

Cohen, J. "Roman Imperial Policy toward the Jews from Constantine to the End of the Palestinian Patriarchate (429)." *Byzantine Studies* 3 (1976): 1–29.

Constantelos, D. "Jews and Judaism in the Early Church Fathers." *Greek Orthodox Theological Review* 23 (1978): 145–56.

Cox, P. *Biography in Late Antiquity: The Quest for the Holy Man.* Berkeley, 1984.

Crone, P. *Hagarism.* Cambridge, 1977.

Dagron, G. *Constantinople Imaginaire: Études sur le recueil des Patria,* [*Bibliothèque byzantine, Études* 8]. Paris, 1984.

———. "Judaiser." *Travaux et Mémoires* 11 (1991): 359–80.

———. *Naissance d'une capitale, Constantinople et ses institutions de 330 à 451.* Paris, 1974.

Dagron, G. and Déroche, V. "Juifs et Chrétiens dans l'Orient du VIIᵉ siècle." *Travaux et Mémoires* 11 (1991): 17–274.

Déroche, V. "L'authenticité de L'"Apologie contre les Juifs" de Léontios." *Bulletin de Correspondence Hellénique* 119 (1986): 655–69.

———. "La polémique anti judaique au VIᵉ et au VIIᵉ siècle. Un mémento inédit, les *Képhalaia*." *Travaux et Mémoires* 11 (1991): 275–312.

Devreesse, R. "La fin inédite d'une lettre de saint Maxime: un baptéme forcé de Juifs et de Samaritains à Carthage en 632." *Revue des sciences religieuses* 17 (1937): 25–35.

Dexinger, F. and Seibt, W. "A Hebrew Lead Seal from the Period of the Sassanian Occupation of Palestine (614–629 A.D.)." *Revue des Études Juives* 140 (1981): 303–17.

Dvornik, F. *Early Christian and Byzantine Political Philosophy*, 2 vols. Washington, D.C., 1966.

Ensslin, W. *Gottkaiser und Kaiser von Gottesgnaden*. Sitzungsberichte der bayerischen Akademie der Wissenschaften, phil.-hist. Abt. Munich, 1943.

Feldman, L. H. "Anti-Semitism in the Ancient World." In *History and Hate: The Dimensions of Anti-Semitism*, ed. D. Berger. Philadelphia, 1986, 15–42.

Frendo, J. D. C. "The Poetic Achievement of George of Pisidia." In *Maistor, Classical, Byzantine and Renaissance Studies for Robert Browning*, ed. A. Moffat, [*Byzantina Australiensia* 5], 159–87. Canberra, 1984.

———. "The Significance of Technical Terms in the Poems of George of Pisidia." *Orpheus* 21 (1974): 45–55.

———. "Special Aspects of the Use of Medical Vocabulary in the Poems of George of Pisidia." *Orpheus* 22 (1975): 49–56.

Frolow, A. "La dédicace de Constantinople dans la tradition byzantine," *Revue de l'Histoire des Religions* 127 (1944): 61–125.

———. "La vraie croix et les expéditions d'Héraclius en Perse." *Revue des Études Byzantines* 11 (1953): 88–105.

Gager, J. *The Origins of Anti-Semitism*. New York, 1983.

Grant, R. *Eusebius as Church Historian*. Oxford, 1980.

———. "Eusebius, Josephus, and the Fate of the Jews." *Society of Biblical Literature 1979 Seminar Papers*, ed. P. J. Achtemeier, vol. 2, 69–86. Missoula, 1979.

———. "War—Just, Holy, Unjust—in Hellenistic and Early Christian Thought." *Augustinianum* 20 (1980): 173–79.

Grayzel, S. "The Jews and Roman Law." *Jewish Quarterly Review* 59 (1968–69): 6–117.

Gregory, T. *Vox Populi: Popular Opinion and Violence in the Religious Controversies of the Fifth Century A.D.* Columbus, 1979.

Grierson, P. *Catalogue of the Byzantine Coins in the Dumbarton Oaks Collection and in the Whittemore Collection*, 2 vols. Washington, D.C., 1966–68.

———. "The Monetary Reforms of Abd al-'Malik." *Journal of the Economic and Social History of the Orient* 3 (1960): 241–64.

Grumel, V. "La reposition de la vraie croix à Jérusalem par Héraclius. Le jour et l'année," *Byzantinische Forschungen* 1 (1966): 139–49.

Haldon, J. "Ideology and the Byzantine State in the Seventh Century: The 'Trial' of Maximus Confessor." *From Late Antiquity to Early Byzantium*, [*Proceedings of the Byzantinological Symposium in the Sixteenth International Eirene Conference*]. 87–91. Prague, 1985.

———. "Some Remarks to the Background of the Iconoclast Controversy." *Byzsl* 38 (1977): 161–84.

Harnack, A. "Die Altercatio Simonis Iudaei et Theophilus Christiani nebst Untersuchungen ueber die antijuedische Polemik in der alten Kirche." *Texte und Untersuchungen zur Geschichte der altchristlichen Literatur* 1 (1883).

———. *The Expansion of Christianity in the First Three Centuries*. Trans. J. Moffatt, 3 vols. New York, [1904] 1972.

———. "Judentum und Judenchristentum in Justins *Dialog mit Trypho*." *Texte und Untersuchungen zur Geschichte der altchristlichen Literatur* 39 (1913): 47–92.

Hruby, K. *Juden and Judentum bei den Kirchenvaetern,* [*Schriften zur Judentumskunde* 2]. Zurich, 1971.

——. "Zum Buch von R. Richardson, *Israel in the Apostolic Church.*" *Judaica* 28 (1972): 30–40.

Hulen, A. "The 'Dialogues with the Jews' as Sources for the Early Jewish Argument against Christianity." *Journal of Biblical Literature* 51 (1932): 58–70.

Hunger, H. *Die hochsprachliche profane Literatur der Byzantiner,* 2 vols. Munich, 1978.

——. *Kaiser Justinian I (527–65),* [*Anzeiger der oesterreichischen Akademie der Wissenschaften,* phil.-hist. Klasse, 102], 339–56. Vienna, 1965.

——. *Prooimion: Elemente der byzantinischen Kaiseridee in den Arengen der Urkunden,* [Wiener byzantinische Studien 1]. Vienna, 1964.

Jaeger, W. *Early Christianity and Greek Paideia.* Oxford, 1961.

Juster, J. *Les Juifs dans l'empire romain.* 2 vols. Paris, 1914.

Karayannopoulos, J. "Der fruehbyzantinische Kaiser," *BZ* 49 (1956): 369–84.

Kaegi, W. E., Jr. *Byzantium and the Decline of Rome.* Princeton, 1969.

——. *Byzantium and the Early Islamic Conquests.* Cambridge, 1992.

——. "Initial Byzantine Reactions to the Arab Invasions." *Church History* 10 (1969): 139–49.

——. "New Evidence on the Early Reign of Heraclius." *BZ* 66 (1973): 308–30.

——. "Two Notes on Heraclius." *REB* 37 (1979): 217–24.

Kasher, A. *The Jews in Hellenistic and Roman Egypt.* Tuebingen, 1985.

Kennedy, G. A. *Greek Rhetoric under Christian Emperors.* Princeton, 1983.

Kitzinger, E. "The Cult of Images Before Iconoclasm." *DOP* 8 (1954): 83–150.

Krauss, S. *Studien zur byzantinisch-judischen Geschichte.* Vienna, 1914.

Krumbacher, K. *Geschichte der byzantinischen Literatur von Justinian bis zum Ende des ostroemischen Reiches (527–1453),* t.2. Munich, 1897.

Lacy, C. "The Greek View of Barbarians in the Hellenistic Age, as Derived from Representative Literary and Artistic Evidence from the Hellenistic Period." Diss., University of Colorado, 1976.

Laga, C. "Maximi confessioris ad Thalassium quastio 64. Essai de lecture." In *After Chalcedon: Studies in Theology and Church History,* ed. C. Laga, J. A. Munitiz, and L. van Rompay. [*Orientalia Lovaniensia analecta* 18], 203–15. Louvain, 1985.

Lévy, I. "Les soixante-dix semaines de Daniel dans la chronologie Juives." *Revue des Études Juives* 51 (1906): 161–90.

Lewis, B. "An Apocalyptic Vision of Islamic History." *Bulletin of the School of Oriental and African Studies* 13 (1949–51): 308–38.

Ludwig, C. "Kaiser Herakleios, Georgios Pisides und die Perserkriege." In *Varia III,* [*Poikila Byzantina* 11], ed. P. Speck, 73–128. Bonn, 1991.

MacCormack, S. *Art and Ceremony in Late Antiquity.* Berkeley, 1981.

Mango, C. *Byzantine Literature as a Distorting Mirror.* Inaugural Lecture, University of Oxford, May, 1974. Oxford, 1975.

——. *Byzantium: The Empire of New Rome.* New York, 1980.

——. "Deux études sur Byzance et la Perse sassanide." *Travaux et Mémoires* 9 (1985): 91–117.

Marrou, H. I. *A History of Education in Antiquity.* Trans. G. Lamb. Madison, 1982.

Martinez, F. J. "Eastern Christian Apocalyptic in the Early Islamic Period: Pseudo-Methodius and Pseudo-Athanasius." Diss., Catholic University of America, 1985.

Matthews, J. "Ammianus' Historical Evolution." In *History and Historians in Late Antiquity,* ed. B. Croke and A. Emmett, 30–41. Sydney, 1983.

McCormick, M. *Eternal Victory: Triumphal Rulership in Late Antiquity, Byzantium and the Early Medieval West.* Cambridge, 1986.

McGiffert, A. C. *Dialogue between a Christian and a Jew entitled Antibolē Papiskou kai Philōnos Ioudaiōn pros monaxon tina.* New York, 1889.

Michel, A. "Les lois de la guerre et les problèmes romains dans la philosophie de Cicéron." *Problèmes de la guerre à Rome,* [*Civilisations et Sociétés* 12], 171–83. Paris, 1969.

Momigliano, A. "Pagan and Christian Historiography in the Fourth Century A.D." In *The Conflict between Paganism and Christianity in the Fourth Century,* ed. A. Momigliano, 79–99. Oxford, 1963.

Moorhead, J. "The Monophysite Response to the Arab Invasions." 51 (1981): 580–91.

Murawski, F. *Die Juden bei den Kirchenvaetern und Scholastikern.* Berlin, 1925.

Nau, F. "Note sur les Mss. de Paris qui renferment la notice bibliographique d'Antiochus, moine de S.-Saba." *ROC* 11 (1906): 327–30.

Nissen, T. "Historisches Epos und Panegyrikos in der Spaetantike," *Hermes* 75 (1940): 298–325.

Nock, A. D. *Conversion: The Old and New in Religion from Alexander the Great to Augustine of Hippo.* Oxford, 1933.

Olajos, T. *Les sources de Théopylact Simocatta historien.* Leiden, 1988.

Olster, D. "Chalcedonian and Monophysite: The Union of 616." *Bulletin d'archéologie Copte* (1985): 93–108.

———. "The Date of George of Pisidia's *Hexaemeron*." *DOP* 45 (1991): 159–172.

———. "Justinian, Imperial Rhetoric and the Church." *Byzsl* 50 (1989): 165–76.

———. "The Politics of Usurpation in the Seventh Century: The Reign of Phocas (602–10)." Diss., University of Chicago, 1986.

———. *The Politics of Usurpation in the Seventh Century: Rhetoric and Revolution in Byzantium.* Amsterdam, 1993.

Ostrogorsky, G. *History of the Byzantine State.* 3d ed. Trans. J. Hussey. New Brunswick, 1969.

Parkes, J. *The Conflict of the Church and the Synagogue: A Study in the Origins of Anti-Semitism.* New York, 1979 [1934].

Peeters, P. "La Prise de Jérusalem par les Perses." *Mélanges de l'Université Saint Joseph* 9 (1923–24): 3–42.

Pertusi, A. "L'attegiamento spirituale della più antica storiografia byzantina." *Aevum* 30 (1956): 134–66.

———. *Giorgio di Pisidia, Poemi: I. Panegirici epici,* [*Studia Patristica et Byzantina* 7], 11–48. Ettal, 1959.

———. "L'encomio di s. Anastasio martire Persiano." *AB* 76 (1958): 5–63.

Peterson, E. *Der Monotheismus als politisches Problem. Ein Beitrag zur Geschichte der politischen Theologie in Imperium Romanum.* Leipzig, 1935.

Podskalsky, G. *Die Byzantinische Reichseschatologie. Die Periodisierung der Weltgeschichte in den 4 Grossreichen (Daniel 2 und 7) und dem tausendjaehrigen Friedensreiche (Apok. 20).* Munich, 1972.

Reichardt, K. "Die Judengestzgebung im Codex Theodosianus." *Kairos* 20 (1978): 16–39.

Reuther, R. *Faith and Fratricide: The Theological Roots of Anti-Semitism.* Minneapolis, 1974.

Ricotti, G. *The Age of the Martyrs: Christianity from Diocletian to Constantine.* Trans. A. Bull. Milwaukee, 1959.

Rike, R. L. *Apex Omnium: Religion in the Res Gestae of Ammianus.* Berkeley, 1987.

Roesch, G. *Onoma Basileias: Studien zum offiziellen Gebrauch der Kaisertitel in spaetantiker und fruehbyzantinischer Zeit,* [*Byzantina Vindobonensia* 10]. Vienna, 1978.

Rokeah, D. *Jews, Pagans and Christians in Conflict,* [*Studia post-biblica* 33]. Jerusalem and Leiden, 1982.

Schreckenberg, H. *Die christliche Adversus-Judaeos-Texte und ihr literarisches und historisches Umfeld (1–11. Jh.).* Frankfurt am Main, 1982.

Sharf, A. "Byzantine Jewry in the Seventh Century." *BZ* 48 (1955): 103–15.

Sherwin-White, A. N. *Racial Prejudice in Imperial Rome.* Cambridge, 1967.

Simon, M. *Verus Israel: A Study of the Relations between Christians and Jews in the Roman Empire (135–425).* Trans. H. McKeating. Oxford, 1986.

Speck, P. *Das geteilte Dossier. Beobachtungen zu den Nachrichten ueber die Regierung des Kaisers Herakleios und seiner Soehne bei Theophanes und Nikephoros,* [*Poikila byzantina* 9]. Bonn, 1988.

——. "Versuch einer Charakterisierung der sogenannten Makedonischen Renaissance." *Les pays du nord et Byzance (Scandanavie et Byzance),* [*Acta universitatis Uppsalensis,* Figura n.s. 19]. Ed. R. Zeitler, 237–42. Uppsala, 1981.

——. *Zufaelliges zum Bellum Avaricum des Georgios Pisides,* [*Miscellanea Byzantina Monacensia* 24]. Munich, 1980.

Starr, J. "Byzantine Jewry on the Eve of the Arab Conquest." *Journal of the Palestine Oriental Society* 15 (1935): 280–93.

——. "St. Maximus and the Forced Conversion at Carthage." *Byzantinisch-neugriechisches Jahrbuch* 16 (1940): 192–96.

Storch, R. H. "The 'Absolutist' Theology of Victory. Its Place in the Late Empire." *Classica et mediaevalia* 29 (1968): 197–211.

Stratos, A. *To Byzantion ston Z' Aiōna,* 2 vols. (Athens, 1965–1966).

Tinnefeld, F. *Kategorien der Kaiserkritik in der byzantinischen Historiographie von Prokop bis Niketas Choniates.* Munich, 1971.

Topping, E. "On Earthquakes and Fires." *BZ* 71 (1978): 22–35.

Treitinger, O. *Die ostroemische Kaiser- und Reichsidee nach ihrer Gestaltung in hoefischen Zeremoniell.* [Jena, 1938], Darmstadt, 1956.

Trilling, J. "Myth and Metaphor at the Byzantine Court: A Literary Approach to the David Plates." *Byz* 48 (1978): 249–63.

Vailhé, S. "Sophrone le Sophiste et Sophrone le Patriarche." *ROC* 7 (1902): 360–85, 8 (1903): 32–69, 356–87.

van Dieten, J. L. *Geschichte der Patriarchen von Sergios I. bis Joannes VI. (610–715)*. Amsterdam, 1972.

Viljamaa, T. *Studies in Greek Encomiastic Poetry of the Early Byzantine Period*, [*Commentationes humanorum litterorum* 42, pt. 4]. Helsinki, 1968.

von Schoenborn, C. *Sophrone de Jérusalem, Vie monastique et confession dogmatique*, [*Théologie historique* 20]. Paris, 1972.

Waegemann, M. "Les traités *adversus Judaeos:* Aspects des relations Judéo-Chrétiennes dans le monde grec." *Byz* 56 (1986): 298–315.

Whitby, M. *The Emperor Maurice and his Historian: Theophylact Simocatta on Persian and Balkan Warfare*. Oxford, 1988.

Wilken, R. *The Christians as the Romans Saw Them*. New Haven, 1984.

——. *John Chrysostom and the Jews: Rhetoric and Reality in the Late Fourth Century*. Berkeley, 1983.

——. *Judaism and the Early Christian Mind: A Study of Cyril of Alexandria's Exegesis and Theology*. New Haven, 1971.

——. "Pagan Criticism of Christianity: Greek Religion and Christian Faith." In *Early Christian Literature and the Classical Intellectual Tradition: In Honorem Robert M. Grant*, ed. W. Schoedel and R. Wilken, [*Théologie historique* 54], 117–34. Paris, 1979.

——. "The Restoration of Israel in Biblical Prophecy: Christian and Jewish response in the Early Christian Period." In *"To See Ourselves as Others See Us": Christians, Jews, "Others" In Late Antiquity*, ed. J. Neusner and E. Frerichs. 443–71. Chicago, 1985.

Williams, A. L. *Adversus Judaeos: A Bird's Eye View of Christian Apologetics*. Cambridge, 1935.

Winkelmann, F. "Aegypten un Byzanz vor der arabischen Eroberung." *Byzsl* 40 (1979): 161–82.

Wortley, J. "The Oration of Theodore Syncellus (BHG 1058) and the Siege of 860." *Byzantine Studies* 4 (1977): 111–26.

Index

University of Pennsylvania Press
MIDDLE AGES SERIES
Edward Peters, General Editor

F. R. P. Akehurst, trans. *The* Coutumes de Beauvaisis *of Philippe de Beaumanoir.* 1992

Peter L. Allen. *The Art of Love: Amatory Fiction from Ovid to the* Romance of the Rose. 1992

David Anderson. *Before the Knight's Tale: Imitation of Classical Epic in Boccaccio's* Teseida. 1988

Benjamin Arnold. *Count and Bishop in Medieval Germany: A Study of Regional Power, 1100–1350.* 1991

Mark C. Bartusis. *The Late Byzantine Army: Arms and Society, 1204–1453.* 1992

J. M. W. Bean. *From Lord to Patron: Lordship in Late Medieval England.* 1990

Uta-Renate Blumenthal. *The Investiture Controversy: Church and Monarchy from the Ninth to the Twelfth Century.* 1988

Daniel Bornstein, trans. *Dino Compagni's* Chronicle *of Florence.* 1986

Maureen Boulton. *The Song in the Story: Lyric Insertions in French Narrative Fiction, 1200–1400.* 1993

Betsy Bowden. *Chaucer Aloud: The Varieties of Textual Interpretation.* 1987

James William Brodman. *Ransoming Captives in Crusader Spain: The Order of Merced on the Christian-Islamic Frontier.* 1986

Kevin Brownlee and Sylvia Huot, eds. *Rethinking the* Romance of the Rose*: Text, Image, Reception.* 1992

Matilda Tomaryn Bruckner. *Shaping Romance: Interpretation, Truth, and Closure in Twelfth-Century French Fictions.* 1993

Otto Brunner (Howard Kaminsky and James Van Horn Melton, eds. and trans.). Land *and Lordship: Structures of Governance in Medieval Austria.* 1992

Robert I. Burns, S. J., ed. *Emperor of Culture: Alfonso X the Learned of Castile and His Thirteenth-Century Renaissance.* 1990

David Burr. *Olivi and Franciscan Poverty: The Origins of the* Usus Pauper *Controversy.* 1989

David Burr. *Olivi's Peaceable Kingdom: A Reading of the Apocalypse Commentary.* 1993

Thomas Cable. *The English Alliterative Tradition.* 1991

Anthony K. Cassell and Victoria Kirkham, eds. and trans. *Diana's Hunt/Caccia di Diana: Boccaccio's First Fiction.* 1991

John C. Cavadini. *The Last Christology of the West: Adoptionism in Spain and Gaul, 785–820.* 1993

Brigitte Cazelles. *The Lady as Saint: A Collection of French Hagiographic Romances of the Thirteenth Century.* 1991

Karen Cherewatuk and Ulrike Wiethaus, eds. *Dear Sister: Medieval Women and the Epistolary Genre*. 1993

Anne L. Clark. *Elisabeth of Schönau: A Twelfth-Century Visionary*. 1992

Willene B. Clark and Meradith T. McMunn, eds. *Beasts and Birds of the Middle Ages: The Bestiary and Its Legacy*. 1989

Richard C. Dales. *The Scientific Achievement of the Middle Ages*. 1973

Charles T. Davis. *Dante's Italy and Other Essays*. 1984

Katherine Fischer Drew, trans. *The Burgundian Code*. 1972

Katherine Fischer Drew, trans. *The Laws of the Salian Franks*. 1991

Katherine Fischer Drew, trans. *The Lombard Laws*. 1973

Nancy Edwards. *The Archaeology of Early Medieval Ireland*. 1990

Margaret J. Ehrhart. *The Judgment of the Trojan Prince Paris in Medieval Literature*. 1987

Richard K. Emmerson and Ronald B. Herzman. *The Apocalyptic Imagination in Medieval Literature*. 1992

Theodore Evergates. *Feudal Society in Medieval France: Documents from the County of Champagne*. 1993

Felipe Fernández-Armesto. *Before Columbus: Exploration and Colonization from the Mediterranean to the Atlantic, 1229–1492*. 1987

R. D. Fulk. *A History of Old English Meter*. 1992

Patrick J. Geary. *Aristocracy in Provence: The Rhône Basin at the Dawn of the Carolingian Age*. 1985

Peter Heath. *Allegory and Philosophy in Avicenna (Ibn Sînâ), with a Translation of the Book of the Prophet Muḥammad's Ascent to Heaven*. 1992

J. N. Hillgarth, ed. *Christianity and Paganism, 350–750: The Conversion of Western Europe*. 1986

Richard C. Hoffmann. *Land, Liberties, and Lordship in a Late Medieval Countryside: Agrarian Structures and Change in the Duchy of Wrocław*. 1990

Robert Hollander. *Boccaccio's Last Fiction: Il Corbaccio*. 1988

Edward B. Irving, Jr. *Rereading* Beowulf. 1989

C. Stephen Jaeger. *The Origins of Courtliness: Civilizing Trends and the Formation of Courtly Ideals, 939–1210*. 1985.

William Chester Jordan. *The French Monarchy and the Jews: From Philip Augustus to the Last Capetians*. 1989

William Chester Jordan. *From Servitude to Freedom: Manumission in the Sénonais in the Thirteenth Century*. 1986

Richard Kay. *Dante's Christian Astrology*. 1994

Ellen E. Kittell. *From Ad Hoc to Routine: A Case Study in Medieval Bureaucracy*. 1991.

Alan C. Kors and Edward Peters, eds. *Witchcraft in Europe, 1100–1700: A Documentary History*. 1972

Barbara M. Kreutz. *Before the Normans: Southern Italy in the Ninth and Tenth Centuries*. 1992

E. Ann Matter. *The Voice of My Beloved: The Song of Songs in Western Medieval Christianity*. 1990.

María Rosa Menocal. *The Arabic Role in Medieval Literary History*. 1987

A. J. Minnis. *Medieval Theory of Authorship*. 1988

Lawrence Nees. *A Tainted Mantle: Hercules and the Classical Tradition at the Carolingian Court.* 1991

Lynn H. Nelson, trans. *The Chronicle of San Juan de La Peña: A Fourteenth-Century Official History of the Crown of Aragon.* 1991

Charlotte A. Newman. *The Anglo-Norman Nobility in the Reign of Henry I: The Second Generation.* 1988

Joseph F. O'Callaghan. *The Cortes of Castile-León, 1188–1350.* 1989

Joseph F. O'Callaghan. *The Learned King: The Reign of Alfonso X of Castile.* 1993

David M. Olster. *Roman Defeat, Christian Response, and the Literary Construction of the Jew.* 1994

William D. Paden, ed. *The Voice of the Trobairitz: Perspectives on the Women Troubadours.* 1989

Edward Peters. *The Magician, the Witch, and the Law.* 1982

Edward Peters, ed. *Christian Society and the Crusades, 1198–1229: Sources in Translation, including* The Capture of Damietta *by Oliver of Paderborn.* 1971

Edward Peters, ed. *The First Crusade: The* Chronicle of Fulcher of Charters *and Other Source Materials.* 1971

Edward Peters, ed. *Heresy and Authority in Medieval Europe.* 1980

James M. Powell. *Albertanus of Brescia: The Pursuit of Happiness in the Early Thirteenth Century.* 1992

James M. Powell. *Anatomy of a Crusade, 1213–1221.* 1986

Jean Renart (Patricia Terry and Nancy Vine Durling, trans.). *The Romance of the Rose or Guillaume de Dole.* 1993

Michael Resler, trans. Erec *by Hartmann von Aue.* 1987

Pierre Riché (Michael Idomir Allen, trans.). *The Carolingians: A Family Who Forged Europe.* 1993

Pierre Riché (Jo Ann McNamara, trans.). *Daily Life in the World of Charlemagne.* 1978

Jonathan Riley-Smith. *The First Crusade and the Idea of Crusading.* 1986

Joel T. Rosenthal. *Patriarchy and Families of Privilege in Fifteenth-Century England.* 1991

Teofilo F. Ruiz. *Crisis and Continuity: Land and Town in Late Medieval Castile.* 1994

Steven D. Sargent, ed. and trans. *On the Threshold of Exact Science: Selected Writings of Anneliese Maier on Late Medieval Natural Philosophy.* 1982.

Robin Chapman Stacey. *The Road to Judgment: From Custom to Court in Medieval Ireland and Wales.* 1994

Sarah Stanbury. *Seeing the* Gawain-Poet: Description and the Act of Perception. 1992

Thomas C. Stillinger. *The Song of Troilus: Lyric Authority in the Medieval Book.* 1992

Susan Mosher Stuard. *A State of Deference: Ragusa/Dubrovnik in the Medieval Centuries.* 1992

Susan Mosher Stuard, ed. *Women in Medieval History and Historiography.* 1987

Susan Mosher Stuard, ed. *Women in Medieval Society.* 1976

Jonathan Sumption. *The Hundred Years War: Trial by Battle.* 1992

Ronald E. Surtz. *The Guitar of God: Gender, Power, and Authority in the Visionary World of Mother Juana de la Cruz (1481–1534).* 1990

William H. TeBrake. *A Plague of Insurrection: Popular Politics and Peasant Revolt in Flanders, 1323–1328*. 1993

Patricia Terry, trans. *Poems of the Elder Edda*. 1990

Hugh M. Thomas. *Vassals, Heiresses, Crusaders, and Thugs: The Gentry of Angevin Yorkshire, 1154–1216*. 1993

Frank Tobin. *Meister Eckhart: Thought and Language*. 1986

Ralph V. Turner. *Men Raised from the Dust: Administrative Service and Upward Mobility in Angevin England*. 1988

Harry Turtledove, trans. *The* Chronicle *of Theophanes: An English Translation of* Anni Mundi *6095–6305 (A.D. 602–813)*. 1982

Mary F. Wack. *Lovesickness in the Middle Ages: The* Viaticum *and Its Commentaries*. 1990

Benedicta Ward. *Miracles and the Medieval Mind: Theory, Record, and Event, 1000–1215*. 1982

Suzanne Fonay Wemple. *Women in Frankish Society: Marriage and the Cloister, 500–900*. 1981

Jan M. Ziolkowski. *Talking Animals: Medieval Latin Beast Poetry, 750–1150*. 1993

This book has been set in Linotron Galliard. Galliard was designed for Mergenthaler in 1978 by Matthew Carter. Galliard retains many of the features of a sixteenth-century typeface cut by Robert Granjon but has some modifications that give it a more contemporary look.

Printed on acid-free paper.